Introduction to Computing
Applications for the Social Sciences

CHARLES M. TOLBERT II
Florida State University

Addison-Wesley Publishing Company, Inc.

Reading, Massachusetts • Menlo Park, California
Don Mills, Ontario • Wokingham, England • Amsterdam
Sydney • Singapore • Tokyo • Mexico City • Bogota
Santiago • San Juan

Photo Credits: *Pages 8 and 9*, Sperry Corporation; *Page 10*, Courtesy Motorola Semiconductor Products Inc.; *Page 11*, Cray Research, Inc.; *Pages 15 and 17 (bottom)*, Control Data Corporation; *Page 17 (top)*, Courtesy Honeywell Information Systems, Inc.; *Page 22*, Courtesy Apple® Computers; *Page 25*, Texas Instruments; *Page 26*, Courtesy Hewlett Packard; *Page 27*, Courtesy Tandy Corporation; *Page 75*, Courtesy Electro General Corporation.

Library of Congress Cataloging in Publication Data

Tolbert, Charles M.
   Introduction to computing.

   Bibliography: p.
   Includes index.
   1. Social sciences--Data processing. I. Title.
H61.3.T64 1984   300'.28'54   84-11178
ISBN 0-201-16488-4

ISBN 0-201-16488-4
ABCDEFGHIJ-AL-898765

Preface

This book is intended to encourage a variety of computing applications in the social sciences. Computing in these disciplines (and most others, for that matter) has generally lacked the coherence that a systematic applications approach could provide. Some in the social sciences use computers mainly for high-speed calculation of statistics. Others use computers primarily to manage large data sets that require some form of automated data processing. Still others use computers only for writing and word processing. In practice, people have learned only what they need to know to carry out a narrow range of applications and have gained little or no perspective on computing. In the pages that follow, some attention will be focused on strategies for quantitative statistical analysis on computers. But there is much more. A variety of nonanalytic applications is discussed which can facilitate instruction, research, and writing in the social science community.

Other than a handful of assignments in methods and statistics courses, formal training in social science computing applications has been virtually nonexistent. Researchers and students alike have relied on a "hands-on" approach in which learning takes place through trial and error. Each computer installation has been viewed as a unique establishment, and far too much emphasis has been placed on particular local techniques at the expense of universal principles underlying computing. There are ample signs now that a systematic approach to instruction in social science computing is warranted. For one thing, the new information technology is advancing at a very fast rate. Students who desire a rudimentary exposure to computing find themselves facing a bewildering array of information sources including books, magazines, retail salespersons, and expert systems analysts. Why not systematize that learning experience in the classroom? Computer instruction is also necessary because of social science curriculum shifts from basic to applied emphases. These new pragmatically oriented programs obviously require some formal training in computing.

This book has been designed for an introductory short course, workshop, or laboratory course in social science computing. The book should also be a welcome supplementary text for social science methods and statistics courses where valuable class time must be devoted to computing basics. Those who want to learn computing on their own should find this book useful as well.

The foremost assumption governing the content of this volume is that the reader has little or no experience in computing or, for that matter, any other statistical or technical background. But others should find the book helpful, too. Those with some computing experience are encouraged to consider some of the advice offered on efficient, economical mainframe analysis. Readers of modest acquaintance with computing are also encouraged to review the variety of applications suggested here. Likewise, the discussion of recent developments in microcomputing will be of interest.

A second assumption made here is that social scientists must have some familiarity with both large and small computers and some (but not all) of the technical jargon of computing. Computer literacy is increasingly a requirement for entry into occupations and the social sciences are no exception. But this is not to say that we all need to be computer programmers. As it happens, most social science computing applications employ user-friendly software packages which require very minimal programming skills. The premise here is that nonprogrammers and programmers alike need to be familiar enough with social science computing applications to identify and use those which may be of value to them.

A third assumption is that there is a common structure underlying most computing operations. Even though a few variations in syntax exist from one system to another, optimal strategies for social science computing are extremely similar across most major brands of computers. Of course, it will be necessary for instructors who use this book as a text to provide students with specifics on local computing procedures and policies. In the process of acquiring "hands-on" experience on a particular system, students will be exposed to generic computing strategies that are employed throughout the social sciences. It is also important to note that the same handful of major software packages can be found in almost every academic, government, or industrial social science research setting. These similarities in computing operations suggest that computing skills are portable—techniques acquired in one computing environment can be readily employed elsewhere.

The fourth assumption here regards the virtually universal software packages just mentioned. The major analysis systems (SPSS, SAS, BMDP, and the like) are documented at great length in large reference manuals and smaller primers. For the most part, the manuals are well written and require little or no programming experience on the part of the user. Consequently the applications languages associated with the software packages are not of great concern here. Instead, portions of this book describe a variety of strategies for accessing these packages, and it is assumed that the software vendors' publications provide adequate detailed information for users.

A fifth assumption made in writing this book is that social scientists need to be aware of the full range of computer applications available to them. When computing is reserved for quantitative statistical analysis, we barely exploit the technology at all. There is much more that can be done with computers and, in view of available applications and promising prospects, the assumption here is that computing can be an integral part of all social scientific research. It should be noted that this emphasis on a range of applications necessarily limits the amount of detail that can be provided on any particular use of computing. When readers encounter applications that appear particularly interesting, they are encouraged to consult the reference materials noted in the text for further information.

Finally, it is assumed that those outside the disciplines typically included in the social sciences may also want to pursue their interests in computing with this book. As it turns out, most of the material discussed here is quite applicable in other fields such as law, business, communications, and the liberal arts. The portions of this book devoted to system architecture, economy, storage media, word processing, record keeping, literature searches, and the like may be useful to virtually all computer users.

Very few fields are changing as rapidly as computing and, no doubt, some material here will be dated quickly. With a basic grasp of the concepts presented here, readers are encouraged to consult more recent issues of periodicals cited in the text for later developments in what is proving to be an exciting and promising technological revolution.

Acknowledgments

Students in methods courses and computer and workshops over the years have contributed much to the organization and content of this book. Their successes, failures, elation and frustration with computing have helped me focus the present volume on material that will be most helpful to their peers in subsequent classes.

My first instructors in computing were Larry Felice and Tom Myers, and they are largely responsible for my early interest. Since then I have made much too frequent use of two consultants whose expertise in social science computing is greater than mine: R. Douglas McLeod and E. Walter Terrie.

Special thanks are due to Richard Briggs, Alice Kemp, and Norman Weatherby for their contributions of appendices to the present volume. Richard Briggs, Alice Kemp, Martin Levin, Gregory Marks, R. Douglas McLeod, and Thomas Myers provided detailed, constructive reviews of a draft of the manuscript. At Addison-Wesley, Peter Gordon's early enthusiasm and encouragement gave impetus to this project and, no doubt, hastened its completion. Cheryl Wurzbacher and Amato Prudente aided in the production stages, and Ellen Hofstadter prepared the indexes.

Finally, thanks to the other Professor Tolbert (Patricia) and Rachel for their support and assistance. They make it all worthwhile.

Tallahassee, Florida　　　　　　　　　　　　　　　　　　　　　　　　　**C.M.T.**
September 1984

Contents

CHAPTER 1   Computing in the Social Sciences   **1**
High Technology and the Socal Sciences   1
Social Science Computing Today   2
Outline of Presentation   3
Suggested Readings   5

CHAPTER 2   Computer Hardware   **7**
The Development of Computer Hardware   7
The Inner Sanctum of a Computer System   12
Today's Large Mainframe   14
Today's Microcomputer   21
Hardware Developments in the Offing   26
Suggested Readings   28
Suggested Exercises   28

CHAPTER 3   Computer Software   **29**
Operating Systems   29
Programming Languages   30
Applications Packages   34
Packages with Social Science Applications   36
Suggested Readings   38

CHAPTER 4   Text Editing Concepts and Procedures   **39**
Editing Procedures   39
Checklist of Editor Features   46
Suggested Exercises   50

CHAPTER 5   Word Processing   **51**
Software Aids for Writers   52
The Text Formatting Process   54
Text Formatting Software   59
Integrated Word Processing Software   61
Printing the Processed Word   65
Report Writing   67
Suggested Readings   68
Suggested Exercises   68

CHAPTER 6   A Variety of Nonanalytic Applications   69
Communications   69
Computer-Assisted Data Collection   71
Computer-Assisted Instruction   76
Online Information   80
Crime, Privacy, and Computers   89
Suggested Readings   90
Resources   90
Suggested Exercises   91

CHAPTER 7   Structures and Sources of Social Science Data   93
Organization of Social Science Data   93
Secondary Data Analysis   106
Suggested Readings   109
Suggested Exercises   110

CHAPTER 8   Strategies for Mainframe Statistical Analysis   111
Basic Modes of Computer Access   111
Batch Access   112
Interactive Time-Sharing Access   116
Which Access Mode?   122
Suggested Exercises   124

CHAPTER 9   Storage, Maintenance and Use of Large Data Files   125
More on Storage Media   125
Maintaining Documentation   132
Economy Considerations   132

CHAPTER 10   Statistical Analysis on Microcomputers   135
Hardware Considerations   135
Microcomputer Analysis Software   138
Prospects for Microcomputing   142
List of Sources for Microcomputer Analysis Packages   143
Suggested Readings   143

APPENDIX I   Applications on an IBM VM/CMS System   145
Norman L. Weatherby
APPENDIX II   Applications on a DEC VAX   165
Richard P. Briggs
APPENDIX III   Applications on a CDC CYBER   177
Charles M. Tolbert II
APPENDIX IV   Applications on a DECSYSTEM 10   193
Alice Abel Kemp
APPENDIX V   Applications on IBM OS/MVS Systems   203
Charles M. Tolbert II

Glossary   213
References   223
Author Index   229
Subject Index   231

CHAPTER ONE

Computing in the Social Sciences

HIGH TECHNOLOGY AND THE SOCIAL SCIENCES

Social scientists have speculated for some time about the nature of post-industrial society. One consistent theme in futurist assessments has been the eventual emergence of a New Class—a social class composed of those who have access to information technology and the ability to exploit it. Hardly the romantic yearnings of some obscure prophets, New Class themes can be found in the work of such prominent writers as Alvin Gouldner, John K. Galbraith, Daniel Bell, and Alvin Toffler.[1] Meanwhile, other writers like Barry Bluestone and Bennett Harrison are chronicling plant closings, relocations, and layoffs in heavy manufacturing. This "deindustrialization" is taking place alongside dramatic growth in the high technology and service sectors.[2] The signals are clear: fundamental skills in computing are likely to be indispensable in the years to come.

Like its counterparts in other fields, the New Class of social science students needs a systematic introduction to computing applications. To

---

1. See Alvin W. Gouldner, *The Future of Intellectuals and the Rise of the New Class* (New York: Seabury Press, 1979); John K. Galbraith, *The New Industrial State* (Boston: Houghton Mifflin, 1967); Daniel Bell, *The Coming of Post-Industrial Society* (New York: Basic Books, 1973); and Alvin Toffler, *The Third Wave* (New York: Random House, 1980).
2. See Bluestone, Barry, and Bennett Harrison, *The Deindustrialization of America* (New York: Basic Books, 1982).

1

be sure, the social sciences have a long-standing tradition of sophisticated computer analysis of large-scale data sets. More recently, social scientists have discovered a number of ways to use the new generation of micro-computers. Small personal computers are becoming indispensable com-panions for writers, researchers, and teachers. The range of applications includes word processing, data collection, instruction, information storage and retrieval, record keeping, and communication. Computers are now commonplace in social science work and it is clearly important to have some exposure to information technology.

SOCIAL SCIENCE COMPUTING TODAY

Word processing, analysis, information retrieval, and data base manage-ment are some contemporary social science computing applications. Public administrators wrestle with ever-present cycles of recession and inflation by computing budget and revenue projections for a variety of fiscal scenarios. School psychologists conduct sophisticated multivariate statistical analyses of students' standardized test scores. Social workers make use of data base management systems to maintain records on their clients and to monitor patterns of interagency referrals. Anthropologists in the field record notes on portable microcomputers. Survey researchers use random digit dialing software and computer-driven interviewer in-structions for telephone surveying. Urban planners use modeling systems to simulate transportation patterns and assess the impact of various land use alternatives. Economists use econometric packages to solve systems of simultaneous equations which model national and state economies.

These are a few computer applications employed routinely in the social sciences. But these kinds of applications are by no means restricted to those fields. Indeed, such analysis and computing skills are in demand in almost every employment setting and are increasingly useful at home. But the basic units of analysis in the social sciences (people) provide some special problems for researchers. Large numbers of subjects are re-quired if samples are to be representative of populations. U.S. Census data files, for example, sometimes contain millions of records. Social scientists thus must have access to large mainframe computers and are not likely to be able to do all of their research on microcomputers. With one or two notable exceptions discussed in Chapter 10, quantitative statistical analysis and management of large social science data sets are most reasonably done on mainframes. Still, it is certainly safe to say that the microprocessor revolution has already had a substantial impact on computing in the social sciences. Indeed, many of the applications suggested in this book are best carried out on microcomputers.

We find ourselves in something of a computing dilemma — although it is a potentially pleasant one. Although one or the other of these types of computer hardware may clearly be the optimal configuration for certain kinds of applications, the choice between large and small computers is not as straightforward as it might be. Nearly all social scientists in academic and research situations have access to mainframe computers, either locally or via telephone networks. But despite the recent proliferation of small machines, the same cannot be said for microcomputer availability. Any consideration of social science computing must discuss large and small devices and, when appropriate, users should be familiar with applications on both types of computers. A major goal of this book is to suggest criteria for choosing between microcomputers and mainframes for a particular application.

OUTLINE OF PRESENTATION

This introductory chapter is followed by chapters on computer hardware (Chapter 2) and software (Chapter 3). In these chapters, basic computing concepts important to the social sciences are identified and explained. In Chapter 2, the history of computing technology is briefly reviewed. Then, the characteristics of contemporary mainframes and microcomputers are discussed. In Chapter 3, various types and uses of software are identified. Special emphasis is placed on the concept of an integrated "package" of software routines, and major packages of use to the social sciences are discussed. Readers with little or no exposure to computing will want to review these chapters carefully since many of the concepts are employed in subsequent chapters.

Assuming a basic grasp of the material in Chapters 2 and 3, we turn to illustrations of social science computing applications in the remaining chapters (4–10). Chapter 4 introduces some of the basics of text editing which is used to prepare programs and text files. In Chapter 5, word processing strategies for preparation of manuscripts, theses, dissertations, and other documents are discussed.

Chapter 6 contains illustrations of nonanalytic social scientific computer applications. Computers are shown to facilitate the gathering of survey data, archival records, and small-group laboratory data. Chapter 6 also covers instructional applications and reviews a variety of online information services. Survey data have long been a mainstay of social science research. The ability to analyze and maintain survey data and other large files on computers has come to be a desirable and highly marketable skill. In Chapter 8, issues in the use and maintenance of machine-readable data sets are discussed, and archival sources for secondary data files are identified. Coding conventions and file structure options available to researchers are also noted.

Chapter 8 details strategies of mainframe statistical analysis. A number of approaches are evaluated in terms of their economy, convenience, and simplicity. Several sample programs and terminal sessions are illustrated. Chapter 9 deals with the computer-assisted maintenance of the large data sets used by social scientists. A modest amount of technical detail on storage media is introduced to aid readers in selecting appropriate storage devices for their data and the associated documentation. In Chapter 10, analysis on microcomputers is discussed. The hardware necessary for analysis is described and several software packages for microcomputer analysis are noted. Emphasis is placed in the chapter on the kinds of analysis that can be done reasonably on a microcomputer.

The core chapters of the book are followed by a number of appendices which provide information for implementing the mainframe analysis strategies detailed in Chapters 8 and 9. Of course, it cannot be guaranteed that the recommended procedures presented here will work in every installation. Instead, readers are provided with suggested analysis procedures which instructors can adapt to a particular mainframe. Ordinarily, readers will only be interested in the one appendix which applies to their installation. But it can be instructive to compare operating system statements from one major brand of computer to another. The recognition of similarity in operations is an important step toward a coherent approach to social science computing.

Throughout the chapters, illustrations and examples are liberally interspersed between explanatory text. For the most part, these illustrations rely on two widely available resources for social science research: the analytical software known as Statistical Package for the Social Sciences (SPSS), and, the machine-readable data files known as the National Opinion Research Center's (NORC) General Social Surveys.[3] Important computer jargon is introduced in boldface and the concepts appear again in the glossary for quick reference. From time to time, suggestions for further reading are provided as are recommendations for

---

3. See Nie, Norman, H., C. H. Hull, J. G. Jenkins, K. Steinbrenner, and D. H. Bent, *Statistical Package for the Social Sciences*, Second Edition (New York: McGraw-Hill, 1975); *SPSSX User's Guide* (New York: McGraw-Hill, 1983); and, Davis, James A., *General Social Surveys, 1972-1982* [machine-readable data file]. Principal Investigator, James A. Davis; Senior Study Director, Tom W. Smith. NORC ed. Chicago: National Opinion Research Center, producer, 1982; Storrs, CT: Roper Public Opinion Research Center, University of Connecticut, distributor. The NORC data used here were acquired through the Inter-university Consortium for Political and Social Research, University of Michigan.

hands-on computing exercises. Readers are strongly encouraged to attempt the exercises before moving on to the next chapter. These instructional aids are intended to systematize the acquisition of computing skills. The mastery of these skills in a coherent fashion can only enhance computing and, ultimately, research and scholarship in the social sciences.

SUGGESTED READINGS

1. The March 30, 1983, *Chronicle of Higher Education* was headlined "Colleges Struggling to Cope with the Computer Age." It contains several good articles on the status of computing at colleges and universities.
2. David Heise has edited a special issue of *Sociological Methods and Research* (May 1981) entitled "Microcomputers in Social Research." Although many of the articles in the issue are cited in the chapters that follow, readers will find the entire collection useful because the papers reflect the diversity of social scientific microcomputer applications.

CHAPTER TWO   Computer Hardware

Until microcomputers began appearing in store windows and became centers of activity in American homes, most people had never seen a computer. For years, television and motion picture scenes focused on tape drives and other auxiliary equipment which at least had flashing lights and moving parts. Even today, the machines constitute a real dilemma for those who would use them for dramatic effect. What could be less exciting than a blue, red, or gray metal box with a few wires here or there? Yet, who can deny the profound influence of these dull-looking boxes on our daily lives?

In this chapter, we will look inside computers and examine external devices often connected to them. At the outset, a brief historical sketch of the development of computer technology is presented. This is followed by an identification of the key components of a computer system. Then, the characteristics of contemporary large- and small-scale computer systems are described in detail. Finally, the promise of the next generation of computing equipment is discussed with emphasis on its implications for the social sciences.

THE DEVELOPMENT OF COMPUTER HARDWARE

By the middle of the nineteenth century, it became obvious that the human potential for rapid hand calculations had reached its limits. At the same time, industrializing societies had increasing requirements for record keeping and accounting. These demands led several inventors to begin experimenting with mechanical counting devices. The curious tabulating contraptions produced in the 1800s were early forerunners of modern computer **hardware**, or the machinery by which computing is accomplished.

The dilemma posed in the late 1880s by massive data collection and tabulation was keenly felt by the U.S. Bureau of the Census. The 1880 Census had been tabulated by hand over a seven-year period. Population increases since 1880 made it unlikely that the 1890 Census tabulation would be complete before the next census at the turn of the century. But a statistician at the Bureau named Herman Hollerith built a device that counted punched cards, and the 1890 Census was tabulated in only two years (Stern and Stern, 1983). Hollerith's coding system for punched cards is still used today, and the company he founded to market his invention was one of several which eventually merged to form IBM. Suffice it to say that important early impetus for automated data processing came from a social science community that already had enormous data sets and required special equipment for data processing.

During the first half of this century, analog computers were used extensively in science and industry. **Analog computers** analyze continuous streams of information such as that provided by a clock with hour, minute, and second hands. An alarm clock with hands is essentially an analog computer because it analyzes a data flow (time) and responds (rings) at an appropriate time. A more sophisticated analog computer is a device like a thermostat which monitors temperature and regulates the operation of a heating system.

In many applications, only segments of a data stream are available. A digital clock, for example, cannot display time in continuous motion; only a "slice" of information is provided. Still other phenomena are inherently discrete; that is, they take on only a few finite states rather than an entire range of conditions. This is especially common in the social sciences where theories specify qualitative variables such as gender (male

The Univac I computer

or female) or political party identification (Democrat, Republican, or Independent). Discrete data can be represented as digits or numerals and **digital computers** were invented to analyze such data. Although analog computers continue to be used for specific technical applications, general-purpose digital computers are more widely used and are the subject of most of the discussion in this book.

The origin of modern digital computer hardware can be traced to a series of developments during and after the second world war when experimental electronic computers were built in a handful of government and university laboratories. Between 1951 and 1958, the first generation of commercial computers was marketed, and the Bureau of the Census was the first organization to purchase such machines (Mandell, 1983). This first generation and later generations of hardware are differentiated by the devices used to control internal operations. The first machines were characterized by the **vacuum tubes** used to control them. To accommodate the unwieldy tubes, hardware cabinets were quite large. Even so, the heat generated by the vacuum tubes plagued the machines. These problems notwithstanding, the early computers proved so valuable that research and development on computer technology proceeded at a feverish pace.

Readers who remember televisions and radios with tubes no doubt also recall the technological revolution brought on by the introduction of transistorized circuitry. In much the same way as household appliances were miniaturized, so was computer hardware. Between 1959 and 1964, manufacturers introduced a second generation of computers internally controlled by **transistors**. These were smaller, faster, more reliable machines, priced to attract an even larger market than their predecessors. But second-generation hardware soon gave way to a third generation which employed **integrated circuits** in lieu of transistors. Appearing between 1965 and 1971, third-generation machines were controlled by tiny rectangular **silicon**

Vacuum tubes like those in early mainframes

Microprocessor built on a silicon chip

wafers or **chips** with dimensions as small as one-eighth of an inch. Hundreds of transistorized circuits were printed or etched onto a single chip. Hardware of this period again proved to be much smaller, faster, and more economical than machines of earlier generations.

By now it should come as no surprise that the third generation of computer hardware was short-lived. Further technological advances resulted in large-scale integrated (**LSI**) circuits which contained thousands of circuits on single silicon chips. Fourth-generation hardware began appearing in 1971, and most large computer installations today house such machines. A few fourth-generation machines have earned the label supercomputers because of their dramatically faster processing speed. **Supercomputer** architecture is based on even further miniaturization of circuitry known as very large scale integration (**VLSI**). These machines are especially valuable in high technology and scientific applications. However, earlier fourth-generation computers have all the ability and processing speed that most applications require, and several research universities report substantial amounts of unused capacity on recently acquired, expensive supercomputers (Magarrell, 1983).

Large fourth-generation machines are a mainstay of social science research. But the real revolution of LSI circuitry is evident in the recent proliferation of microcomputers. Third-generation machines were almost exclusively the property of corporations and other institutions.

In contrast, fourth generation computers are smaller, faster and—for the first time—priced well within the reach of professionals, small businesses, and consumers. It is far too early to assess the significance of fourth-generation computers in any conclusive fashion. Nevertheless, it is interesting to make an analogy to the transportation revolution of the late nineteenth and early twentieth centuries. As nineteenth century railroads provided industries and companies with cost-effective transportation, twentieth century automobiles provided an economical means of transportation for the general population. Fourth-generation computers have the potential for a parallel revolution in computing. Whereas large mainframe computers offer corporations and other institutions tremendous computing power, microcomputers offer everyone enormous potential for enhancing the completion of routine chores and creative tasks.

In view of the rapid technological changes of the 1950s and 1960s, it may seem unusual that a decade should pass without the proliferation of a fifth generation of hardware. The fifth generation is expected to be yet another radical departure in technology which will involve a blurring of the distinction between hardware and software. One important result will likely be artificial intelligence unlike any we have known (Markoff, 1983). The term **artificial intelligence (AI)** is usually reserved for applications that involve complex simulations of logical analysis such as a physician's diagnosis of a patient's malady or a mental health coun-

Supercomputer

selor's evaluation of a client's emotional problems. Experimental fifth-generation computers already have shown incredible capacities for problem-solving and generally emulating human thought and reasoning processes. But fifth-generation machines remain more on drawing boards than on computer center floors because of the severity of the recessions of the 1970s and the reluctance of Western societies (except Japan) to commit large amounts of resources to research and development. The prospects for fifth-generation equipment are discussed further in the concluding section of this chapter. In the section that immediately follows, the basic components of a computer are identified. Then, large and small fourth-generation systems used by social scientists are examined in detail.

THE INNER SANCTUM OF A
COMPUTER SYSTEM

When this writer was first introduced to computers, Professor Thomas Myers drew an analogy between a computer system and a stereo component system. Over the years, this analogy has been useful in explaining how a computer system is structured. A **configuration** refers to the pattern of interrelationships among parts in a system, and the configurations of stereo and computer systems are strikingly similar.

A stereo component system is made up of specialized parts, each of which serves a different function. Consider the model stereo system in Figure 2.1, where a turntable, tape deck, speakers, radio tuner, and amplifier are depicted. The turntable, tape deck, and tuner provide electronic signals which are transformed into sound by the amplifier and then reproduced through the speakers. Note the central role the amplifier plays in this stereo system: all of the other parts can be reached only by passing through the amplifier. Indeed, the other parts are of little value without being linked to the amplifier. Note also that some parts are only capable of reproducing the sound. The tape deck, however, can send electronic signals to the amplifier or receive and record the signals (note the connections pointing both ways in the figure).

A basic computer system is typically configured in much the same way. **Input** devices channel incoming information into the system and **output** devices receive outgoing information which has been processed by the system. Still other devices are capable of both input and output (**I/O**) functions. Like a stereo system, a computer system has a central component through which all other parts are interfaced. This key part is known as a **central processing unit** (**CPU**) and, although its technical functioning is not the same as a stereo amplifier, the symbolic role of the CPU in the

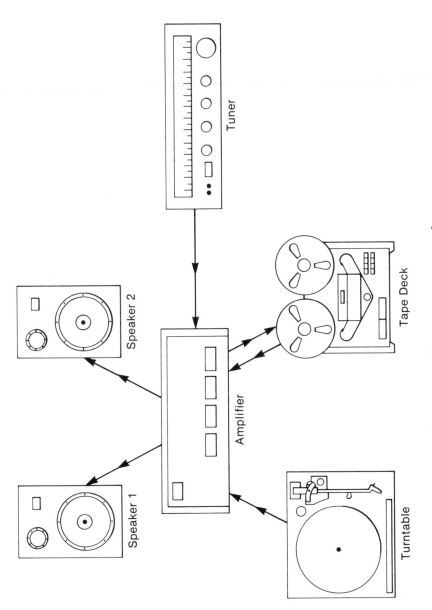

Fig. 2.1 Model Stereo Component System

Tuner

Speaker 2

Amplifier

Speaker 1

Tape Deck

Turntable

13

configuration is the same. The CPU houses a control unit which governs the operation of the system by synchronizing its components. The CPU includes an arithmetic and logic unit which does calculations and makes logical comparisons. It also houses a primary storage unit which stores data and instructions. Unlike the stylish cabinets of contemporary stereo amplifiers, all of this is contained inside the unimpressive metal boxes of a large computer.

But other computer hardware units have external appearances that are more interesting. Returning to our stereo analogy, recall that the components included a turntable, tuner, tape deck, and speakers. A computer system has a number of very similar I/O devices which are classified as **peripheral units** because they are free-standing accessories to the CPU. A **tape drive** works in much the same fashion as a reel-to-reel tape recorder. The user may record (**write**) or play back (**read**) something stored previously on magnetic tape. Another common device is a **disk drive** which does not look like a turntable, but operates in a similar manner. Like a phonograph record, a disk is a flat, circular medium consisting of concentric rings or **tracks** which contain data. The tracks are read (or written on) by an extending sensor which resembles the tonearm on a turntable. Some disk drives contain several disks that are stacked on top of each other resembling a stack of records on a turntable.

A speaker in a stereo system is strictly an output device. Similarly, a printer only produces outgoing computer information. Input-only devices for computers include **console keyboards** manned by operators and **optical character recognition devices** which read specially coded forms. By now the purpose of the stereo analogy should be clear. Both computer and stereo systems have central units and peripheral units, some of which are reserved for input or output and others which have I/O capabilities. Both large and small fourth-generation computers have many of these units configured in similar ways. The following sections contain detailed considerations of contemporary mainframe and microcomputer systems.

TODAY'S LARGE MAINFRAME

Social scientists ordinarily encounter large fourth-generation computers in institutional settings such as universities, government, or private industry. The computer (including the CPU) in such large-scale systems is referred to as a **mainframe**. Most mainframes are the anchors for **distributed data processing systems**. That is, they serve as centers of large computer networks which link central sites with numerous remote facilities and many individual users. In contrast, most microcomputers are single-user devices.

Fourth generation mainframe

The Central Site

The central site houses a CPU that is typically augmented with **auxiliary memory** devices as illustrated in Figure 2.2. These enhanced CPUs are capable of simultaneously handling many sets of instructions generated by large user communities. A number of peripheral devices including several disk and tape drives complete the central site configuration. A large installation can have many tape drives and may require a number of operators to mount tape reels according to instructions issued by the CPU. Whereas some disk drives contain permanent disk packs and need no operator intervention, others accept removable packs which must be mounted by operators. The operators oversee the system from a console which consists of one or more screens and typewriter-like keyboards for issuing commands.

High-speed **line printers** provide output printed a line at a time (as opposed to a character at a time). To save paper and reduce storage costs, very long output is sometimes reduced to microforms such as **microfiche** or **microfilm**. Other printing devices can provide higher quality printing. Such machines include graphic **plotters** for scientific figures and versatile **laser printers** for camera-ready copy. Still other peripheral units include high-speed **card readers** and **card punch devices**.

16

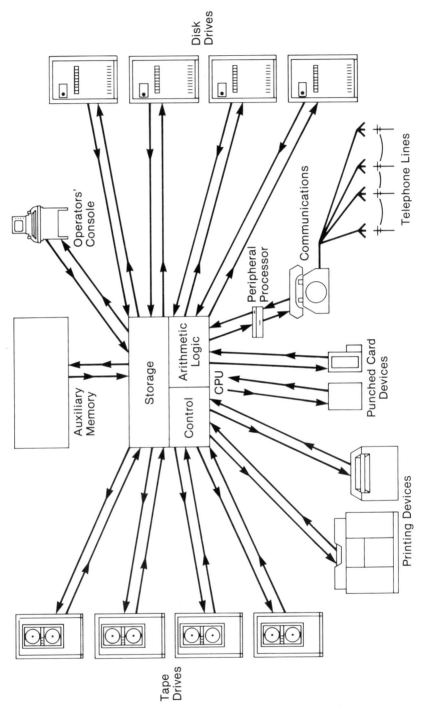

Fig. 2.2 Fourth-Generation Mainframe Configuration

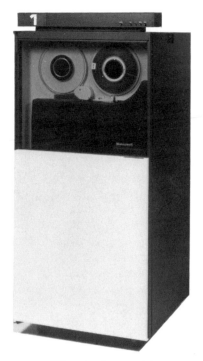

Nine-track tape drive

Mainframe disk drive

Although the large peripheral units are the most obvious "boxes" at a central site, other smaller devices enhance the functioning of the computer system. In some instances, small computers known as **peripheral processors** are used to facilitate the connection of peripherals with the mainframe. There may be hundreds of incoming telephone lines to provide access to users at remote sites across the street or many miles away, and sophisticated **communications equipment** is required to regulate this network.

And what of the human element required to keep the hardware functioning? Of course, operators are needed to monitor the system, mount tapes, and perform other routine tasks. But the important computer center personnel for most users are the consultants who aid users in accessing the computer and who provide advice on computing applications. Social science users can expect mixed results in working with these consultants. On the one hand, computer center employees are well versed in a system's particular characteristics and operations. On the other hand, it is less common that computer center personnel have much experience with social science applications. The best advice for novice users is to find those consultants (if any) who are designated as the computer center's social science contact persons.

Those involved in social science computing for years will recall many routine journeys to computer centers in the days before the telecommunications revolution. Now distributed systems are the rule, and most social science computing is done at remote sites which can be far removed from a central site.

The Remote Site

The most common piece of hardware at a remote site is a **terminal** which allows users to enter and receive information from the mainframe. Most terminals have typewriter-like keyboards which resemble the one in Figure 2.3. One important difference between a typewriter and a terminal keyboard console is the control key (**CTRL**), located in this case on the left end of the second row of keys. Like the shift key, holding the CTRL key down and hitting another key produces a result that differs from striking that key by itself. One common use of the CTRL key is in conjunction with the H key to produce a backspace. This allows the user to back up and type over the space(s) again with correct information. Note also the number keys to the right of the keyboard in Figure 2.3. This is called a **numeric pad** and is very useful when numerical data are being entered from a terminal. Some terminals also have **special function keys** which are used to issue specific system commands. Unfortunately no standard for terminal keyboards has emerged, and terminals differ with

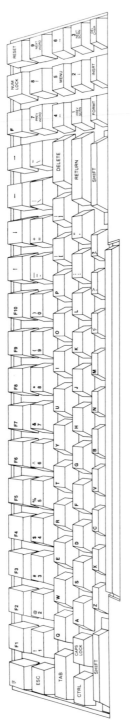

Fig. 2.3 Terminal Console Keyboard

respect to the placement of some keys and the presence of numeric pads and special function keys. If you have never learned to type, there is really no reason to despair. There are a number of tutorial software packages designed to teach people to type on terminal or microcomputer consoles.

One important distinction among terminals is how they display information received from the mainframe. Some terminals employ screens resembling televisions and are called cathode ray tubes (**CRT**) or video display terminals (**VDT**). Other terminals print information on paper and are referred to as **hardcopy** terminals. Some users prefer hardcopy terminals since they provide a complete record of the interaction with the computer. Others note that CRT terminals can be significantly faster in displaying information, and that they have fewer moving parts and are thus more reliable. A compromise approach involves a **slave printer** attached to a CRT. When printed output is needed, the printer is activated.

Remote sites may also house line printers which eliminate the need for trips to a central facility to pick up printed output. In such situations, users can elect to have their output routed to remote station printers or to central site printers. Another convenient device at a remote site is a small **floppy disk drive** which is connected to a mainframe. These disk drives accept **diskettes** from microcomputers and can provide for rapid data transfer between large and small machines. As will be noted in Chapter 10, the capacity to transfer data between mainframes and microcomputers is essential for routine analysis of social science data on microcomputers.

Telecommunications technology allows remote facilities to be connected to central installations. A **modem** is one important piece of hardware which facilitates telecommunications by connecting a terminal and computer via a telephone line. Several terminals can be connected to a mainframe over a single phone line with a device called a **multiplexer**. The speed at which these remote telecommunications between terminals and computers take place is referred to as a **BAUD** rate. A BAUD rate of 300 means that 30 characters per second are transmitted across the line. Where hardware will permit, rates of up to 9600 BAUD are used for video terminals. Still another option for terminal-computer interface is hardwiring which is a direct connection without the use of a phone line.

Mainframes in Perspective

In sum, large fourth-generation mainframes are typically configured in a distributed fashion. Computing can be so decentralized, in fact, that users never visit the central site. Such a computer system is actually a computing network which is limited only by the outreach of telephone lines. A number of manufacturers produce large fourth-generation systems, and examples include the IBM-370, CDC-CYBER, DECSYSTEM-10, and Burroughs Large Systems.

These large capacity mainframes are particularly well suited for the analysis and maintenance of large data sets typically used by social scientists. The massive central memory and auxiliary storage provided by a number of peripheral devices facilitate processing and statistical analysis of large files. The high speed at which input/output operations take place can rarely be duplicated by other kind of hardware. Moreover, the distributed configurations allow many users to do their work simultaneously. It would be inconvenient indeed if only one user could use the entire computer system.

One major disadvantage of fourth-generation mainframes is that they are difficult to use. In sharp contrast to user-friendly microcomputers, mainframes cannot be used by novices without some instruction or coaching. Another disadvantage of mainframes is that word processing is not generally cost-effective when compared to similar microcomputer applications. Further innovations in microcomputing may make other applications such as management and analysis of modest size data files less cost-effective on mainframes as well.

Promising microcomputer developments notwithstanding, large mainframes are here to stay. Many scientific applications including work with large data files cannot easily or efficiently be done on microcomputers. Also, social scientists in academic settings do more computing on mainframes because of a current shortage of microcomputers. Most of the applications illustrated in subsequent chapters can be carried out on fourth-generation mainframes as well as on microcomputers. It is imperative that social scientists be prepared to use both types of hardware.

TODAY'S MICROCOMPUTER

Perhaps the best way to introduce microcomputers is to refer again to the stereo analogy employed earlier in this chapter. Since a typical microcomputer configuration has only a few peripheral devices, the system diagrammed in Figure 2.1 is a better representation of a small-scale computer than a large one. Despite this numerical difference in external devices, there is a fundamental parallel between mainframe and microcomputer hardware in that both systems have CPUs and peripheral devices. Where the systems obviously differ is in capacity, size, cost, and the number of users that they can support. As employed in this book, the term **microcomputer** refers to small fourth-generation systems that can be used by no more than a few persons at any one time and that are quite inexpensive in comparison to large mainframes.

Desktop microcomputer

Bits, Bytes, and Chips

Like a mainframe, the heart of a microcomputer is a CPU. The micro-computer CPU, however, is typically a single LSI chip known as a **microprocessor**. One way to comprehend the diversity of microcom-puters available today is to classify them according to the type of microprocessor that they use (see Table 2.1). The basic units of computer memory are binary storage areas known as **bits**. In the tradition of main-frames, the first widely marketed microcomputers had microprocessors organized around sets of 8 bits called **bytes**. The 8-bit microprocessing chips can address up to approximately 64,000 bytes of memory (64k). Two families of microprocessors account for 95 percent of 8-bit com-puters: the Motorola 6500 and 6502 chips used by Apple, Commodore, and Atari; and, the Intel 8080 and Zilog Z80 chips used by Tandy (Radio Shack), Osborne, Kaypro, and many others (Osborne, 1982).

An important advance in microcomputer CPU technology involves the use of a 16-bit microprocessor such as the Intel 8086 or 8088. These chips can be significantly faster than their 8-bit counterparts and can address at least 1000K, or one **megabyte** of memory (Heywood, 1983). Probably the most successful machine to date with a 16-bit micro-

Table 2.1 Bit Architectures, Microprocessors, and Manufacturers

Architecture	Microprocessor	Microcomputer Manufacturer
8-bit	Motorola 6500, 6502	Apple, Commodore, Atari
	Intel 8080, 8085; Zilog Z80	Tandy (Radio Shack), Xerox, Osborne, Kaypro, Heath, Sanyo, Morrow
16-bit	Intel 8088	IBM, Compaq, Columbia, Corona, Eagle, Sanyo
"Super" 16- and 32-bit	Motorola M68000, Intel 80230, National 16032, Zilog Z8000	Apple, Hewlett-Packard

processor is the IBM Personal Computer. The introduction of 16-bit architecture has generated some technical controversy among microcomputer experts because the remainder of the circuitry has generally remained 8-bit in design. Later entries in the microprocessor market are now characterized as "super" 16-bit chips because the overall design takes more advantage of 16- and 32-bit technologies (Wong, 1983). The power of the 16-bit chips leads many observers to conclude that 16-bit processing will be the industry standard very soon. As Lemmons (1983) reports, there are now a number of IBM "clones" and other 16-bit machines vying for a share of the market.

Although each family of microprocessor chips requires its own specific instruction set, there is much potential for standardization among microcomputers. One example of standardization involves the 8-bit 8080 and Z80 processors which are used by many computer manufacturers (Osborne, 1982). Similarly, quite a few machines are built around the 8088 chip. Standardization is also enhanced by having **dual microprocessors** or **coprocessors** which means that a microcomputer is equipped with two or more different CPU chips. Such an arrangement allows the use of software developed for each of the microprocessors. The DEC Rainbow and the Zenith Z-100 are examples of microcomputers that have both 8-bit and 16-bit microprocessors. These hardware considerations aside, the potential standardization of microcomputers rests ultimately on common operating system software discussed in Chapter 3.

A Typical Configuration

Figure 2.4 illustrates a typical microcomputer configuration. The microprocessor is housed in a central unit and is linked to a low-profile, detached keyboard designed to reduce operator fatigue. The micro-

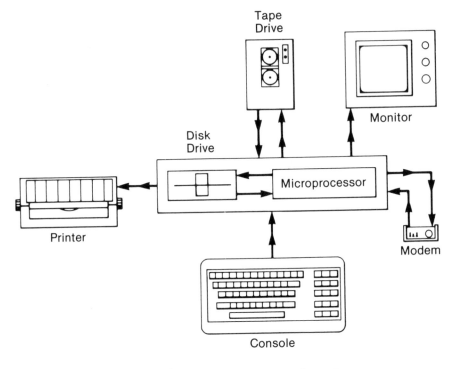

Fig. 2.4   Fourth-Generation Microcomputer Configuration

processor functions in much the same way as a mainframe CPU – storing programs and data, performing logical and arithmetic calculations, and governing the operation of the system. Output devices include a printer and a CRT monitor. I/O devices on microcomputer systems can include tape drives which use cassette tapes and disk drives which employ single diskettes sized at approximately 3, 5, or 8 inches in diameter. The modem illustrated in the figure is the same kind of communications device that interfaces terminals with mainframes. Other peripherals can be configured into an elaborate microcomputer system and these will be discussed in Chapter 10. On a substantially smaller scale, the peripheral devices function in a microcomputer system just as they do in large mainframe configurations.

Microcomputing in Perspective

These little machines have generated much excitement and optimism among computing enthusiasts in the social sciences. Many of the routine

Diskette and disk drive

applications that were once confined to mainframe systems are now carried out on microcomputers. Word processing, data collection, record keeping, bibliographic filing, and literature searches are in many cases more easily and economically done on microcomputers. Social scientists are also discovering the tremendous potential of communications. Microcomputers are communicating with other microcomputers, mainframes, word processors, electronic bulletin boards, and information retrieval systems.

Despite the advantages of this new generation of smaller hardware, it is not likely that social scientists will ever use microcomputers exclusively. Although the advertised costs of micro systems seem very inexpensive, the price of a system configured with a printer, two disk drives (one for reading while writing on the other), a modem, CRT monitor, and software remains substantial. It is conceivable that social science agencies, departments, and organizations can purchase a few of these systems, but hardly enough to satisfy the demand. Even when available, only sophisticated (and expensive) configurations allow more than one user to work at any given time. Finally, it should be reiterated that analysis of large social science data sets such as Census files containing hundreds of thousands of records is best done on large mainframes.

HARDWARE DEVELOPMENTS IN THE OFFING

If it is assumed that social scientists are likely to continue using mainframes and microcomputers, then it is important to consider the innovations in such hardware which are likely to be introduced in the next few years. Fifth-generation machines are expected to provide a tenfold improvement in computing speed and to be highly innovative in simulating human intelligence. Social scientists should certainly consider the social, economic, and political implications of the fifth-generation computer. For instance, what are the implications for world economic and political organization when a single country like Japan invests heavily in the development of fifth-generation computers? Will one country emerge as a clear leader in technology at the expense of others? Similarly, what will artificial intelligence mean for the way work is organized? Will automation make substantial inroads into professional and technical occupations as Markoff (1983) suggests? These are but a few of the interesting social issues involved in the introduction of fifth-generation computers.

Of course, improvements in microcomputer hardware are likely as well. Indeed, first-generation portable microcomputers are now typically referred to as **transportables** because of their weight and bulky size. Transportables are quickly giving way to the first **briefcase computers** which have many of the same features at a fraction of the older portables'

Transportable microcomputer

Briefcase microcomputer

size and weight. Likewise, enhancements in system memory and storage capacities are likely as 32-bit microprocessors become more commonplace and as mass storage technology is refined.

Perhaps the most interesting development in the near future will involve innovations in distributive configurations including both mainframes and microcomputers. Microcomputers double nicely as terminals for large mainframes. Indeed, the small computers are actually superior to common computer terminals because they can be programmed to send (**upload**) or receive (**download**) and store information from mainframes. Microcomputers with appropriate software are **intelligent** or smart terminals, capable of executing many instructions themselves. A distributive system with many smart terminals could prove to be very economical since much routine computing could be done by the terminal and only larger tasks referred to the mainframe. The necessary hardware exists and such configurations are clearly in the offing. The major task that remains is the modification of existing software; in this case, creation of operating systems that allow local or remote processing depending on the magnitude of the task. As the foregoing suggests, even the most advanced hardware is useless without operating instructions (software). Software of significance to social science computing is the topic of the next chapter.

SUGGESTED READINGS

1. Stern and Stern (1983) have written an excellent social history of the development of computer technology (see especially Chapter 2).
2. Persons contemplating a microcomputer purchase will want to read a regularly updated review of available hardware by Gregory Marks (1983) of the Inter-university Consortium for Political and Social Research, University of Michigan.
3. Which four universities had supercomputers and what were they doing with them in 1983? The answers can be found in Magarrell's (1983) survey of the prospects for supercomputers at U.S. colleges and universities.
4. A clear and brief comparison of 8- and 16-bit microprocessors has been written by Shea (1983).
5. Preliminary speculation on the social implications of the microcomputer revolution has been done by one of the industry's most quoted gurus, Adam Osborne. His *Running Wild: The Next Industrial Revolution* contains a number of predictions about social conditions in a microprocessor-oriented society. One social scientist who has made a similar assessment is Calhoun (1981). Among the possibilities he notes are growth in the number of persons working at home, elimination of jobs in labor intensive service industries, and important changes in educational technology.

SUGGESTED EXERCISES

1. Arrange a visit and tour of a nearby mainframe installation. Note the correspondence of the machine room configuration to that described here. Also, pay special attention to tape library rules and regulations, location of output bins, and whereabouts of consultants. Are there public terminals available around the clock? Users of a mainframe will want to be acquainted with all of these aspects of a central site.
2. Visit a computer store and study the various microcomputers on the market. Which microprocessors are used in which models? What are the options in central memory capacity? How inexpensively could you assemble a configuration like that in Figure 2.4?

CHAPTER THREE   Computer Software

Every computer application requires **software** which directs the computer hardware to carry out specified tasks. Computer software consists of **programs** or sets of instructions written in a variety of codes or languages. **Operating system** software exists primarily to coordinate and enhance the overall functioning of a computer system. **Programming languages** and other **applications software** give users access to the power of the computer. Operating systems, programming languages, and applications packages are discussed in the following sections. In the final section of the chapter, some major software packages with social science applications are identified.

OPERATING SYSTEMS

An operating system manages an entire computer system. Advances in operating system software have greatly reduced the amount of human intervention necessary to keep a computer system functioning in an optimal manner. The operating system distributes the resources of the system among the active programs and determines which instructions will be executed next. The operating system issues cues to peripheral devices at appropriate times when a program requires I/O devices. For example, an operating system instructs an operator to mount a tape and then controls the tape drive while the tape is in use. In addition, operating systems allow **multiprogramming** which means simultaneous execution of numerous programs. These features greatly enhance the efficiency of computing, and all computer users must learn something of their particular operating system. Like most computer applications, social science ones are initiated through interaction with an operating system. Although users may be unaware, this interaction with the operating system continues as applications software is used.

It is unfortunate that each company manufacturing large mainframes has developed its own operating system software for these purposes. Companies frequently market more than one operating system; some IBM facilities operate under OS/MVS, some CDC configurations use NOS, some UNIVAC systems use VS, and so on. Hence, working with the same brand of computer is no guarantee that this important systems software will be the same from one system to the next. In using different computer installations, social scientists (and anyone else for that matter) will likely find it necessary to acquaint themselves with different operating systems. Note that there is more to this lack of standardization than mere inconvenience. It means that certain data sets cannot easily be interchanged between computers. Fortunately there is some consistency in programming and other applications languages across most mainframes. Before turning to this software, some discussion of microcomputer operating systems is in order.

Since several manufacturers use the same microprocessors, some standardization of microcomputer operating systems has been apparent. The most successful compatibility efforts to date have centered on the 8080 and Z80 chips and the **CP/M** operating system. The increasing popularity of the 8088 microprocessor is creating a new *de facto* standard in microcomputer operating systems for IBM and compatible machines. These machines' operating systems (**MS-DOS** and related systems) are now commonplace. In contrast to the mainframe situation, user demand and market forces make it likely that operating systems used on one microcomputer will be encountered on other brands as well.

PROGRAMMING LANGUAGES

Machine and Assembly Languages

Programming software consists of a variety of languages, some of which are binary codes (patterns of zeros and ones) known as **machine language**. Machine language is the native code of digital computers, and programs written in binary code are the most versatile and powerful of program types. One level higher, **assembly language** contains some recognizable characters (other than ones and zeros) and even a few words. For a computer to execute an assembly language program, the code must be translated to machine language with another software program known as an **assembler**. Systems experts and professional programmers use machine and assembly languages for complex applications that require very precise control over memory locations. Since a great deal of technical expertise is required to use these **low-level** languages, most routine programming is done with **high-level** languages which are far removed from binary code. Thus the user can be less concerned with details of hardware operation and write programs in languages that are easier to learn.

High-level Languages

High-level languages include English-like statements that typically represent a series of computer instructions. To be run by a computer, the high-level program must be translated into machine language. Two types of software that do this translation are a **compiler** which translates the entire program and an **interpreter** which translates one instruction at a time (Cole, 1983).

Readers who want to learn a high-level language should try **BASIC** which is an acronym for Beginner's All-purpose Symbolic Instruction Code. An easy language to learn, some version of BASIC is found on most computers, and it can be used for any modest task. BASIC is somewhat similar to another language called **FORTRAN** which stands for Formula Translator. The oldest of the high-level languages, FORTRAN is best suited for scientific and mathematical problems. Although more difficult to learn than BASIC, FORTRAN is the choice of many technicians and experts in quantitative analysis and modeling.

Other high-level languages that social scientific users will encounter include COBOL, Pascal, PL/I, APL, and C. **COBOL** is an acronym for Common Business Oriented Language. As its name suggests, COBOL is primarily used in business applications such as maintaining inventories and accounting. **Pascal** is a relatively new language named after the French scientist Blaise Pascal who developed one of the first calculating devices in the seventeenth century. The Pascal language encourages a coherent structure in programs organized around versatile, inter-changeable components or modules. **PL/I** is a high-level language which combines the computational power of FORTRAN with the data management features of COBOL. **APL** stands for A Programming Language and it is intended for rapid calculations, turning the computer terminal with a special keyboard into a very high-powered calculator. **C** is a relatively new language that has much of the power of low-level code along with high-level language convenience. Many C programs are proving to be highly portable from one system to another.

Programming

Some simple principles are associated with the construction of high-level language programs. First, the instructions are executed one after another in what is called **sequential execution**. The computer does not skip statements or take them out of order unless specifically directed to do so. When instructions are executed in nonsequential fashion, it is typically because of **branching statements** which channel program execution in more than one direction. Branching is often accomplished by logical or arithmetic evaluation. That is, branching statements alter the sequential flow of instructions depending on a specified value checked by the computer. Program statements or sets of statements can be repeated any number of times with a **loop**. Looping causes the computer to re-execute commands inside the loop an appropriate number of times. A final aspect of a typical program involves **input** and **output** of data. If no provisions were made for retrieving the results of calculations, the use of the computer would be pointless. Likewise, if there were no way to get information to the program, the utility of the computer would be quite limited. Thus, programs are typically written to read data and write results.

Sample BASIC Program

At this point, a concrete example is overdue. A BASIC program is illustrated here which analyzes data on the annual earnings of 100 male and female labor force participants, chosen at random from the National Opinion Research Center's 1982 General Social Survey (Davis, 1982). The first ten lines of the file (named DATA) are listed in Figure 3.1. In the file, there are a pair of numbers on each line. The first entry represents the sex of the respondent and is coded zero for males and one for females. The second figure is the earnings of each individual expressed in dollars.

```
0, 3500
1,11250
1, 1500
1,13750
1,11250
1, 7500
1, 3500
0, 9000
0, 9000
0,13750
```

Fig. 3.1   First Ten Lines of Data File

A BASIC program which reads the data file is listed in Figure 3.2. The first line (10) opens the data file (The B:DATA means that the file resides on a disk drive designated as B.) Lines 20 and 30 initialize the variables SUMF and SUMM which will be used to sum women's and men's earnings, respectively. **Initialization** of a variable refers to the introduction (naming) of a variable and the assignment of an initial value (here the value is zero). Similarly, lines 40 and 50 initialize variables which will count the number of females and males.

Line 60 commences a loop (LOOP1) and indicates that the commands within the loop (through line 140) are to be executed 100 times — once for each person (or row) in the data file. The next line (70) reads the variables SEX and EARNINGS from DATA and thus serves as an input statement. Line 80 is a branching statement which sends cases with a sex code of

PROGRAM:

```
10  OPEN "I",#1,"B:DATA"
20  SUMF=0
30  SUMM=0
40  NFEMALE=0
50  NMALE=0
60  FOR LOOP1=1 TO 100
70     INPUT #1,SEX,EARNINGS
80     IF SEX=0 THEN GOTO 120
90         NFEMALE=NFEMALE+1
100        SUMF=SUMF=EARNINGS
110        GOTO 140
120      SUMM=SUMM+EARNINGS
130      NMALE=NMALE+1
140  NEXT LOOP1
150  CLOSE #1
160  MEANF=SUMF/NFEMALE
170  MEANM=SUMM/NMALE
180  PRINT"MEAN FOR FEMALES= $"MEANF
190  PRINT"MEAN FOR MALES= $"MEANM
200  END
```

Output:

```
MEAN FOR FEMALES= $ 11701.9
MEAN FOR MALES= $ 18296.9
```

Fig. 3.2 BASIC Program and Output

zero (males) directly to line 120. Those cases with values other than zero continue to line 90 where the count of females (NFEMALE) is incremented by one to indicate that another value of one has been encountered in the data file. Then, line 100 computes a running sum of females' earnings (SUMF). Next, line 110 routes female cases to the end of the loop (line 140) where the value of LOOP1 is augmented by one and the loop continues. The sums for males are computed on lines 120 and 130, and the next instruction in sequence returns to the starting point of the loop. After 100 such passes through the loop, line 160 is executed and the mean earnings for females (MEANF) is computed. Likewise, the male mean (MEANM) is computed on line 170. Finally, the two means are output on lines 180 and 190, and the program terminates at line 200. The actual output from the program is reproduced in the lower portion of Figure 3.2.

This is a simple example of a high-level language program. Instructions are executed sequentially unless a branch is encountered. Data are input and output, and arithmetic and logical statements are included. These same principles apply to most applications packages, although the packages are typically much more tolerant of our propensity to use English words and phrases.

APPLICATIONS PACKAGES

A **software package** is an integrated collection of general-purpose, high-level programs. Written in such a way that nonprogrammers can use them, these packages are mainstays of many computing applications, including those in the social sciences. Just as a high-level language statement substitutes for several machine language commands, an applications package instruction represents a number of high-level language statements. Consider the following program written for the software package SPSS:

```
DATA LIST       FIXED (1)/1 SEX 1 EARNINGS 3-7
VALUE LABELS    SEX (0) MALE (1) FEMALE
BREAKDOWN       TABLES=EARNINGS BY SEX/
```

These commands open the data file excerpted in Figure 3.1 and compute the descriptive statistics for males' and females' earnings shown in Figure 3.3. Thus, the 20-line, high-level language program in Figure 3.2 is replaced by a three-line package program which provides the user with considerably more information. To be sure, the package commands invoke lengthy, sophisticated FORTRAN program components or sub-

```
                                        84/01/12. 20.38.55. PAGE   2

FILE - NORC82    (CREATED - 84/01/12)

- - - D E S C R I P T I O N   O F   S U B P O P U L A T I O N S  - - -
CRITERION VARIABLE    EARNINGS
    BROKEN DOWN BY    SEX
- - - - - - - - - - - - - - - - - - - - - - - - - - - - - - - - - - -

    VARIABLE            CODE      MEAN    STD. DEV.     N VALUE LABEL

FOR ENTIRE POPULATION        14867.500  10208.647   100

SEX                    0    18296.875  10290.418    48 MALE
SEX                    1.   11701.923   9133.948    52 FEMALE

   TOTAL CASES =      100
```

Fig. 3.3   Sample of SPSS Breakdown Procedure

routines written by professional programmers. But the great advantage of the package is that novice users can avail themselves of the power of thousands of programmed code lines by issuing a few simple commands. Indeed, some refer to package syntax as **applications languages**, meaning that these languages are a step higher or even further removed from machine code than high-level languages.

Social science programming tasks in the early 1960s required different FORTRAN programs for each analysis. When one researcher would perfect a routine for say, a *t*-test, the analyst would swap it with colleagues for any programs they might have. Thus, the 1960s saw a proliferation of special-purpose programs, like the one in Figure 3.2, which were written by a number of persons. Each program required that a researcher learn a new syntax or customize the code.

Fortunately, several groups of researchers began putting together packages composed of several of the older, special-purpose routines. At that point, some coherence began to emerge as a common syntax was employed across the programs incorporated in a package. Data base management features were included and this gave the packages added advantages over single programs. By the early 1970s, social science researchers were enjoying the luxury of integrated statistical analysis packages which employed simple, English-like syntax and were capable of sophisticated statistical computations. The availability and ease of use of these packages attracted nonprogrammers as well, permanently altering routine methods of data analysis in the social sciences.

Much has happened, then, in the last twenty years of social science computing. Software packages are employed today in a variety of ways by social scientists. Mainframe analysis packages continue to be the primary vehicles for conducting sophisticated statistical computations. But microcomputer software packages are available which are capable of statistical analysis once reserved for mainframes. Data base management is a frequent need and several software packages provide excellent means for doing this. Still other types of software are used to facilitate word processing, data collection, record keeping, instruction, and simulations. In the final section of this chapter, some software packages of importance to the social sciences are identified.

PACKAGES WITH SOCIAL SCIENCE APPLICATIONS

Some common social science applications packages are mentioned in this section. The discussion is organized by type of application: statistical analysis, data base management, and word processing. Some illustrations of this software are included in subsequent chapters on word processing, analysis, and other applications.

Statistical Analysis

Several popular software packages are used routinely by social science researchers for statistical analysis on mainframes. The most widely known of these is the Statistical Package for the Social Sciences (**SPSS**) which was introduced in the mid 1960s at Stanford. Written in FOR-TRAN, SPSS is quite simple to use and can perform very powerful statistical computations. People from many disciplines other than the social sciences use SPSS, and it is frequently the most accessed package at a computer installation. Because versions of SPSS are available for nearly every major mainframe, this particular package will be illustrated at several points in this book.

Despite its success and general acceptance, SPSS has a number of competitors. The Statistical Analysis System (**SAS**) is used by a sizable segment of the social science research community. SAS is preferred by many because of its efficient statistical algorithms, variety of advanced multivariate procedures, and data manipulation facilities. Unfortunately, SAS is currently not available on all types of mainframes. The Biomedical Data Programs (**BMDP**) developed at UCLA are also used by some social scientists as is **OSIRIS**, a University of Michigan product. Other university products include Princeton's **P-STAT** and Pennsylvania's **Mini-Tab**. In Chapter 8, strategies of mainframe statistical analysis with these kinds of applications packages are discussed at length.

If microcomputers are limited in any way, it is in their *present* capacity to analyze and manage large social science data sets such as Census data or large survey files. But, where the units of analysis are not persons or where the number of individuals is small (i.e., a few hundred), a number of promising microcomputer analysis packages are now available. SPSS and BMDP are two mainframe package vendors who are marketing microcomputer versions of their products. Other firms have developed packages exclusively for the smaller machines and these packages include **ABC, ABSTAT, AIDA, DSSA, ELF, MATHSTAT, STATPAK, SYSTAT,** and **STATPRO**. Athough such software will be discussed at length in Chapter 10, it is important to note here that many of the microcomputer analysis packages run only on one or two brands of machines and no industry standards have emerged. Moreover, sophisticated analysis packages require a substantial investment in additional hardware (central memory and mass storage). Nevertheless, researchers with small- to medium-size files will find microcomputer analysis packages quite satisfactory for most purposes.

Data Base Management Systems

These applications packages have provisions for data base management such as updating, sorting, and modification of files. They are most useful on **relational** or **hierarchical** files where records are related to one another in some systematic fashion. For example, Census data on individuals are often organized by households which, in turn, are grouped in geographic units. On mainframes, very powerful data base management systems (**DBMS**) such as the Scientific Information Retrieval (**SIR**) system are available. Size problems inhibit microcomputer data base management of large social science data files. However, smaller files can easily be accommodated by software such as **Condor, dBase II, DataStar,** or **Personal Pearl**. Where the microcomputer data base managers may hold the most promise is in the organization and storage of qualitative data. These packages can greatly facilitate data entry and subsequent retrieval. They also can be used to produce impressive reports on the information contained in a data base. Researchers will find microcomputer data base managers useful for maintaining bibliographic data such as references and lists of citations. These and similar nonanalytic applications are discussed in Chapters 5 and 6.

Word Processing

Social scientists use computers for preparing manuscripts, reports, and other documents. Software packages such as **SCRIPT, SCRIPTSIT, RUNOFF,** and **PROSE** can be used to format previously entered text in an attractive manner. Most university computing centers support mainframe word processors, and graduate students preparing theses and dissertations have traditionally passed these skills on to succeeding generations of students. It is interesting to note that a number of schools now accept computer-printed copies of theses and dissertations. Several excellent software packages are marketed for word processing on microcomputers including **Final Word**, **Multimate**, and **WordStar** which is illustrated in Chapter 5.

Other Software

Social scientists have found still other ways to use computer software and some of these are illustrated in Chapter 6. Computers are assisting in the collection of telephone survey data by displaying questions for interviewers and recording respondents' answers as they are typed by the interviewer. These procedures completely circumvent the once tedious task of coding and cleaning survey data. Small-group laboratory experiments and simulations are being run by computer software which monitors subjects and records data as experiments progress. Still other software packages and services allow electronic mail to be sent and manuscripts to be exchanged over phone lines without postal delay. These various applications typically require that the user enter text into a computer and produce a final product according to prevailing conventions. This is done with text editing and word processing software packages, and these are the subjects of the next two chapters.

SUGGESTED READINGS

1. Jerry Pournelle's "The Micro Revolution" in the June 1984 *Popular Computing* is a candid and informative account of the development of microcomputer operating systems and the potential for standardization.
2. The September 1983 issue of *Popular Computing* is devoted to historical sketches and overviews of the major programming languages.

CHAPTER FOUR

Text Editing Concepts and Procedures

A **text editor** is a software package that allows the computer user to create and modify files. Text editors are used in many applications. One common strategy for statistical analysis involves the editing of a program file for a package such as SPSS. Word processing applications typically require the building of text files, and this can be done with text editors. Editors are also useful when original research data are entered for subsequent computer analysis. This range of applications places text editors among the most widely used software packages.

Text editors display information and operate on files in a number of ways. Some are **line-oriented editors** which access one line of information at a time according to commands issued by the user. To edit any given line, the user positions an invisible **pointer** at the line to be edited. **Full-screen** editors access as many lines as can be displayed on a CRT screen. These editors are controlled by commands or by moving a **cursor** about the screen. This latter feature is most convenient and is accomplished by certain keystrokes on a console or by rolling movements of a **mouse** attached by a cable to the keyboard. Basic line and screen editing procedures are discussed and illustrated in the following section.

EDITING PROCEDURES

Editors are used to build, display, modify, and store files, and these tasks are illustrated in the following sections. Emphasis is placed on fundamental text editing procedures without reference to any specific editor. Of course, readers will need to consult documentation for the editor they plan to use. In doing so, however, they will most likely find the generic editor illustrated here very similar to their editor. A few conventions are used in the figures which accompany the text in this chapter. Where appropriate, commands issued by the user are displayed in lowercase letters and responses by the editor are presented in uppercase. Also, the symbol < **cr**> indicates a carriage return.

Building Files

Entering Text and Commands.   All editors must have some way of distinguishing between information to be entered into a file and editor commands that modify the file. Some editors have **input** and **edit modes** which serve these purposes. When an editor is in input mode, everything typed on the keyboard becomes part of the data set. Under edit mode, the editor expects commands which include listing, modifying, or storing the file. One of the basic features of any editor is the invoking of input and edit modes. Sometimes this is done by merely hitting a carriage return as the first character of a line. **Modeless editors** preface commands with a special symbol such as @ or a designated keystroke such as the CNTL key. All text entered without one of these special signals is assumed to be

in this example of a modeless editor, a '@' distinguishes a command from input text

```
This  is  a  line  of  text
aThis  is  an  editor  command
This  is  another  line  of  text
```

here hitting the CNTL key and a T (^T as it is sometimes symbolized) is a command which deletes the word indicated by the cursor.

```
This  is  a  line  of  of  text

This  is  a  line  of  text
```

this is an example of a toggle into and out of input mode with carriage returns (indicated by <CR>)

```
INPUT
This  is  a  line  of  text<cr>
This  is  another  line<cr>
<cr>
EDIT
<cr>
INPUT
Text  entry  continues
```

Fig. 4.1   Ways of Distinguishing Commands from Input Text

input data. These various ways differentiating commands from input text are illustrated in Figure 4.1.

Word Wrapping.   Some editors include a feature known as word wrapping which is especially useful in word processing applications. Word wrapping eliminates the need for the typist to be concerned with exceeding the right-hand margin. If a word will not fit in the remaining space, it is automatically hyphenated or moved to the next line. Ordinarily, carriage returns are only used to indicate places where word wrapping is not appropriate such as the ends of paragraphs. Because the typist does not have to watch the screen as text is entered, word wrapping can increase typing speed substantially. In Figure 4.2, word wrapping eliminates the need for all but one carriage return.

Tabs.   Editors frequently make use of tabs like those on typewriters. A special function key is sometimes designated as a tab key, or an editor

```
I------------------------I
This is an example of
word wrapping.  Notice
that words which will not
fit on the remainder of a
line appear on the next
line.  Note also that the
only carriage return
entered is at the end of
this paragraph.<cr>
```

Fig. 4.2   Building Text with Word Wrapping

	INPUT

file built with semicolons indicating tabs to column 16	`run name;sample spss job<cr>`
	`get file;norcdata<cr>`
	`condescriptive;rincome,educ<cr>`
	`statistics;1,2,5<cr>`
	`<cr>`
	`EDIT`

when file is displayed in edit mode, effects of tabs are apparent	`RUN NAME       SAMPLE SPSS JOB`
	`GET FILE       NORCDATA`
	`CONDESCRIPTIVE RINCOME,EDUC`
	`STATISTICS     1,2,5`

Fig. 4.3   Building Text with Tabs

may reserve an input character as a tab indication. This latter feature is illustrated in Figure 4.3 where a file is built that contains an SPSS program. In input mode, the editor interprets semicolons (;) as tab commands, and the resulting file is structured accordingly.

Displaying and Locating Text

Once files have been created, text editors can be used to display file contents and to locate specific lines or sections. All or a portion of a file can be listed as illustrated in the upper panel of Figure 4.4. Full-screen editors often have a paging feature which displays as much of a file as will fit on a CRT screen. Such features typically involve special function keys or commands in edit mode. A single line or similar small segment of a file is easily located and displayed by a **search command** such as the one shown in Figure 4.4.

Modifying Text

Upon displaying and initially reviewing text, it is usually necessary to make some modifications to eliminate typing errors or make revisions. One major advantage of a text editor is that the edited file does not have to be retyped. Instead, the editor provides sets of commands that make it simple to alter the original text, insert additional text, and delete unwanted material. Such modifications rely on the user's positioning of a line pointer or screen cursor at the place in the file where a change is to be

beginning in edit mode, user   EDIT
instructs editor to list file   list
                                     RUN NAME   SAMPLE SPSS JOB
                                     GET FILE   NORCDATA
                                     CONDESCRIPTIVE   RINCOME,EDUC
                                     STATISTICS   1,2,5

from edit mode, user instructs   EDIT
editor to search for the first oc- find /get/
currence of the string of text   GET FILE   NORCDATA
indicated within the delimiters
(slashes)

Fig. 4.4   Displaying File Contents by Listing and Searching

in edit mode, user moves pointer	```EDIT```
to line needing correction by	```find /fiel/<cr>```
using search command; then	```GET FIEL NORCDATA```
change command is issued	```change /fiel/file/<cr>```
	```GET FILE NORCDATA```
cursor is moved with command	```GET FIEL NORCDATA```
keystrokes to location of typo;	
the correct letters are typed over	```GET FILL NORCDATA```
incorrect ones.	
	```GET FILE_ NORCDATA```

Fig. 4.5 Methods of Making Corrections

made. Figure 4.5 illustrates the correcting of a typo with an editor that employs a line pointer concept. Note that the editor **verifies** or redisplays the line, indicating the results of the modification. Figure 4.5 also shows a similar change with an editor that uses a cursor that can be located anywhere within a line.

Insertions made between lines are illustrated in Figure 4.6. In the figure, several lines of text are inserted between two existing lines. Insertions of text within a line are accomplished by the use of change commands. Deletions are accomplished in a similar manner either by deleting portions of lines or entire lines. In Figure 4.7, an entire line of text is deleted by moving the pointer to a line and then issuing a delete command. Two ways of deleting text within a line are shown in Figure 4.8. The first makes use of a search command to move a pointer and then a change command to alter the contents of a line. The second approach illustrates a special function key which deletes a character where the cursor is positioned.

Saving Edited Files

If edited files are to be reused, they must be saved as permanent files. To speed the editing process, text editors usually operate on files (or copies of them) which reside in central memory or RAM. The final edited product must be moved to disk for storage or the effort that has gone into constucting the file will be lost. An example of permanent file storage is provided in Figure 4.9. The save command(s) are among the most important instructions for any editor. In the event of a power outage or other problem, editing work done since the last save command is usually lost. Thus there is no substitute for frequent use of save commands while editing a file.

search command is used to position pointer at line below which insertion is to be made; insert command invokes input mode and insertion continues until input mode is terminated by <CR> on otherwise blank line; listing of file verifies that insertion has been made.

```
find /file/<cr>
GET FILE        NORCDATA
insert<cr>
INPUT
compute         college=educ<cr>
recode          college (0 thru 12=0)<cr>
                (13 thru 20=1)<cr>
var label       college college attendance (1=yes)/<cr>
<cr>
EDIT
list<cr>
RUN NAME        SAMPLE SPSS JOB
GET FILE        NORCDATA
COMPUTE         COLLEGE=EDUC
RECODE          COLLEGE(0 THRU 12=0)
                (13 THRU 20=1)
VAR LABEL       COLLEGE COLLEGE ATTENDANCE (1=YES)/
CONDESCRIPTIVE  RINCOME,EDUC
STATISTICS      1,2,5
```

Fig. 4.6 Insertion Between Existing Lines

in edit mode, line to be deleted is
located and deleted command
issued; line immediately above is
listed by editor to verify deletion.

```
EDIT
find /sta/<cr>
STATISTICS      1,2,5
delete<cr>
CONDESCRIPTIVE RINCOME,EDUC
```

Fig. 4.7   Deletion of Line of Text

in the examples below, both a
cursor and a pointer are used to
remove the ',5' from the
STATISTICS line of the SPSS
program.

```
STATISTICS      1,2,5
```

1. *Pointer moved to appropriate*
   line by search command;
   change command used to
   eliminate string of text (note
   the adjacent delimiters);
   change is verified.

```
EDIT
find /stat/<cr>
STATISTICS      1,2,5
change /,5//<cr>
STATISTICS      1,2
```

2. *Cursor is positioned where*
   deletion is to be made; special
   function key hit twice to
   delete ',5'.

```
STATISTICS      1,2,5

STATISTICS      1,25

STATISTICS      1,2_
```

Fig. 4.8   Inline Deletion of Text Strings

from edit mode, save command is
issued which causes the editor to
save the file under the name
given it at the beginning of the
editor session; editor verifies
save.

```
EDIT
save<cr>
SAVED

(edit session continues)
```

Fig. 4.9   Saving Edited File as Permanent File

These basic editing tasks—building, displaying, modifying, and saving—are common to virtually all editors. Many editors closely resemble the one illustrated here. Typically several editors are available for any particular computer. Some editors are capable not only of these basic tasks, but also more complicated functions which add considerably to the power of the software. The final section of this chapter is intended to be a guide in choosing a versatile text editor which accomplishes the basics as simply as possible and which is capable of sophisticated text and file manipulations.

CHECKLIST OF EDITOR FEATURES

It is rare that any editor will have all of the desirable features noted here. In choosing among available editors, it is best to weigh the convenience and versatility of a sophisticated editor against the additional time required to learn to use the advanced features. Almost any editor will suffice for computer applications of very short duration. The longer and more frequent the anticipated usage, the more useful a powerful and sophisticated editor will be.

Command Syntax Features

Abbreviation.   In repeated usage, the ability to abbreviate commands saves time and lowers the probability of syntax errors.

Examples

```
C = Change
S = Save
D = Delete
```

Consistency.   Various editor commands should have a consistent syntax.

Examples

```
LIST,1,10        (lists first through tenth lines)
DELETE,1,10    (deletes first through tenth lines)
```

Edit-Input Transition.   The transition between edit and input functions should be as simple as possible (preferably a single keystroke).

Examples

```
@CHANGE      (a command)
CHANGE        (input text)
```

Concatenation of Commands.   Issuing multiple commands on the same line can expedite the editing process by reducing the number of prompts supplied by the editor and reducing the frequency of responses required on the part of the user.

Examples

`EDIT`	(save command issued by user)
`save`	(editor reports that file has been saved)
`SAVED`	(user terminates edit session)
`end`	(editor confirms end of edit)
`END`	(operating system ready for further commands)
`READY`	

`EDIT`	(user concatenates save and end commands)
`end save`	
`SAVED`	(editor saves and terminates edit session)
`END`	(operating system ready for further commands)
`READY`	

Optional Verification. The user should be able to activate and deactivate the verification feature at his or her discretion.

Examples

`VERIFY ON`	(user requests verification)
`VERIFY OFF`	(user does not desire verification)

Repetition and Looping. Commands should affect many or all lines of text.

Example

`change /old/new/1,*,g`   (changes all 'old' to 'new' from first through last line of file as indicated by '*'; 'g' indicates global change meaning every occurrence in every line—not just the first occurrence in each line)

Similarly, there should be ways to execute sets of editor commands. Many editors have looping features which allow programs of editor commands or **macros** to be executed repetitively.

Access to Other Command Systems. The ability to communicate with the operating system during an edit session can be useful. Such a feature aids the user who is carrying out multiple tasks on a computer system.

Example

```
EDIT                    (while editing, user queries operating system about
status                  status of other jobs belonging to user in system)
NO JOBS FOUND
EDIT
```

Wildcard Characters. It is convenient to be able to enter wildcard characters in search and change operations.

Example

```
find /chapter #/1,*     (searches entire file for the word
CHAPTER 1               CHAPTER, a blank space, and any
CHAPTER 2               character and finds three such text
CHAPTER 3               strings; in the example, the '#' is the
EDIT                    wildcard character)
```

Undo Command. Another useful command is an undo feature which returns the text to its status immediately prior to the last command issued.

Example

```
EDIT
change /old/new/        ('old' is 'changed' to new)
THIS IS THE NEW TEXT.   (editor verifies change in sentence)
undo                    (user decides to undo change)
THIS IS THE OLD TEXT.   (editor verifies return to old text)
```

File Manipulation Features

Merging. Merging is a useful feature which allows two or more files to be joined together. While editing a file, the user instructs the editor to add the contents of another file at the position of the cursor or pointer.

Example

```
EDIT                    (files named a1 and a2 are
merge,a1,a2             added to the file being edited)
MERGE COMPLETE
```

Copying. Copying allows the user to reproduce some portion of a file elsewhere in the same file.

Example

```
EDIT
list                   (file is listed and it contains three lines)
THIS IS LINE 1
THIS IS LINE 2
THIS IS LINE 3
copy,1,3,4             (first three lines are copied to line 4)
list
THIS IS LINE 1
THIS IS LINE 2
THIS IS LINE 3
THIS IS LINE 1         (the result is a copy of lines 1-3 at lines 4-6)
THIS IS LINE 2
THIS IS LINE 3
```

Block Moves. Sometimes called "cutting and pasting" commands, block moves reorganize files by rearranging portions or blocks of text. As the examples indicate, line-oriented editors move lines and some cursor-oriented editors move blocks of text that may or may not be entire lines.

Examples

```
Edit                        (a block of lines is moved
list                        with a line-oriented editor;
THIS IS PARAGRAPH ONE.      move command moves lines
IT IS ONLY TWO LINES        1-3 to lines 4-6)
LONG.
THIS IS PARAGRAPH TWO.
IT IS ALSO ONLY TWO
LINES LONG.
move,1,3,4                  (moves lines 1-3 to line 4 and
list                        adjusts of other lines)
THIS IS PARAGRAPH TWO.
IT IS ALSO ONLY TWO
LINES LONG.
THIS IS PARAGRAPH ONE.
IT IS ONLY TWO LINES
LONG.
```

```
This is line 1.  This          (file is listed with cursor-
is line 2.  This is line        oriented editor)
3.  This is line 4._
```

```
This is line 1.  <B>This        (now, block to be moved is
is line 2.<B>  This is line     marked with special func-
3.  This is line 4._            tion key; cursor is posi-
                                tioned where block will go)
```

```
This is line 1. This is        (move block command results
line 3.  This is line 4.        in line being moved to end of
This is line 2.                 file)
```

Versatile commands such as these facilitate text editing. Editing is one of the most fundamental computing skills and is required for many applications. Not the least of these applications is the use of text editors to create files for word processing. The software that transforms edited files into polished, printed documents is the subject of the next chapter.

SUGGESTED EXERCISES

1. Before getting on the computer:
   a. Consider text editors available to you in terms of the checklist of features in Chapter 4. Compare the editors' syntax and advanced features. In view of applications you are likely to undertake, which editor is the optimal choice?
   b. Study available documentation for the editor you plan to use. How are the four basic editing tasks (text building, displaying, modifying, saving) accomplished? Experiment with the syntax by forming commands to carry out these basic functions.
2. On the computer:
   a. Practice using a text editor by making an exact copy of a long paragraph from a book. Continue to modify the file until it is an exact replica of the original. In doing so, you will be forced to use most, if not all, of the basic editing functions.
   b. Save the paragraph as a permanent file. It will be useful for exercises in conjunction with the next chapter on word processing.

CHAPTER FIVE   Word Processing

In their early days, computers proved so valuable in data processing that their designers quickly began to consider processing words and text as well as numbers. The resulting word processing technology is now common-place in the social sciences and nearly every other field. Word processing is accomplished on microcomputers, mainframes, and **dedicated word processors** (which turn out to be well-disguised computers).

Word processing can be defined as the manipulation of words with computers to produce neatly organized textual output. Two related procedures are involved: text editing and text formatting. As discussed in Chapter 3, the welcome advantage of text editing is that original text is typed only once. Corrections and revisions do not mean that a document has to be retyped. **Text formatting** is the arrangement of edited text according to user-supplied criteria such as margins and numbers of lines per page. Once text has been formatted with word processing software, it is ready to be printed according to conventions for finished copy chosen by the writer.

In some applications, text formatting is a distinct, second phase of word processing. **Text formatting software** is used to format files that have been created previously with a text editor. Other word processing applications combine text entry and formatting into a single step. These **integrated word processing packages** are sometimes referred to as "what you see is what you get" word processors because the text displayed on the screen has already been formatted to a certain extent. Contemporary word processing technology has eliminated much of the burdensome work associated with producing printed material. With this barrier removed, writing specialists have found that people write more and revise more often (Hennings, 1981; Bradley, 1982; Watt, 1984).

This chapter on word processing begins with a discussion of recent software innovations such as spellers and electronic thesauruses which facilitate writing and composing. Next, the text formatting process is described in detail. The discussion of formatting is followed by illustrations of a text formatter and an integrated word processing package. Options for printing are considered in the next section. Finally, the inclusion of quantitative data summaries in written reports is discussed.

SOFTWARE AIDS FOR WRITERS

Recently, a new generation of software products has appeared which assists in the text production process. These packages include spelling checkers that search for misspelled words, electronic thesauruses that provide lists of synonyms for specified words, grammar checkers that search for questionable or incorrect grammar, and electronic notecard files that serve the same reference and bibliographic functions as files of 4 × 6 cards did in the past. A brief discussion of each of these writers' aids follows.

Spelling Checkers

Spelling checkers typically work by comparing every word in a text file against a dictionary of correct words (Jones, 1984). The user's attention is directed to any word that cannot be found in the dictionary on the chance that it is misspelled. Given this mode of operation, it follows that the larger the dictionary, the more useful the spelling checker. A dictionary in excess of 50,000 words is a reasonable minimum for academic writers. Some packages allow secondary dictionaries which contain words added by the user. This is a must in fields such as the social sciences where technical terms and jargon are frequently employed. Jones (1984) argues for a method of identifying and correcting misspellings which is done automatically by the package under the user's guidance. Some spelling checkers merely flag suspect words and require the user to re-edit the file manually and make corrections.

Electronic Thesauruses

Writers always struggle to find appropriate substitutes for frequently used terms, and thesauruses have proved invaluable over the years. Now, the same help is available with software packages that are essentially electronic thesauruses. In a recent issue of *The Atlantic*, writer James Fallows described his use of such a package:

> With this program, you can pause at any point while working on a text, select one word, push a certain button twice, and in a little more than one second, a list of possible synonyms appears at the top of the screen. It is so easy to use that I find myself using it all the time. Most often it convinces me that I had the right word to begin with. But at other times it has helped me find the *mot juste* that I knew was just out there but that I could not recall. (Fallows, 1983:107)

As convenient as an electronic thesaurus may be, it is important that the overall text entry process not be disrupted or—worse—temporarily terminated. It is one thing to have suggested synonyms displayed in a matter of seconds. It is something else altogether to terminate an edit session, run a separate program, and then initiate yet another edit session to replace words with synonyms. For this reason, Jones (1984) recommends using a thesaurus which can be integrated with existing word processing software.

Grammar Checkers

Grammar checkers search for common errors such as suspect punctuation, subject-verb agreement, consistency in tenses, and sexist language. Some packages can be instructed to search for frequently used words and phrases and substitute equivalent wording. The most important difference among these packages is—once again—the extent to which the checking process is integrated into text entry and other word processing procedures. Grammar checkers that must be run separately may be so inconvenient that users forgo them to save time and effort.

Electronic Card Files

Most of us learned to write term papers and manuscripts by assembling notecard files that serve as data bases for organizing material found in the library. These card files contain the information on which manuscripts are based and detail the sources for that material. Of course, the latter information includes items such as authors, journals, and publishers and appears in bibliographies constructed according to prevailing conventions.

Electronic card files automate the process of storing, retrieving, and documenting such information. Some packages can be programmed to search manuscripts for citations and assemble bibliographies tailored to specifications of professional journals. Scholars can revise the electronic files over time by adding newly published material to their existing file. Note that these card file packages are a special case of the general concept of a data base management system. As such, general-purpose data base systems should also be adequate as electronic card files.

These writers' aids are early entrants into a growing market of products that can enhance writing. Watt (1984) discusses some experimental software which promises further sophistication and convenience. Once text files have been checked and proofed by writing enhancement software, the files are ready for formatting and printing. Aspects of the formatting process are discussed in the following section.

THE TEXT FORMATTING PROCESS

The simplest way to convey what is meant by text formatting is to provide an example. Consider the text in the upper panel of Figure 5.1 which is not formatted. Note that the lines are of various lengths and that much

```
The simplest way to convey what is meant
by text formatting is to provide an example.  Consider the
text in the upper
panel of Figure 5.1 which is not
formatted.
Notice that the lines are of various lengths and
that a good deal of space has been
wasted on several
lines.  In contrast, the text in the lower panel of
Figure 5.1 is formatted.  It is readily apparent that the line
structure has been reorganized
quite a bit.  After further revisions, the text
can easily be reformatted to
adjust for any subsequent insertions or deletions
that may be necessary.
```

```
The   simplest way to convey what is meant by   text
formatting is to provide an example.  Consider the
text in the upper panel of Figure 5.1 which is not
formatted.    Notice    that  the lines are of various
lengths   and   that a good deal of space  has  been
wasted on several lines.  In contrast, the text in
the lower panel of Figure 5.1 is formatted.  It is
readily   apparent that the line structure has been
reorganized quite a bit.  After further revisions,
the   text can easily be reformatted to adjust   for
any  subsequent  insertions or deletions that may be
necessary.
```

Fig. 5.1   Unformatted and Formatted Text

```
The   simplest way to convey what is meant by   text
formatting is to provide an example.  Consider the
text in the upper panel of Figure 5.1 which is not
formatted.     Notice   that the lines are of various
lengths   and   that a good deal of space   has   been
wasted on several lines.  In contrast, the text in
the lower panel of Figure 5.1 is formatted.   It is
readily   apparent that the line structure has been
reorganized   quite a bit.    The text   now   appears
neatly aligned within the margins.  After further revisions,
the   text can easily be reformatted to adjust   for
any subsequent insertions or deletions that may be
necessary.
```

```
The   simplest way to convey what is meant by   text
formatting is to provide an example.  Consider the
text in the upper panel of Figure 5.1 which is not
formatted.     Notice   that the lines are of various
lengths   and   that a good deal of space   has   been
wasted on several lines.  In contrast, the text in
the lower panel of Figure 5.1 is formatted.   It is
readily apparent that the line structure has   been
reorganized   quite   a bit.    The text now   appears
neatly aligned within the margins.   After further
revisions,   the text can easily be reformatted   to
adjust   for any subsequent insertions or deletions
that may be necessary.
```

Fig. 5.2   Insertion and Reformatting of Text

space has been wasted on a couple of lines. In contrast, the text in the lower panel of Figure 5.1 is formatted. It is readily apparent that the line structure has been reorganized quite a bit. The text now appears neatly aligned within the margins. After further revisions, the text can easily be reformatted to adjust for any subsequent insertions or deletions that may be necessary.

In the upper part of Figure 5.2, the text has been changed by adding a long phrase. Since the text is no longer properly aligned, it is reformatted and the results displayed in the lower portion of the figure. The luxury of word processing software is that text formatting can be invoked with only a few keystrokes or commands (sometimes only one). The number and extent of revisions is limited only by the user's perseverance. A number of options are to be considered in text formatting, and these are detailed in the following.

Margins and Justification

The user can specify the upper, lower, right, and left margins within which text will be set. Most word processing packages have convenient standard settings (**defaults**) which correspond to conventional typewritten pages and will suffice for most manuscripts and documents. **Justification** refers to the alignment of text at the right and left margins. Nearly all textual material begins at the same left-hand margin and is said to be **left-justified**. As is evident in the lower panels of Figures 5.1 and 5.2, word processing software offers the user the option of also having the text **right-justified** as well, producing exact alignment on both sides.

Hyphenation

Hyphenation is a standard feature of many word processing packages. Dividing words enhances the product of the formatting process by allowing more text to be placed on a single line. This is especially useful when justified text is desired because the number of midline blanks is minimized. In the upper portion of Figure 5.3, note the gaps between words

```
Hyphenation   is a standard feature of many   word
processing  packages.    Dividing  words   enhances
the    product   of   the   formatting   process    by
allowing   more   text to be placed   on   a   single
line.    This  is  especially useful when justified
text   is   desired because the number of   midline
blanks   is  minimized.    In  the  upper  portion   of
Figure   5.3,   note   the gaps between   the   words
which   are necessary in order to align the   text
at  the  right margin.    With a hyphenation option
invoked,  however,  the  text can be formatted more
neatly   as  indicated in the lower panel of   that
figure.
```

```
Hyphenation   is a standard feature of many   word
processing   packages.    Dividing words   enhances
the   product of the formatting process by allow-
ing   more   text to be placed on a   single   line.
This is especially useful when justified text is
desired because the number of midline blanks   is
minimized.    In  the  upper  portion of Figure 5.3,
note  the gaps between the words which are neces-
sary   in   order  to align the text  at   the   right
margin.    With   a  hyphenation   option   invoked,
however,   the   text  can be formatted more neatly
as  indicated in the lower panel of that figure.
```

Fig. 5.3   Nonhyphenated and Hyphenated Text

which are necessary to align the text at the right margin. With an hyphenation option invoked, however, the text can be formatted more neatly as indicated in the lower panel of that figure. Some word processing packages hyphenate automatically, but users may prefer to oversee the hyphenation process so that words are divided only at appropriate intervals. Some packages employ a **soft hyphen** at the ends of lines. This means that the hyphen will only appear in the final printed product only if the divided word remains at the end of a line after all subsequent revisions.

Paging

Word processing packages typically adhere to established conventions for typewritten documents including numbers of lines per page and vertical widths of headings and footings. The default settings assume 66 lines per page, with top and bottom margins of six blank lines each. Lines can be single or double spaced depending on the desired final format of the document. At the user's option, page numbers calculated by the computer can be inserted at the top or the bottom. Full-feature word processing packages support **conditional paging** which means that a designated block of text is put on a page only if the entire block will fit on the remainder of a page. Text formatting can also observe the conventions which hold that new paragraphs should not begin at the bottoms of pages and that last lines of paragraphs should not be carried over to a new page. This type of formatting option is known as **widowing**.

Headings

Headings include titles, subtitles, subheadings, and the like. Some formatting packages construct headings according to academic conventions. For example, the IBM mainframe package Waterloo SCRIPT can be instructed to produce headings and subheadings according to the *Publication Manual of the American Psychological Association* (1974). That is, manuscript and chapter titles are centered on a new page in uppercase letters. Section titles are centered and underscored, whereas headings within sections are underscored and presented at the left margin. This and other features of Waterloo SCRIPT will be demonstrated later in this chapter.

Indexing

One of the least enjoyable tasks in writing a book is compiling an index. This typically involves identifying key concepts, names, and topics, and then noting every reference to them in the text. This very laborious chore once required large stacks of index cards with many handwritten entries on each card. Fortunately the new word processing technology has eliminated much of the human effort required to prepare an index. Sophisticated word processing packages have simple methods for identifying key words and, once these designations are made, an index is assembled automatically.

Tables of Contents

In much the same way as an index is created, a table of contents can be prepared for longer documents such as books, dissertations, or theses. Instead of searching for key words, a contents program notes the page numbers associated with chapter titles, section headings, and subheadings. The table of contents is produced in a matter of a second or two instead of an hour or two by hand. Moreover, subsequent versions of tables of contents can easily be produced as editing and revisions continue.

Multiple Columns

There are few restrictions on the formatting process. Some word processing software can produce multiple columns like those found in newspapers and magazines. Although such formatting is usually not required for documents in the social sciences, the multiple column capacity serves as yet another indication of the power of word processing.

Print Control Commands

Most word processing packages have provisions for identifying text that is to be printed in some special format. This designation is usually done by embedding print control commands in the text. These commands affect the formatting and printing process but do not appear in the printed output. Desirable print controls include underscoring, subscripting, superscripting, and boldface printing. Some of the word processing packages recently introduced for the new generation of 16-bit microcomputers take control of printing a step further by displaying the effects of such commands on the monitor screen as the command is issued.

Automatic Footnoting

Yet another luxury of a sophisticated word processing package is automatic footnoting. Footnotes are input at any point in the text and they are inserted at the bottom of the appropriate pages during the formatting process.

Proportional Spacing

Proportional spacing refers to printed text in which the characters take up differing amounts of horizontal space on a line. For example, the thin letter "i" would be allocated less space than the wider letter "m". When used in conjunction with justification, proportional spacing makes occasional embedded blanks in lines unnecessary. The final printed product resembles professional typesetting.

Boilerplate Documents

Letters, contracts, and other documents can be personalized by the use of boilerplate word processing features which insert material from other files at appropriate locations. After the inserting, the text is reformatted to adjust for variable widths of inserted material. Some packages can handle quite complex sets of instructions to insert not only names, addresses, and other relevant information, but also optional phrases or paragraphs.

In the sections that follow, text formatting packages and integrated word processing software are illustrated which have many of these features.

TEXT FORMATTING SOFTWARE

Once a file has been edited, a formatting package is used to read the original text file and write a new, formatted file. The formatted output file can then be viewed at a terminal and printed if the finished product appears satisfactory. Ordinarily another round of revisions will be necessary, and it is then that the luxury of word processing becomes apparent. The user simply makes the necessary changes on the original text file and uses the word processing software to create yet another formatted file. The revision process continues until a final version has been produced.

The key to such word processing is formatting software and the quality and capacity of these packages vary widely. Among the packages are SCRIPT, SCRIPTSIT, FORMAT, RUNOFF, and PROSE. Not all formatting packages have the desirable features noted earlier. Hyphenation can be cumbersome, and facilities for larger documents such as indexing and tables of contents are not always supported. Those planning to process large documents such as manuals, theses, and dissertations will want to use formatting packages that include any advanced features that may be required. In the next section, one package with several advanced features is illustrated.

Formatting Illustration

Waterloo SCRIPT is a sophisticated word processing software package that operates on IBM mainframes. Although a thorough illustration is beyond the scope of this book, a few of SCRIPT's features are described here. As was noted, an initial step is required in which a text file is edited. Such a text file is depicted in Figure 5.4 along with line numbers provided by the editor. The entries in the file prefaced by colons control the formatting process.

The results of formatting with SCRIPT appear in Figure 5.5. By comparing the unformatted version in Figure 5.4 with the formatted text in Figure 5.5, the reader can see how the embedded commands affected the formatting process. The formatting was controlled by SCRIPT's Generalized Markup Language (GML). The APA4 version of GML is a set of document characteristics (i.e., chapter titles, subheadings, and the like) specifically for academic manuscripts (APA stands for American Psychological Association).

Text formatting packages can obviously be extremely valuable in word processing. But there is also much to be said for integrated word processing packages which combine the text editing and formatting steps into a more unitary process.

```
00010 :H1.word processing with SCRIPT
00020 :H2.About Waterloo SCRIPT
00030 :P.Waterloo SCRIPT was written at the University of Waterloo, Ontario.
00040 It is the most versatile mainframe
00050 word processing package I have ever used.
00060 SCRIPT incorporates some of the desired features indicated above plus
00070 others too numerous to mention.
00080 This package will greatly facilitate the handling of any large
00090 document.
00100 :H2.Tips on Keying-In Text for Processing
00110 :P.Remember, the format of the original text has nothing to do
00120 with the appearance of the final product.
00130 In fact, it is recommended that sentences be kept as separate lines
00140 so that revisions will be easier.
00150 Notice also that the editor QED is providing line numbers.
00160 These expedite editing and they will be stripped from the file before
00170 it is formatted.  As always,
00180 it is wise to save frequently so that all entered text will be preserved.
00190 :H2.Running SCRIPT
00200 After the text has been prepared, corrected, and revised, SCRIPT is
00210 used to format the file.
00220 The original file is read and a formatted version is written to a new
00230 output file. This leaves the original file intact for subsequent revision.
```

Fig. 5.4   Unformatted Text

WORD PROCESSING WITH SCRIPT

About Waterloo SCRIPT

Waterloo SCRIPT was written at the University of Waterloo, Ontario. It is the most versatile mainframe word processing package I have ever used. SCRIPT incorporates some of the desired features indicated above plus others too numerous to mention. This package will greatly facilitate the handling of any large document.

Tips on Keying-In Text for Processing

Remember, the format of the original text has nothing to do with the appearance of the final product. In fact, it is recommended that sentences be kept as separate lines so that revisions will be easier. Notice also that the editor QED is providing line numbers. These expedite editing and they will be stripped from the file before it is formatted. As always, it is wise to save frequently so that all entered text will be preserved.

Running SCRIPT

After the text has been prepared, corrected, and revised, SCRIPT is used to format the file. The original file is read and a formatted version is written to a new output file. This leaves the original file intact for subsequent revision.

Produced with the **Generalized Markup layout GMLAPA4** by Waterloo SCRIPT - Version 84.0 (84FEB1).

Fig. 5.5   Text Formatted with Waterloo SCRIPT

INTEGRATED WORD PROCESSING SOFTWARE

The sequence of steps involved in the use of integrated word processing software includes the building of a text file (usually with a full-screen editor) and the formatting of the file. Although these may seem very much like the steps involved in the use of a text editor followed by a formatting package, there are some differences and these will be detailed.

Entering Text

In using an integrated package, text entry is typically accomplished with a full-screen editor. Since the ends of lines are arbitrary, text is entered without carriage returns. Carriage returns are only issued when a definite end of line is to be placed in the file.

Formatting with an Integrated Package

Some formatting takes place simultaneously via word wrapping as a file is initially built. This feature produces a "what you see is what you get" effect, as the final product takes shape on the screen. Still, some realignment may be in order because of revisions, insertions, and deletions. The formatting procedure is quite straightforward and may involve only a single keystroke to reformat and redisplay the file on the screen. Some packages stop and query the user with regard to the hyphenation of certain words. Other packages use a few simple rules of thumb such as syllable structure to hyphenate words. Still other packages do not hyphenate at all.

Justification can also be invoked at the user's option. One important difference between formatting packages and integrated word processing is that the latter typically operates directly on the original text file. As the file is altered, the integrated package constantly redisplays the resulting text. Some of these features are detailed in the following section on the popular word processing package **WordStar**. Although the illustration focuses on WordStar, there are many other similar packages such as **Multimate**, **The Final Word**, **AppleWriter**, **EasyWriter**, and **PerfectWriter**. There is even a word processing package for children called **The Bank Street Writer** created at the Bank Street School in New York.

Word Processing with WordStar

WordStar is a widely used integrated word processing software package that operates on many different microcomputers, including those that employ the MS-DOS and CP/M operating systems. Because WordStar uses a full-screen editor, readers should bear in mind that illustrations here will not indicate the spontaneity of interactions and responses between the user and the microcomputer. Potential users are encouraged to seek out demonstrations of the full features of WordStar and other microcomputer software. WordStar is a modeless editor and commands are differentiated from input text by combining a single letter representing a command with the CTRL key. A carat (ˆ) is sometimes used to indicate that the command syntax requires pressing the CTRL key plus the appropriate letter.

Positioning the Cursor. The cursor is moved about with some simple commands. For example, typing ˆS moves the cursor one character to the left. The cursor can be quickly moved horizontally through a line, skipping across entire words (instead of single characters). ˆF moves the cursor to the end of the next word to the right, and ˆA moves to the begin-

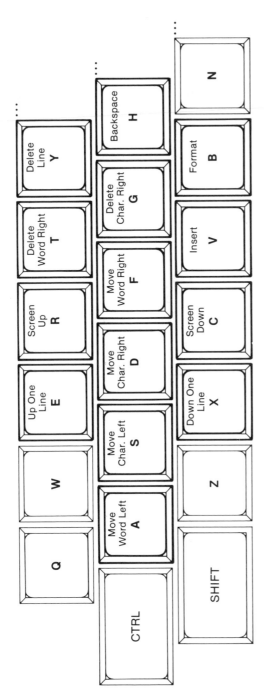

Fig. 5.6 WordStar Cursor Movement

ning of the next word on the left. To be sure, some skeptics complain about these different command combinations, but there is some method to the apparent madness. Figure 5.6 focuses on the keys used to move the cursor about a WordStar text file. Note they are logically arrayed in a manner that corresponds to the direction of cursor movement, and that they can be easily reached with the left hand. After a few minutes of practice, first-time users find themselves zipping around a file.

Deletions.   Deleting existing text in a WordStar file is merely a matter of positioning the cursor and issuing one of several commands. For example, consider the following line of text and the position of the cursor:

        The <u>l</u>lazy brown fox

Issuing ˆG produces

        The <u>l</u>azy brown fox

Although the spontaneous nature of the revision cannot be accurately demonstrated here, imagine issuing a ˆG key stroke and seeing the extraneous "l" instantly disappear and the remaining text slide to the left to fill the space the unwanted letter occupied. Entire words can be deleted with a single command (ˆT).

        The <u>l</u>azy lazy brown fox
        The <u>l</u>azy brown fox

Insertions.   When insert mode is on, any typed text is inserted at the cursor position, and all text to the right is moved further to the right to accommodate the new material. Note the position of the cursor and that insert mode is on.

        The <u>b</u>rown fox

Typing the word "lazy " with a space at the end produces

        The lazy <u>b</u>rown fox

If insert mode were not on, the same sequence would result in

        The lazy<u>n</u> fox

Formatting.   Word wrapping at the ends of lines occurs by default in WordStar. But revisions typically make it necessary to format the file once it has been entered. WordStar formats from one paragraph to the next or, technically, from one carriage return embedded in the file to another. When a ˆB is issued at the beginning of a paragraph, a paragraph is reformatted according to parameters specified by the user. Formatting options include word wrapping, justification, and hyphenation. Although any of these commands could be issued, the default settings will usually suffice. For example, the text in the upper panel of Figure 5.1 was formatted in WordStar with a single ˆB command.

When formatting a paragraph, WordStar occasionally pauses and asks the user to specify the appropriate place (if any) to hyphenate a word. This is precisely how the formatting in Figure 5.3 was accomplished. Some persons find this annoying and turn the hyphen-help off. When this is done, the final formatted product will not use the space on each line as efficiently as it could have.

Print Commands. Like a formatting package, WordStar has a number of dot commands for controlling printing. The user may also invoke a number of special printing features by embedding certain characters in files. Some of these control subscripting, superscripting, shifts from pica to elite characters, and bold printing. Although the options for printing are quite versatile in WordStar, the printed product is no better than the device used to print the material. The important issue of printing and word processing is discussed in the following section.

PRINTING THE PROCESSED WORD

Despite widespread applications of word processing, printing technology has lagged somewhat behind. Ideally, documents should be **letter quality**; that is, they should be printed at least as well as standard business typewritten documents. In contrast to computer printers in general, printers that produce letter quality output tend to be very slow. Faster printers produce a lower print quality sometimes referred to as **draft quality**. This dilemma has existed for mainframes, dedicated word processors, and microcomputers. Fortunately, some recent developments aimed at a compromise have resulted in a middle range called **correspondence quality**. A discussion of the means of obtaining these different print qualities follows.

Draft Quality Printing

Mainframe users can get draft quality output from high-speed line printers that are equipped with upper- and lowercase printing capabilities. But not all line printers have lowercase letters, and some delays can be experienced by users who opt for this mode of printing. Microcomputer users can purchase fairly fast, reliable printers in the $200–350 range which will handle most draft printing needs. These printers are of the **dot matrix** variety, which means that they use a matrix of dots to represent printed characters.

Correspondence Quality Printing

A new generation of dot matrix printers is now available which produces print somewhere between draft and letter quality. The correspondence quality printers are attracting a good deal of attention and many users are rethinking their need for slower, more expensive letter quality printers. These printers work at speeds up to 100 **CPS** (characters per second) when printing in correspondence mode. The better quality printing is achieved through higher resolution of dots (i.e., they are closer together) and by overstriking or double-striking each letter. Some of these printers offer the user a choice of faster draft quality (160-200 CPS) or slower correspondence quality (80-100 CPS). This option is highly desirable.

Letter Quality Printing

Some mainframe users have access to **laser printers** which constitute an important innovation in computer printing. These devices are capable of fast letter quality printing on letter- or legal-sized paper. The character sets are virtually unlimited and include Greek, Arabic, and mathematical symbols. Many types of printing which would be complicated or impossible on a line printer are quite straightforward on a laser printer. Special effects include subscripting, superscripting, varieties of boldfaced printing, and variations in the size of letters. The Waterloo SCRIPT examples in Figures 5.4 and 5.5 were printed on a laser printer. The drawback associated with a laser printer is that its cost is not currently competitive with other types of printers. Financial considerations notwithstanding, laser printers are clearly the preferred mode of printing when word processing is done on a mainframe. As the laser technology becomes more commonplace, the cost will likely become reasonable enough for microcomputer users.

Although slower, daisy wheel printers and terminals are another source for letter quality printing. A **daisy wheel** typing element is round and edged with impressions of alphanumeric characters. Since each letter or symbol can be exactly reproduced, the representation of characters is far superior to draft quality dot matrix. Examples of the various printing

```
This is correspondence quality priting.

This is draft quality printing.

This is letter quality printing.
```

Fig. 5.7   Letter, Correspondence, and Draft Quality Printing

formats—dot matrix, correspondence, and letter quality—appear in Figure 5.7.

Letter quality printing of the highest caliber is now routinely available through data transfer between computers and phototypesetting devices. For example, this book was produced in part by using the author's WordStar diskettes in a typesetting machine. Such typesetting services are frequently advertised in computer magazines.

REPORT WRITING

Thus far our coverage of word processing has focused on using computers to produce neatly organized text. There are numerous occasions, however, when social scientists need to summarize numerical data in their written reports. Most mainframe statistical analysis packages have **report writers** or **report generators** which do for numbers what word processing packages do for words. That is, they facilitate the orderly presentation of summary statistical information in tables and charts. The standard tables and graphics produced by these packages can be used along with text formatted by a word processing package to complete a manuscript.

One example of a mainframe report generator is the SPSS procedure REPORT. Software packages now exist that integrate word processing, data base management, and information retrieval in single, versatile operating environments. Packages such as **Lotus 1-2-3** and **Context MBA** are becoming very popular because they facilitate the tasks involved in report writing. Such packages make it easy to construct tables and graphs from information stored in a data base. It is equally straightforward to annotate the numerical reports with paragraphs of explanatory material. Final versions of reports can be augmented with tables of contents, lists of figures and tables, and the like.

As these new report writing packages suggest, integration has become a key concept among software developers. It is no longer necessary to learn a different language or package for each computing task. This longstanding computer schizophrenia is giving way to a new generation of software which integrates routine tasks such as word processings and report writing. Indeed, it will be apparent in the next chapter on nonanalytic applications that the potential exists to integrate virtually every phase of scholarly work into easy-to-use operating environments.

SUGGESTED READINGS

1. Writer James Fallows has been using word processing software on microcomputers for some time. His recent discussions of word processing (Fallows, 1982; 1983; 1984) in *The Atlantic* are excellent introductions to fundamental procedures and concepts.
2. A good review of microcomputer word processing software has been written by Shuford (1983). Although he reviews all of the packages on an IBM PC, most packages are available for other computers as well.
3. The January 1984 *Popular Computing* has a number of articles on word processing. The issue contains a brief overview by Michael Miller (1984) and several reviews of word processing software packages.

SUGGESTED EXERCISES

1. Before getting on the computer:
   a. Examine documentation associated with the word processing software available to you. How many of the desirable features listed in Chapter 5 does each package have? Is the software a formatting package, or is it an integrated editing and formatting package?
   b. What printing options do you have? In terms of print quality and speed, what is the optimal printing procedure for you?
   c. Suppose that you had $1500 for purchasing word processing equipment. What would you buy and why? (*Hint*: A good answer to this question would begin with a listing of likely word processing applications.)
2. On the computer:
   a. Edit a paragraph or so of text or use the paragraph edited in conjunction with the exercises in Chapter 4. Experiment by processing the paragraph with formatting and integrated packages. Which do you prefer and why?
   b. If possible, print some processed text on both letter and draft quality printers. How easy will it be for you to get printed output when you need it quickly? Turnaround time on mainframe printing may be several hours or overnight. It is best to schedule word processing tasks accordingly.

CHAPTER SIX   A Variety of Nonanalytic Applications

Communications, data collection, instruction, and online information—these are computer applications that do not necessarily involve statistical analysis. As suggested at the outset, one important purpose of this book is to note the wide variety of computer uses available to the social science community. Hence, the applications included in this chapter are as diverse as posting one's vita in a national electronic resume bank and downloading current economic indicators from an information service. The chapter begins with a discussion of the general topic of communications. Then the use of computers in research data collection is considered. The third section of the chapter centers on computer-assisted instruction (CAI) and, finally, a section is included on online information resources.

COMMUNICATIONS

Much of what follows would not be feasible without contemporary communication technology. The capacity exists to transmit information across great distances with telephone lines, radio waves, microwaves, fiber optic cables, and satellite transmitters and receivers. In most cases, this communication technology makes the locations of the host computer and the user unimportant. All that really matters is access to a communication network, and that can simply be accomplished with a household telephone. This communications capability has led several writers including Toffler (1980) and Calhoun (1981) to suggest that the next wave of industrial development will include cottage industries in which workers never leave their homes and transact work related functions on terminals or microcomputers. The topic of communications encompasses a dizzying array of terms, conflicting definitions, and competing transmission standards. Fortunately only a handful of concepts are important to beginners and these are introduced below.

Basic Communication Concepts

Communications are commonly classified as asynchronous or synchronous. **Asynchronous communications** are based on random exchanges of information across a communications link. Such communications typically include lower BAUD rates such as 300 or 1200. Most terminals and microcomputers serving as terminals employ asynchronous procedures. **Synchronous** communications can take place at much faster speeds because two (or more) communicating devices are synchronized or timed by a clocking signal (Mier, 1984). Considerable precision is introduced, and BAUD rates of 9600 are not uncommon. For example, line printers at remote sites can print quite rapidly when they are linked synchronously with a mainframe. Were it not for the special phone lines or other sophisticated linkages required, synchronous communications would be the optimal choice. Still, there is much that can be done through asynchronous communications over an ordinary telephone line.

The rationale for communication is the exchange of information. Almost any terminal or microcomputer with a modem can communicate in a line-by-line fashion with other computers. But many times multiple lines (or entire files) need to be transmitted. Such file transfers require a **communications protocol** or, simply, a set of rules for data interchange. To complicate things, both (or all) devices in communication with one another must employ the same protocol. Otherwise, data may be lost or transmission errors can invalidate portions of the exchanged data. Protocols are established by **communications software** which provides instructions for receiving and sending data, stopping and starting transmissions, and for checking errors. One versatile public domain communications package, KERMIT, is discussed by Weatherby in Appendix I of this book. The key to successful file transfers, then, is selection of a protocol that can be implemented by software on both (or all) devices that are to be linked. And, where there is an option, the precision and speed of synchronous communications are to be preferred.

Communications Networks

One important part of the growth in communications has been the establishment of national networks through which many mainframe computers can be accessed (provided, of course, that the user has permission to do so). Known as **packet switching networks**, these services have greatly expanded communications capabilities. One such network is the U.S. Department of Defense's Advance Research Projects Agency network **APRANET** which links 400 computers at research organizations, universities, and military bases (Turner, 1983). Three commercial networks are **Telenet**, **Tymenet**, and **Uninet**. These systems can be accessed by local telephone lines in metropolitan areas or, elsewhere, by toll-free lines. Once connected to a communication system, the user can access any subscribing computer system regardless of its location. Contemporary communication technology thus places a variety of resources no further away than the nearest telephone. Information resources of particular value to social scientists are discussed throughout this chapter.

COMPUTER-ASSISTED DATA COLLECTION

Mainframes and microcomputers are routinely used to collect data in a variety of research designs. The purpose of this section is to outline some of the diverse data collection strategies now assisted by computers. Computer-assisted surveying is considered first. Subsequent topics include gathering archival data, content analysis, and computers in small-group laboratories. Finally, a number of interesting uses of computers in field and observational research are outlined. In each case, it will be apparent that researchers are employing mainframes and, increasingly, microcomputers in a variety of ingenious ways that facilitate the gathering of basic social science data.

Survey Data Collection

One significant use of computers in survey data collection is computer-assisted telephone interviewing (**CATI**). Shanks, et al. (1981) describe a system in which telephone interviewers read questions as displayed on monitors. Shanks (1983) notes two general advantages of CATI which are cost-efficiency and data quality. When interview schedules contain complicated branching instructions, the computer assures that the correct pattern of questioning is followed. All questions are displayed in appropriate order and the interviewer need not be burdened with complex branching directions. As Bailey (1982) notes, the respondent's answers to survey questions are keyed-in by the interviewer, eliminating the necessity of coding and other data entry. Moreover, the quality and the accuracy of data are enhanced as the computer reviews each entry and rejects invalid responses (Babbie, 1983). In comparison to traditional survey interviews, Freeman (1983) argues that CATI has several other distinct advantages. Words, phrases, or even languages can be substituted as situations warrant. Furthermore, it is quite straightforward to ask questions in random order or to vary systematically the order of items.

CATI systems have been designed on mainframes, minicomputers, and networks of microcomputers (Shanks, 1983). Although there are some limitations on the complexity and length of interview schedules, the sytems have automated and substantially refined survey data collection procedures. Indeed, the U.S. Bureau of the Census has a CATI project of its own underway (Shanks, et al., 1981).

Some CATI systems also generate lists of random telephone numbers and dial them with random digit dialing (**RDD**) software. RDD software is also used in non-CATI telephone surveys as are a number of other computer-assisted applications. Coding and data cleaning are expedited by various automated data entry devices such as optical character recognition (**OCR**) equipment. This hardware facilitates the conversion of handwritten and coded survey data to machine-readable formats for data processing.

Shanks (1983) suggests that CATI could be combined with direct data entry (**DDE**) systems for self-administration of questionnaires by respondents as they use terminals or microcomputers. One development along these lines is Heise's (1982b) program for presenting semantic differential items to research subjects. The respondent controls a cursor-like check mark displayed on a monitor screen to indicate responses. Some of the advantages of this system include an implied continuous response scale, a repeated measures facility with randomization, and simultaneous recording of responses.

Archival Data Collection

Libraries and other archives house a wealth of social science data in the form of records, manuscripts, government documents, and the like. In Chapter 7, it will be noted that considerable archive information exists in machine-readable formats. But many researchers must rely on data in original handwritten or printed forms. One problem with the analysis of such data is the tedious transfer of information to a machine-readable medium. It is not uncommon for researchers to spend hours copying data from historical sources such as books, manuscripts, and microfilm. After

```
INDUSTRY:   -------------------------------

SIC CODE:   --------      NUMBER OF FIRMS:   ---------

NET PROFIT:   ---------------

COST OF SALES AND OPERATIONS:   ---------------------

PAYROLL:   -----------------

CONTRIBUTIONS TO EMPLOYEE BENEFIT PLANS:   ----------
```

Fig. 6.1 DBMS Form for Data Entry

the coding process is complete, the obtained data must still be entered into a computer.

The new generation of portable hardware can greatly facilitate the collection of such archival data. A number of electronic typewriters and similar devices are now marketed which store alphanumeric data until it can be transferred to a computer or word processor. The most straightforward solution is to use a portable microcomputer with cassette or diskette storage. Many briefcase microcomputers have battery-powered memories which can be used to store information until it can be transferred to a permanent mass storage device.

Microcomputer data base managers are very useful in data entry and the production of data files for analysis by statistical packages. A DBMS package can be used to construct a form on the monitor screen for direct data entry. Suppose, for example, that a researcher is collecting data on characteristics of industries from the IRS annual summaries of corporate tax returns (see, e.g., U.S. Internal Revenue Service, 1972). The form depicted in Figure 6.1 is designed with a DBMS and then displayed on the screen for data entry purposes. As each field (line) on the form is completed, a carriage return moves the cursor directly to the next field for further input. Upon completion of the form, the information is added to the data base and a blank form appears on the screen to accept the next set of information. In some instances, researchers may be able to reproduce the printed form from which they are coding. Any of the above strategies can substantially reduce the amount of time and tedium associated with the transformation of printed or written archival data to some machine-readable medium.

Content Analysis

Content analysis is a special case of archival analysis which involves quantification of verbal data (typically documents). Following Bailey

(1982:312), content analysis can simply be considered "counting" the occurrences of certain words or phrases. The utility of computers in collecting data from machine-readable text should be readily apparent. Simple procedures can be written which use text editors to search files for certain words and phrases. More elaborate software can be designed to sample the amount of space devoted to a certain topic or to search for thematic material. Pioneering efforts by Phillip Stone and his colleagues (Stone, et al., 1966; Stone, 1968) resulted in a software package known as **The General Inquirer**. Stone summarizes the package as follows:

> The General Inquirer is a set of computer programs to (a) identify systematically, within text, instances of words and phrases that belong to categories specified by the investigator; (b) count occurrences and specified co-occurrences of these categories; (c) print and graph tabulations; (d) perform statistical tests; and (e) sort and regroup sentences according to whether they contain instances of a particular category or combination of categories. (Stone, et al., 1966:68)

The potential contribution of content analysis is illustrated in Naisbitt's (1981) runaway bestseller *Megatrends*. Naisbitt's consulting firm uses content analysis of newspapers and magazines to identify trends in society which could well indicate imminent social change.

Computers in the Small-Group Laboratory

One of the earliest systematic uses of computers in social science data collection was in small-group experimental laboratories. Cooperband (1966) reports on research in which he used a terminal connected to a mainframe to run an experiment, control the various contingencies, and analyze the collected data. Johnson (1967:484) describes a similar experiment in which a mainframe was used:

> The Subject communicates his trial solutions to the computer by typing them on a computer-linked typewriter in ordinary English. The computer processes the hypotheses and responds by typing on the same typewriter, also in English. The end product is thus a written dialogue between S and the mechanical experimenter, containing S's step-by-step solution to a problem. Additionally, the computer controls all phases of the experiment. It explains the task to S, evaluates his hypotheses for errors, and provides him with continual feedback concerning his progress toward a solution.

Computers have played an important role in experimental research for some time. Large laboratories have been designed with twenty or more stations for subjects (Shure and Meeker, 1969). More recent examples of computer-assisted experiments and games can be found in Orcutt and Anderson (1977) and Molm (1981). The analog-to-digital capability of microcomputers means that streams of data generated by measures such as galvanic skin response can be monitored and analyzed constantly. With the advent of the inexpensive microcomputer, these kinds of applications will doubtless continue to be an important aspect of experimental research.

Field and Observational Research

Structured observation can be facilitated by portable recording devices. These recorders are used to enter coded data and, subsequently, to transfer the coded data to a computer. One such device is the **Datamyte 1000** which records codes and the times at which codes are entered. Sykes (1977) provides an overview of the development of these devices and suggests a variety of applications in behavioral research. One interesting research project detailed by Sykes called for the collection of data on the routine behavior of policemen. Conger and McLeod (1977) report on a study in which observers coded behaviors such as verbal and

Portable data entry device

physical contacts, emotional affect, commands, and compliance. Kirk (1981) suggests a number of ways that anthropologists can use Datamytes in the field.

Portable hardware is now durable enough to be taken virtually anywhere. Kline (1983) chronicles his travels with an Osborne microcomputer and a roving band of Afghan rebels. In the same article, Kline writes about a zoologist who uses a portable computer to track elephants in the Zambian bush. Kirk (1981) mentions several computer applications which may be of interest to social science researchers working in remote locations. He advocates taking microcomputers into the field to store data and to serve as terminals. He also suggests using microcomputers for daily management of research and for on-site analysis capability. Kirk notes that microcomputers are particulary valuable as storage devices in remote settings because it may not be feasible to transfer data to a mainframe for extended periods of time. Kline (1983) recommends that world travelers purchase an **acoustic coupler** modem which has rubber cups that accept a standard telephone handset. This advice is offered because the small modular jacks used for direct connect modems are not likely to be found in remote places. Although there are occasional technical problems of this sort, it should be clear that most social science data collection can be enhanced by computers. Indeed, computer-assisted data collection is likely to increase dramatically in years to come. As we shall see in the next section, the same can be said for the use of computers for instruction in the social sciences.

COMPUTER-ASSISTED INSTRUCTION

Computers can be used to enhance social science instruction in a variety of ways. There are software packages which provide learning experiences for students through drill and practice, games, and simulations. Other software can aid in managing instruction by expediting grading and record keeping. With respect to the former type of software, it is useful to differentiate between simple computer-assisted drill and practice and more elaborate gaming and simulation systems.

CAI Drill and Practice

As the microcomputer boom sweeps U.S. schools, the use of drill and practice software as part of computer-assisted instruction (**CAI**) is rapidly increasing (Coburn, et al., 1982). Becker (1982:16) has characterized these drill and practice programs as follows:

The element common to all CAI is repetition of similar exercises and immediate reinforcement (cognitive and affective feedback regarding performance). The more elaborate drill programs divide the instructional program into discrete tasks where progress from one task to another depends on a student's prior performance.

Although most CAI is centered in elementary and secondary classrooms, there are now a few drill and practice packages available for introductory-level college social science texts. These packages serve as automated study guides, providing drill and practice on basic concepts and even some sample test questions.

To be sure, there is no concensus among educators about the value of CAI drill and practice. Coburn, et al. (1982) provide a positive evaluation, suggesting that cleverly designed software can eliminate some of the tedium and boredom associated with routine practice. Becker (1982) summarizes CAI research and criticism and concludes that too much emphasis may be placed on rote learning at the expense of higher-level intellectual skills. Thus, there is reason at this point to question the utility of CAI drill and practice, particularly for college students. But this is certainly not to suggest that computers are of little value in instruction in the social sciences. Game and simulation packages can be designed to aid students' understanding of social processes and several important contributions have been made by social scientists in this type of instruction.

Instructional Games and Simulations

Many computerized versions of games and simulations have been developed which address important substantive issues. For example, Wieting's (1975) SIMSEARCH is a package designed for undergraduate research methods courses. The program simulates a number of steps in the research process, including research problem selection, research design strategies, and sampling procedures. There are also a number of packages that provide instruction in demography, including population projections, growth, and development issues. Still other software packages dealing with crime, mate selection, and life in the inner city are reviewed by Anderson (1981).

Heise (1982a) provides the code for a simple basic program which can be used to illustrate the Central Limits Theorem. Heise (1982b) has also developed a program that teaches students about the semantic differential technique while prompting them to respond to a series of the attitude measures. The program displays the results of the inventory so that the student can analyze the data. Other social science instructional programs can be obtained through **CONDUIT**, which is a nonprofit educational software distributor. Wallace (1983) recommends CONDUIT's Diffusion Game which simulates the role of diffusion in social change. (The addresses of CONDUIT and other resource organizations are listed at the end of the chapter.)

Since most social science computing has been done on mainframes up to now, it is not surprising that most of the games and simulations were originally written for mainframes. Likewise, it should come as no surprise that many of these are being converted to microcomputers. One example of this conversion is the mainframe package Dynamo which produces dynamic models of systems by computer simulation (see Roberts, et al., 1983). A new version of this package, called Micro-Dynamo is now available. It incorporates many of the same features of the original package. Users can develop a DYNAMO model and then vary the assumptions about relationships within the model. The package produces impressive color graphics of the baseline model and its variations. Practitioners concerned about the implications of various intervention strategies will find system dynamics modeling with DYNAMO very informative. The *Social Science Micro Review* ordinarily includes at least one interesting simulation in each issue (with optional diskettes). Some recent examples include a simulation of the 1984 national elections and a policy-making simulation of a community mental health program (Garson, 1983a). In years to come, microcomputers promise to make simulations and games more available to students in the social sciences.

Instructional Data Analysis

Another increasingly popular use of the computer in social science curricula is instruction in data analysis (Anderson, 1981). Davis (1978) argues that students should be introduced to the social sciences by encouraging them to pose and answer research questions with appropriate data. And, as Sobal (1981) has noted, a wealth of secondary data exists with which students can research a great variety of issues. Perhaps the best curriculum package is SETUPS (Supplementary Empirical Teaching Units in Political Science) developed by the American Political Science Association. The packages are designed to provide students with opportunities to follow the logic of the research enterprise from basic hypothesis formulation through data analysis and, finally, interpretation of results (Sobal, 1981). Microcomputer-based instructional analysis software is also being distributed by the *Social Science Micro Review*. As the expense of instructional computing continous to decline, we can expect an increase in these laboratory-like additions to social science courses.

Computer Assistance for Instructors

Students are not the only ones who profit from instructional computing applications. Mainframes and microcomputers provide assistance in managing instruction in general and grading in particular. Since most universities have OCR devices that read standardized test forms, instructors use computers to score and analyze tests. Bassis and Allen (1977) report on a sophisticated computer-managed instruction (**CMI**) system in which students take tests by computer and are quickly provided with feedback on their performance. **PLATO** is a mainframe CMI system that contains an enormous data base of lessons for students as well as a performance monitoring system for instructors. Although PLATO has been confined to Control Data installations, versions of certain learning modules are now being marketed for microcomputers.

One recent software innovation is the electronic spreadsheet package such as **VisiCalc** or **SuperCalc**. Designed as elementary accounting packages for managers and small businesses, these microcomputer products work well as computerized gradebooks (Tolbert and Tolbert, 1983).

	A	B	C	D	E
1	SOC 101				
2	Fall, 1984				
3					
4	Name	Test I	Test II	Test III	Final Average
5	-------	-------	-------	-------	-------------
6	Adams, R.	82	72	92	AVERAGE(B6:D6)
7	Baker, A.	80	76	91	AVERAGE(B7:D7)
8	Charles, A.	83	79	82	AVERAGE(B8:D8)
9	Daniels, R.	89	85	79	AVERAGE(B9:D9)
10	Jones, E.	72	83	72	AVERAGE(B10:D10)
11	Smith, T.	91	93	94	AVERAGE(B11:D11)
12	-------	-------	-------	-------	-------------

	A	B	C	D	E
1	SOC 101				
2	Fall, 1984				
3					
4	Name	Test I	Test II	Test III	Final Average
5	-------	-------	-------	-------	-------------
6	Adams, R.	82	72	92	82.00
7	Baker, A.	80	76	91	82.33
8	Charles, A.	83	79	82	81.33
9	Daniels, R.	89	85	79	84.33
10	Jones, E.	72	83	72	75.67
11	Smith, T.	91	93	94	92.67
12	-------	-------	-------	-------	-------------

Fig. 6.2 Spreadsheets Used as Gradebooks

The spreadsheets consist of rows and columns which form cells into which data are entered. To use a spreadsheet as a gradebook, names are entered in the first column and test scores in other columns as illustrated in Figure 6.2. One powerful feature of a spreadsheet is that formulas can be built into cells as has been done in column E of the upper portion of the figure. Ordinarily, it is desirable to have the rightmost column display the average (not the formula from which it is computed) like the spreadsheet in the lower part of Figure 6.2. When a new set of scores is entered, a column is simply inserted between the average column on the far right and the remaining columns. Formulas are automatically adjusted and averages are instantly recalculated as the data are entered. Thus, current averages are always displayed and can be printed for posting purposes. In short, there is clearly much that can be done with existing computer applications to enhance instruction in the social sciences.

ONLINE INFORMATION

Much information of importance to social scientists is readily available on computers. Whether it be bibliographic information on a book, a listing of articles on a certain topic, or a file of time series data, it is likely that the information is available online. **Online** simply means that information can be immediately obtained by communicating with a computer. In this section, a number of information resources are noted, including data bases, information retrieval systems, and general-purpose information systems.

Data Bases

A data base is a collection of machine-readable information organized in a systematic fashion that facilitates retrieval of the data. The data bases of most general interest to social scientists are those that contain bibliographic information and those that include research data. Bibliographic data bases are grouped here as library card catalogs, indices, and abstracts. Although each of these tools is invaluable to the researcher in printed form, their use is substantially expedited when computers are used to manage the data bases.

Library Card Catalogs.   Many libraries have computerized their card catalogs, and users enjoy online access to these data bases (Beckman, 1982). In the example in Figure 6.3, a book's title is typed by a user and a

```
Title?   ,power elite$


MILPELI980
E169.1M64-1959
Mills, Charles Wright
The power elite.    •
New York, Oxford University Press,[1959]
A Galaxy book, GB-20


   KEY
MILPELI98

MC          ED

MAIN        3    ON SHELF
```

Fig. 6.3   Sample Online Library Catalog Query

computer responds with information on the whereabouts and status of the library book. Some of these systems allow remote access by telephone so that the researcher can locate items without traveling to the library.

Indices.   An index organizes key pieces of information such as book titles, authors, and subjects so that a researcher can quickly locate an item of interest. As the listing in Table 6.1 suggests, many indices of pertinence to the social sciences exist as online data bases.

Abstracts.   Abstracts constitute yet another source of online information that can be accessed by researchers. An abstract is a brief summary of a research paper, journal article, or other periodical item. Most social science students learn literature search procedures by manually leafing through collections of abstracts. Fortunately the use of such resources has been considerably improved by storing abstracts in data bases. As the list in Table 6.2 indicates, there is no shortage of such online compendia.

Research Data.   Basic research data contained in several data bases is available online. The machine-readable information includes a wide variety of political, social, economic, and historical indicators (see Table 6.3). Although Data Resources, Inc., is known for its economic forecasting, the organization has recently joined with VisiCorp, the makers of the spreadsheet package VisiCalc, to provide online data services to the business community. Machine-readable data for economic research are available online. Also, Data Resources distributes time series data on

Table 6.1   Indices Available as Online Data Bases

Index	Source
CIS (Congressional Information Service)	CIS, Washington, DC
Criminal Justice Periodical Index	University Microfilms, Ann Arbor, MI
Economic Literature Index	American Economic Association, Pittsburgh, PA
Family Resources	National Council of Family Relations, Minneapolis, MN
Foundation Grants Index	The Foundation Center, New York, NY
GEOARCHIVE	Geosystems, London, England
Health Planning and Administration	U.S. National Library of Medicine, Bethesda, MD
International Software Database	Imprint Software Ltd., Ft. Collins, CO
LABORLAW	Bureau of National Affairs, Washington, DC
Legal Research Index	Info Access Corp., San Diego, CA
National Newspaper Index	Info Access Corp., San Diego, CA
NCJRS (National Criminal Justice Reference Service)	NCJRS, Rockville, MD
NEWSEARCH	Info Access Corp., San Diego, CA
NTIS (National Technical Information Service)	NTIS, Springfield, VA
PAIS International (Public Affairs Information Service)	PAIS, New York, NY
Population Bibliography	Carolina Population Center, Chapel Hill, NC
Social Science Citation Index	Institute for Scientific Information, Philadelphia, PA
U.S. Political Science Documents	University of Pittsburgh Center for International Studies, Pittsburgh, PA

diskettes that are formatted for analysis with VisiCalc. The convenience and utility of this integrated program for data acquisition and analysis suggest that much more basic research data is likely to be available in the near future.

Most online data bases have searching facilities that aid the user in finding items of interest. These facilities notwithstanding, many users prefer information retrieval packages with enhanced searching capabilities. These systems are discussed in the next section.

Table 6.2   Abstracts Available as Online Data Bases

Abstracts	Source
Congressional Record Abstracts	Capitol Services International, Washington, DC
Dissertation Abstracts Online	University Microfilms, Ann Arbor, MI
Economics Abstracts International	Learned Information, Ltd., London, England
ERIC (Educational Resources Information Center)	National Institute of Education, Washington, DC
Federal Register Abstracts	Capitol Services International, Washington, DC
Historical Abstracts	ABC-Clio, Inc., Santa Barbara, CA
Language and Language Behavior Abstracts	Sociological Abstracts, San Diego, CA
Mental Health Abstracts	National Institute of Mental Health, Rockville, MD
PSYCINFO (formerly Psychological Abstracts)	American Psychological Association, Washington, DC
Sociological Abstracts	Sociological Abstracts, San Diego, CA

Table 6.3   Some Online Research Data Bases

Data Base	Source
America: History and Life	ABC-Clio, Inc., Santa Barbara, CA
BI/Data Forecasts	Business International Corporation, New York, NY
BI/Time Series	
BLS/Employment, Hours, and Earnings	Bureau of Labor Statistics, Washington, DC
BLS/Consumer Price Index	
BLS/Labor Force	
BLS/Producer Price Index	
Dunn's Market Identifiers	Dunn's Management Services, Parsippany, NJ
EIS/Industrial Plants	Economic Information Systems, Inc., New York, NY
EIS/Manufacturing Establishments	
PTS/International Time Series	Predicasts, Inc., Cleveland, OH
PTS/Time Series	

Information Retrieval Systems

Much social science research is interdisciplinary, and searching a single data base may reveal only a portion of the available information.

```
DIALOG:  call connected


ENTER YOUR DIALOG PASSWORD                            (logon sequence)
         LOGON File1 Fri 20jan84 9:20:39 Port096

?b139                                                 (data base identified
    20jan84 9:20:58 User845                           and opened)
    0.007 Hrs File1*
    Tymenet

File139:Economic Literature Index - 1969-83/Dec
         Set Items Description
         --- ----- -----------

?ss labor(w)market?/ti or labor(w)market?             (search terms selected
                                                       and combined; 336 entries
        1    336 LABOR(W)MARKET?/TI                    in title (set 1); 6564
        2   6564 LABOR(W)MARKET?                       with terms in text (set 2))
        3   6564 1 OR 2

?ss local?/ti or definition/ti or county/ti or        (more terms selected
regional/ti or defined/ti or classif?/ti or geograph?/ti   and combined)

        4    690 LOCAL?/TI
        5    136 DEFINITION/TI
        6     54 COUNTY/TI                             (numbers of entries with
        7   1148 REGIONAL/TI                           terms in titles)
        8      9 DEFINED/TI
        9    135 CLASSIF?/TI
       10    124 GEOGRAPH?/TI
       11   2271 4 OR 5 OR 6 OR 7 OR 8 OR 9 OR 10

?c 1 and 11                                           (finds 16 entries that
                                                      appear in both set 1
       12     16 1 AND 11                              and set 11)

?c 3 and 11                                           (finds 157 entries common
                                                      to sets 3 and 11)
       13    157 3 and 11

?s labor(w)market?/de                                (searches for 'labor market'
                                                      as descriptor or keyword
       14   6509 LABOR(W)MARKET?/DE                    associated with biblio-
                                                      graphic entry)
?s labor market/de or labor markets/de
```

Fig. 6.4 Sample DIALOG Search

Moreover, there is no guarantee that search command syntax will be consistent across different data bases. An information retrieval system is designed to search multiple data bases according to a common set of instructions provided by the user. The use of such integrated packages reduces to a matter of seconds a literature review process that once took days or weeks. Most information retrieval systems are structured around certain identification components which are used to link similar items in the data bases. Users specify descriptors and keywords, or terms that represent the central concepts of their research. Information in a bibliographic archive can be retrieved by matching these keywords, authors' names, manuscript titles, and the like. The information

```
                    O LABOR MARKET/DE
                    O LABOR MARKETS/DE
         15         O LABOR MARKET/DE OR LABOR MARKETS/DE
?ss local(w)labor(w)market? or regional(w)labor(w)market?        (selects and combines items)

         16        13 LOCAL(W)LABOR(W)MARKET?                     (results of search)
         17         0 REGIONAL(W)LABOR(W)MARKET?
         18        13  16 OR 17

?c 12 or 18                                                      (finds 16 entries common
                                                                 to sets 12 and 18)
         19        16  12 OR 18

?ss py=1979;py=1984                                             (selects only items
                                                                published from 1979–
         20 35016  PY=1979:PY=1984                               1984; n = 35,016)

?c 20 and 13                                                    (combines those items which
                                                                appear in both sets 20
         21        62 20 AND 13                                  and 13; n = 62)

?c 19 or 21                                                     (combines items in sets 19
                                                                or 21 to get final total
         22        73 19 OR 21                                   of 73)

?& 22/3/1-73                                                    (73 items in set 22 printed
                                                                offline; to be mailed to
Printed22/3/1-73  Estimated Cost: $5.48 (To cancel,             researcher)
enter PR-)

?type 19/3/1-2                                                  (first 2 items in set 19
                                                                printed at terminal)
19/3/1
   134032
   Inflationary Expectations, Taxes and the Political
   Business Cycle: A Local Labor Market Perspective
   Izraeli, D.; Kellman, M.
   Urban Studies,  February 1982,  19 1,  33-41

19/3/2
   124185
   On the Integration of Labor Markets:  A Definition and
   Test of the Radical-Segmentation Hypothesis
   Amacher, Ryan C.; Sweeney, Richard James
   Journal of Labor Research,  Spring, 1981,   2 1,   25-37

?logoff                                                         (search concluded)
```

Fig. 6.4 (continued)

retrieval process can be further enhanced by **videotex** which refers to two-way transmission of textual data between a host computer and a micro-computer or terminal (Miller, 1983). In a videotex system, the online user not only identifies an item of interest, but can request that the entire text of a document be displayed. In the paragraphs that follow, large systems primarily used by libraries and institutions are discussed as are some smaller information retrieval systems that are available to in-dividual subscribers at modest cost.

Libraries and other institutional subscribers routinely use retrieval systems such as **DIALOG** and **BRS**. These systems can access enormous amounts of information from many data bases. DIALOG, for example,

```
->upi

  ..UPI DATANEWS... IS ON-LINE!

HELP or QUIT at any time...

(N), Regional (R), or State (S) news, Features (F) or STOP?
n

Select General (G), Business (B), or Sports (S) news, Miscellaneous
(M) or STOP:
g

Key words (press return for all stories):
computer

Enter starting & ending date - or press return for today:
<cr>

Pick a starting story number - from 1 (the earliest) to
    7 (the latest):
1

Read forward in time (RF), read backward (RB), scan forward (SF) or
scan backward (SB)?
sf

1 -23-84 04:05 aes

New Apple computer: as common as the  "telephone"
By PETER COSTA
UPI Senior Editor
   NEW YORK (UPI) - Apple Computer Inc. hopes the "Macintosh" - a
personel computer that can be mastered in two hours and produce human
or music - will become as common as the telephone and win back
Apple's market lead from IBM.

2 23-84 04:11 aes=

adv for sun., jan. 29 or thereafter
(HORIZONS)
(biz 1,500 - may end at 3 em dashes)

3 -23-84 04:10 aes

xxx in the subject
In the study commissioned by Control Data, the company found that
attitudes by, and about, women in relation to computers  "is a major
problem."

4 -23-84 04:10 aes

for sun, jan. 29 or thereafter
(HORIZONS)
(biz 600)
```

Fig. 6.5   Sample UPI Data Base Search

links 170 data bases, and thus encompasses some 75 million records of information (DIALOG Information Services, Inc., 1983). Figure 6.4 contains excerpts from a DIALOG search of the Economic Literature Index on the topic of local labor markets. The search proceeds by narrowing down the more than 6000 entries that use labor market in titles or elsewhere in the information associated with them. By requiring certain combinations of

```
Computer just part of best managed U.S. farm

5 23-84 04:18 aes=

adv for sun dec 4 or thereafter
(HORIZONS)
(Living-Leisure 620-Picture)

6 -23-84 07:38 aes

 (fixing type - personal sted personel)
 New Apple computer: as common as the  "telephone"

7 23-84 12:14 pes=

WASHINGTON (UPI) - Deputy Transportation Secretary Jim Burnley has
told the chairman of the U.S. Railway Association that  "personal
invective"  will not stop the transportation department's inquiry into
the association's operations.

Pick a starting story number - from 1 (the earliest) to
7 (the latest):
1

Read forward in time (RF), read backward (RB), scan forward (SF) or
scan backward (SB)?
r f

1 - Apple Computer Inc. hopes the  "Macintosh"  - a
personel computer that can be mastered in two hours and produce human
speech or music - will become as common as the telephone and win back
Apple's market lead from IBM.
    Apple unveils the new 32-bit computer - selling for $2,495 and
aimed at  "knowledge workers"  too busy to spend 40 hours learning how
to operate a computer - at its annual meeting in California Tuesday.
    "Our vision is that we want to bring the personal computer to tens
of millions of people. It is analogous to the telephone," Apple
chairman Steven Jobs said in an interview with UPI.  "The Macintosh is
the first telephone in the computer industry, in that, in addition to
passing information, it lets you 'sing."
    Jobs said Apple currently is producing 10,000 Macintoshes a month.
"And that is just the start up stage. The Macintosh is designed to be
produced in the millions," he said.
    He said Apple is initiating a $15 million advertising campaign to
coincide with the introduction of the computer.
The Macintosh is based on technology developed for the Lisa, the
business computer Apple introduced in 1983 with a $10,000 price tag that
is blamed for its disappointing sales record.
    Jobs said the Macintosh is targeted for what he calls knowledge
workers - people who use and process information but who do not have the
time or interest to spend an average of 20 to 40 hours reading a
400-page computer user's manual.
```

Fig. 6.5 (continued)

terms and specifying publication dates between 1974 and 1984, the scope of the search is narrowed to 73 bibliographic entries. These items are printed (offline) and two are listed to confirm their contents.

Although it is difficult to comprehend the size and scope of these compound data bases, the potential of information retrieval systems for enhancing research and instruction is readily apparent. All of the data bases listed in Tables 6.1, 6.2, and 6.3 are available online on either DIALOG or BRS (there is some overlap in data base coverage). The costs associated with use of information retrieval systems depends on particular data base(s) accessed and minutes of telephone connection (connect time) with the mainframe on which the systems operate.

Using these enormous information retrieval systems can be expensive. It may also be necessary for a researcher to travel to a library in order to conduct a search. Thus, there is a market for similar systems that can be accessed by individuals from their personal computers or terminals. Recognizing this, both BRS and DIALOG operate systems oriented toward individual users. **Knowledge Index** and **BRS/After Dark** access subsets of the data bases available in the larger systems and make use of the systems after hours at substantial discounts. Like their more comprehensive cousins, these smaller systems allow the user to search data bases and to display abstracts on a monitor. Advertisements refer to the BRS service as: "Your own university library online at home." The clever marketing of these services directly to personal computer users may well revolutionize the research habits of many in university and research settings.

General Information Systems

The online information sources discussed thus far have largely been sponsored by academic and research organizations. But consumer-oriented online systems have a good deal to offer as well. Personal computer owners have access to general-purpose information systems that amount to national personal computing networks. Reached by Telenet and other packet switching services, two of these systems are **The Source** and **CompuServe**. Consumer emphasis notwithstanding, a number of features on these systems are useful to social scientists. The Source and CompuServe provide electronic mail services through which persons can communicate with one another by leaving messages on the central system or actually "chatting" with one another. A number of teleconferences for social scientists have been held using these and similar communication facilities, saving travel time and expense. Users can also access the U.S. Postal Service's electronic mail system **E-COM**. After the text for a letter is entered by the user, E-COM prints the letter on a computer near the destination, cutting transit time dramatically. Book orders can be placed, and buyers are promised shipment of their selections within 48 hours. Several electronic bulletin boards are included which offer tips for computer users, advertise new computing products, and announce research services. A number of journals and periodicals can be searched and printed as well.

Social scientists who collect data on current events will find The Source's United Press International files very valuable. Figure 6.5 is an illustration of a UPI file search in which the user scans the first few lines of all stories for the week related to the keyword "computer." Those without access to a mainframe can use statistical libraries and avail themselves of the analysis power of a mainframe. Job seekers can read national employment ads, post their own resumes, and respond to specific job notices. Travel is expedited by the ability to peruse flight schedules and make one's own airline and hotel reservations.

The obvious intent of CompuServe and The Source is to put the power of a mainframe and the knowledge contained in a massive general-purpose data base at the disposal of the personal computer owner. In doing so, these services provide yet another useful source of online information for social scientists. These technological conveniences aside, there is always a chance that online information sources can be abused. This is discussed briefly in the final section below.

CRIME, PRIVACY, AND COMPUTERS

It is important to note that communications networks and online services increase the potential for computer crime and for violations of privacy. Adam Osborne has written about the potential for security violations and outright computer theft (Osborne, 1979). More recently, the news media have highlighted a number of cases of mischievous youngsters accessing major institutional mainframes. But these sensationalized cases detract attention from very real potential for serious abuses of computer technology. The increasing capacity of mainframes and associated communications advances makes it more likely that huge government and private data files can be merged. Stern and Stern (1983) note the potential for abuse of privacy represented by data bases such as the FBI's National Crime Information Center and the National Security Agency's files. Similarly, much confidential information could be obtained by merging health insurance data bases with credit bureau information systems. Even when such data bases are shared for legitimate reasons, the possibility for an invasion of privacy is very real.

Even if appropriate safeguards for privacy are maintained, the potential for criminal activity will continue to exist. Columbia University officials recently sued a student at another school for nearly $300,000 for allegedly altering Columbia's operating system through a security breach in APRANET (Turner, 1983). We will likely hear much more about the critical issues of computer crime and privacy as federal and state governments attempt to establish regulations governing the use and merging of large data bases. In the meantime, we are faced with a classic example of Ogburn's (1922) concept of culture lag: communication and information technologies have advanced far ahead of our society's values, norms, and laws pertaining to the protection of private records.

Thus, there are many computer applications for social scientists other than statistical analysis. Indeed, the survey of nonanalytic applications in this chapter addresses one major objective of this book. But another goal is to consider ways of facilitating analysis of social science data with computers, and that is the theme of the remaining chapters.

SUGGESTED READINGS

1. On communications:
   a. The January 1984 issue of *Popular Computing* contains several articles on the topic of communications. Topics include micro to micro and mainframe to micro communications.
   b. Alfred Glossbrenner has written a good introduction to communications. *The Complete Handbook of Personal Computer Communications* (New York, St. Martins Press, 1983) is highly recommended as a nontechnical primer on the subject.
2. The November 1983 issue of *Sociological Methods and Research* is devoted to the topic of Computer-Assisted Telephone Interviewing (CATI).

RESOURCES

1. Information Retrieval Systems
   a. BRS/After Dark
      200 Route 7
      Latham, NY 12110
   b. Knowledge Index
      DIALOG Information Services
      Marketing Department
      3460 Hillview Avenue
      Palo Alto, CA 94304
2. General-Purpose Information Services
   a. CompuServe
      CompuServe Information Service
      5000 Arlington Centre Blvd.
      P.O. Box 20212
      Columbus, OH 43220

b. The Source
   The Source
   1616 Anderson Road
   McLean, VA 22102
3. Periodicals of Interest to Social Scientists
   a. *ICPSR MicroNews*
      Inter-university Consortium for Political and Social Research
      P.O Box 1248
      Ann Arbor, MI 48106
      Editor: Greg Marks
   b. *Social Science Micro Review*
      Link 212 NCSU
      Raleigh, NC 27650
      Editor: G. David Garson

SUGGESTED EXERCISES

1. Many libraries sponsor training sessions on the use of information retrieval systems. Persons planning to make use of these information services should find these workshops very useful. The expense associated with online searches can be minimized when the user has some knowledge of searching strategies and procedures.
2. There is no substitute for "hands-on" experience with an online system. The Source and CompuServe occasionally offer an hour or so free usage as part of promotional offers. Readers who access The Source are encouraged to send comments and other messages to the author (Source ID STG752).
3. The instructional system PLATO has a number of fascinating learning packages. Some of the programs employ a special touch-sensitive screen which allows small children and nontypists to interact with the PLATO system. If PLATO is available locally, readers should arrange a sample terminal session. Only then will the enormous potential of this system be apparent.

CHAPTER SEVEN

Structures and Sources of Social Science Data

We have two tasks in this chapter. One is to introduce the reader to conventions and options in the structure of research data that are analyzed by computer. The second task is to illustrate the wide variety of data that already exists in machine-readable form for use by the social science community. Whether using original data or someone else's, the researcher must fashion a data file that can be processed by the computer. The basics of file construction follow.

ORGANIZATION OF SOCIAL SCIENCE DATA

Data files are composed of **variables** which, as the name suggests, are entities that vary or take on different values. A **case** is a set of variables associated with a particular unit of analysis. In the social sciences the cases often represent individuals about whom a number of different pieces of information (variables) have been gathered. Another example of a social science data file is a set of nations (cases) containing a number of characteristics (variables) on each of the countries.

File Structure Options

Two primary options are available for building and storing data sets: "raw" data and system files. These options are most often employed because they are appropriate for analysis packages such as SPSS. **Raw data** files contain unprocessed research data (most often, only numbers). The information is not described, labeled, or embellished in any way. Raw data files can be built with text editors or entered into the computer from a tape or other medium. **System files** are created by software packages and can contain a lot of useful information about a file. System files are formatted so that the files can be processed by software packages more efficiently than raw data. Several factors influence the researcher's decision on whether to maintain data files in raw or system formats. The advantages of each storage option are detailed in the following discussion of various file structures.

Rectangular Data Files. The most straightforward file structure is a rectangular data file which means that the data form a simple two-dimensional array of rows and columns. The rows of the file represent cases and the columns represent variables. Suppose a researcher has surveyed 10 persons and asked them nine questions that can be answered yes or no. The survey data could be represented as the hypothetical rectangular data file in Figure 7.1. Each row represents one case (person) and

```
0 1 2 1 2 1 2 1 2 1

1 1 1 2 2 2 1 1 1 2

2 1 2 1 2 2 2 2 1 2

3 1 1 2 2 2 1 1 1 1

4 1 1 1 1 2 2 1 2 1

5 1 1 1 2 2 1 2 1 2

6 1 2 1 2 2 2 1 2 2

7 1 1 2 1 2 1 2 2 1

8 1 2 1 2 2 1 2 1 1

9 1 1 2 2 2 2 1 2 2
```

Fig. 7.1 Simple Rectangular Data Array

01	1	11111000011010000001100000011001100100211200000000004110101000001100110000100 11
01	2	11111000111111001101010111111100010010000000100100001000000110011010110010010010
01	3	00110000000110000000000000001112111121010211111111111110001010110100111111110010
02	1	11012111200000011011122100000000000000011101101111012100000000000000000000000111
02	2	11111111111110000000000011111111111110000000111111100001010011000000000001121121
02	3	01210000011010000000000001101000019001000101111111111111000000000101010100101
03	1	10001010010100101101010102100010110000000101111111001010101021000100201009100
03	2	10100000001110000000000000010011111101010111111111111111000000001100010910000 0
03	3	11111100000001212100000000000001101110000000101000000000000011110000000000011010
04	1	01100000000000000011911011001111111001010001110000000111111111110000000011001
04	2	11111100000000110101000111212910001210000000000000101012100000000000000000000101
04	3	10100011010000000000012100000100201200000000901200100000110100110000000010111110

Fig. 7.2 Data Array with Three Deck Structure

each column contains codes representing values on one variable. The cases are identified in the first column by a sequencing variable (0-9) and the responses to the nine questions (coded 1 for yes and 2 for no) are listed in columns two through ten. Thus, there are ten variables in this simple array and ten cases, resulting in a 10 × 10 rectangular file. The width in columns of the data array depends on the number of variables and the number of columns reserved for each variable. It is important to note that variables need not be restricted to single column widths. The length of the array depends on the number of cases which, for Census data, can run into the millions. Whatever the dimensions, each row and column always has the same width and length; hence, the file is said to be rectangular.

In deference to the tradition of the punched card, researchers occasionally limit the width of any row of a rectangular file to 80 columns (**card image data**). In doing so it may be necessary to use multiple rows (cards) to include all the data associated with each case. The corresponding row for each case in a rectangular file is referred to as a **deck**, and the researcher must be careful to keep track of which deck and which column(s) contain the variables of interest. Figure 7.2 illustrates another hypothetical data file in which there are three 80-column rows of information for each of four respondents. To enhance the illustration, vertical lines have been inserted in the figure; they are not actually part of the file. The first two columns on each deck contain a sequence number for identification and this code remains the same for all three records associated with the same case. The third column contains a sequential deck number and varies within each case. It should be noted that this practice of restricting the width of rectangular files to 80 columns is rapidly going the way of the punched card. Where software and hardware will permit, the width of rectangular data files stored on disk or magnetic tape should simply be equal to the number of columns that contain data. In this way, complications in file structure due to multiple decks can be avoided.

Hierarchical Data Files.   A more complex type of data file is a hierarchical file which organizes cases so that some are grouped under others. Many U.S. Census files are organized in hierarchical fashion. For example, data are grouped by certain areas such as states or Standard Metropolitan Statistical Areas (SMSAs). Preceding each geographic group is a record that summarizes information for all the person records that pertain to the area. Within these geographic groups, data on persons are organized into household and family subgroups. Each of these groups of records on persons is preceded by a record that summarizes information on the group. Thus the rows of a hierarchical data file can pertain to different units of analysis.

A data file organized in hierarchial fashion is illustrated in Figure 7.3. The indexing variables are separated from one another by vertical lines

```
1 | 0001 | 01 | 03 | 01110000001100010001
2 | 0001 | 01 | 03 | 45123123938
3 | 0001 | 01 | 01 | 00100104600000001100000000110191001001001
3 | 0001 | 01 | 02 | 00100010009011100110011100110001001
3 | 0001 | 01 | 03 | 0110100350121000020111010000000011010010
1 | 0002 | 02 | 04 | 01101111100201001000
2 | 0002 | 01 | 02 | 54121332839
3 | 0002 | 01 | 01 | 1012100000000000011001000000001110011000
3 | 0002 | 01 | 02 | 0101011110100100100000001011000000000110
2 | 0002 | 02 | 02 | 36130232938
3 | 0002 | 02 | 01 | 1010000001101010101000000000001101100111
3 | 0002 | 02 | 02 | 0110110000000000110101010101000000110110
```

Fig. 7.3   Sample Hierarchical Data Structure

for purposes of illustration. The first column is a record flag which indicates whether the record is for a household (code = 1), a family (code = 2), or a person (code = 3). The second variable contained in columns 2 through 5 is a unique household identification number. The meaning of the third indexing variable depends on the record type. On household records, the value in columns 6 and 7 represents the number of families within the household. On family and person records, the third index variable indicates the sequence number of the family within the household. Similarly, the fourth indexing variable takes on different meanings depending on the type of record. On household records, columns 8 and 9 indicate the number of persons in the entire household. On family records, the fourth indexing variable represents the number of individuals in the family. On person records, the last index variable index indicates the sequence of individuals within the family.

Regardless of record type, the remainder of variables associated with each case begins in column 11. Note that the file does not appear rectangular, and it would not be classified as such. This is because different types of records have completely different coding schemes and layouts. It would clearly be incorrect to treat each row in Figure 7.3 as an equivalent case; some are records for households, some for families, and some for individuals. The record flag in column one indicates that the first record is a household record. Hence, its index variables indicate a household sequence number (0001), the number of families within the household (1), and the number of persons residing in the household (3). The second record has a 2 in the flag column, indicating that it is a family record for household (0001). According to the other index variables for the family, it is the first to be encountered in the household and there are three person records to follow. Accordingly, the individuals living in household 0001, family 01, are represented in sequence on the next three records. Moving on to the next household record it is apparent that household 0002 houses two, two-member families.

Hierarchical files thus allow the researcher to choose among two or more levels of analysis. Nonrectangular files are valuable to social science researchers because they lend themselves nicely to multilevel analyses and studies of contextual effects (see, e.g., van den Eeden and Huttner, 1982).

System Files.   System files are by-products of analysis of raw data files by software packages such as SPSS, SAS, and BMDP. To appreciate system files, it is necessary to introduce some fundamentals about the structure of programs written for these analysis packages. Package programs typically consist of two parts: a **data definition** section and a **task definition** section. Although the terminology used here is that of the SPSS system, parallel programming structures are used with other analysis packages. In the data definition section of a package program, the user provides necessary information about the data file that is to be analyzed. The task definition section consists of analysis instructions. At a minimum, data definition of raw data involves naming each variable and specifying its location in the data file. In addition, data definition usually involves extensive labeling of variables and transformations of original variable values (**recodes**). In a system file, all the data definition information supplied by the user, including variable names, explanations, labels, recodes, and file documentation, is stored along with the data.

In other words, everything the researcher needs for subsequent work is conveniently stored in a system file. The data definition section of later programs may only consist of a single command to identify the system file. Repeated data definitions or **passes** through a raw data file can represent a tremendous waste of time and money. And, the greater the number of variables in the data file, the greater the waste. This is especially true for analysis programs that require recoding or other routine transformations. These must be repeated each time a pass is made through the same raw data file.

Once the variables have been identified and documented in a system file, all that is required to reuse them is the name that was assigned when the system file was created. Suppose, for example, that a user wants to read the variables RACE, SEX, and AGE from a rectangular raw data file. In an initial program which creates a system file, it is necessary to identify the variables by name and to indicate the columns they occupy in the data array. An extensive data definition step is not required in any subsequent analysis because the variables have been defined and the information stored as part of a system file. To use the RACE, SEX, and AGE variables, the user need only mention them by name.

Despite this convenience and economy, the use of system files has some drawbacks. The additional information stored with the data increases the size of the file. Also, a file formatted for optimal use on one computer may not be at all useful on another machine. System files are frequently not portable; that is, they cannot be used by different brands of computers. Users may also experience difficulty in using software packages other than the one originally used to create the system file. Fortunately, interfacing of various package system files has been enhanced with features such as the SAS procedure CONVERT which transfers system files from other packages into SAS system files.

The user must weigh the advantages and disadvantages of the system file option. Generally, a system file is preferred when all data analysis is done on the same computer with a single software package. Although a system file is created each time raw data are read, it may or may not be useful to save the system file as a permanent file. If the system file is to be saved for subsequent analysis, this is easily done by issuing a few instructions to the operating system. Most analysts begin their research with either rectangular or hierarchical raw data files. Once they are confident that the data are clean (i.e., free of invalid variable values), researchers typically store working versions of data files as system files. Over the course of a research project, multiple generations of system files are typically created as modifications of original variables and redefinitions of the analysis files are made. An analysis that maximizes the use of system files can be convenient, economical, and efficient.

Coding Conventions

The values that variables take on are represented by coding schemes that usually consist of numbers. In the case of most quantitative variables, the codes represent actual values of the variables. For example, if a person earns $12,000 a year, the corresponding earnings variable can be simply coded as 12000. Qualitative variables are typically coded with arbitrary numerical values that represent the various categories of the variables. For example, survey questions requiring yes or no answers can be coded 1 if the respondent's answer is yes and 2 if the respondent's answer is no. Although computers are certainly capable of reading yes and no variable values, it is customary to code qualitative variables in a numeric fashion. One reason for this is that it takes less memory space to store a single digit than it does to store several letters. In addition, some software packages will not process alphanumeric data for analysis purposes.

Social science data files may contain many qualitative variables, and potential users must have access to documentation on data sets to determine the meanings of the codes. Researchers typically assemble codebooks which describe their data files in very great detail, noting all the variables and explaining the coding scheme. Codebooks ordinarily also

DECK 1   -36-
COLS. 74-76
Qs. 18-20

18. RESPONDENT'S MOTHER'S (SUBSTITUTE MOTHER'S) DEGREE

[VAR: MADEG]

RESPONSE	PUNCH				YEAR						COL. 74
		1972	1973	1974	1975	1976	1977	1978	1980	1982	All
Less than high school ..	0	832	768	817	796	811	807	781	727	707	7046
High school	1	390		420	451	422	437	512	488	497	4032
Associate/Junior											
college	2		12	13	11	13	14	27	10	16	132
Bachelor's	3	3ː	41	44	51	45	48	49	55	74	446
Graduate	4	13	14	16	8	9	16	11	20	17	124
Not applicable (no											
mother/mother											
substitute)	7	80	67	55	38	51	53	51	62	53	510
Don't know	8	96	76	98	125	136	141	92	88	127	979
No answer	9	147	111	21	10	12	14	9	18	15	357

19. RESPONDENT'S SPOUSE'S DEGREE

[VAR: SPDEG]

RESPONSE	PUNCH				YEAR						COL. 75
		1972	1973	1974	1975	1976	1977	1978	1980	1982	All
Less than high school ..	0	403	379	373	315	336	319	268	250	222	2865
High school	1	568	500	526	524	483	478	508	469	457	4513
Associate/Junior											
college	2	10	20	20	17	21	27	29	24	21	189
Bachelor's	3	92	100	95	92	79	97	90	82	101	828
Graduate	4	37	53	42	50	50	45	55	56	47	435
Not applicable (not											
married)	7	453	428	419	488	525	555	571	579	652	4670
Don't know	8	15	2	5	3	2	4	7	2	3	43
No answer	9	35	22	4	1	3	5	4	6	3	83

Figure 7.4 Sample Pages from *General Social Surveys, 1972-1982: Cumulative Codebook*

contain information on how and when the data were collected, the order of the variables in the file, the number of cases, and so forth.

In Figure 7.4 portions of codebook pages from the *Cumulative Codebook* of the National Opinion Research Center's (**NORC**) General Social Surveys (Davis, 1982) are reproduced. Information is provided in the figure on the survey's SEX and RACE variables. In the column labeled "Punch" are the codes for the various categories. With respect to the SEX variable, male respondents are coded 1 and female respondents are coded 2. On the RACE variable, whites are coded 1, blacks are coded 2, and others are coded 3. A very useful and convenient feature of this codebook is that a frequency distribution for each variable is provided immediately to the right of the code. Since the NORC surveys have been repeated over a number of years, the codebook indicates the frequencies by year. Note

20. CODE RESPONDENT'S SEX

[VAR: SEX]

CODE	PUNCH				YEAR					COL. 76
		1972	1973	1974	1975	1976	1977	1978	1980	1982	All
Male	1	807	701	691	670	669	693	643	641	639	6154
Female	2	806	803	793	820	830	837	889	827	867	7472

REMARKS: Interviewer coded. See Appendix O, GSS Technical Report No. 17.

Deck Number ⟶ DECK 1
COLS. 77–80
Q. 21

21. CODE WITHOUT ASKING ONLY IF THERE IS NO DOUBT IN YOUR MIND.

What race do you consider yourself? RECORD VERBATIM AND CODE

[See REMARKS]   *Variable*   *Column*

[VAR: RACE]   *Name*   *Number*

                Codes

RESPONSE	PUNCH					YEAR					COL. 77
		1972	1973	1974	1975	1976	1977	1978	1980	1982	All
White	1	1348	1308	1304	1323	1361	1339	1358	1318	1323	11982
Black	2	261	183	173	163	129	176	158	140	156	1539
Other (SPECIFY) [See REMARKS]	3	4	13	7	4	9	15	16	10	27	105

REMARKS: Interviewer coded except in 147 cases where question suggested was asked.
Punch 3 in Col. 77 (Other SPECIFY) included 20 American Indian, 12 Asian,
3 Chinese, 1 Creole, 13 Filipino, 1 Guayanese, 4 Hawaiian, 3 Hindu, 2 Indian
(Asian), 8 Japanese, 1 Korean, 6 Mexican, 3 Mulatto, 12 Oriental, 3 Polynesian,
4 Puerto Rican, 1 Thai, 1 Vietnamese, and 1 "Yellow."

DECK NUMBER .... COL. 80, PUNCH 1

Fig. 7.4 (continued)

also that the columns and decks in which variables appear are listed. The codes for question number 20 (SEX) are located in column 76, deck 1. Likewise, in deck 1, column 77, the codes for responses to item 21 (RACE) appear. Thus, a codebook identifies variables, possible responses, codes, and locations in the data file. It should be amply evident that, without a codebook, the researcher is lost.

Building a System File

An SPSS-X program that creates a system file using the NORC General Social Survey data for 1982 is presented in this section. The execution of this and similar programs is illustrated further on a variety of mainframes in the appendices. Veteran SPSS users making the transition to SPSS-X will want to read Brigg's tips on the new package in the section on VAX computers (Appendix II). The 1972–82 Cumulative File of the NORC survey data is organized in rectangular, card image fashion with 11 decks (i.e., 11 records of information) for each of 13,626 respondents. To read the raw data file, the researcher must know the deck and column number(s) of each variable to be included in the file.

Table 7.1   Variables from NORC Data To Be Included in System File

Variable	Variable Label	Deck	Columns	Value Labels	Missing Values
MARITAL	Marital status	1	23	1 = Married 2 = Widowed 3 = Divorced 4 = Separated 5 = Never married 9 = NA	9 = No answer
AGE	Age	1	56–57	(actual years) 98 = Don't know 99 = No answer	0 = Not applicable
EDUC	Highest year of school complete	1	64–65	(actual year)	98 = Don't know 99 = No answer
SEX	Sex	1	76	1 = Male 2 = Female	none
RACE	Race	1	77	1 = White 2 = Black 3 = Other	none
REGION	Region of interview	2	65	1 = New England 2 = Middle Atlantic 3 = E. Nor. Central 4 = W. Nor. Central 5 = South Atlantic 6 = E. Sou. Central 7 = W. Sou. Central 8 = Mountain 9 = Pacific 0 = Foreign	none
RELIG	Respondent's religious preference	5	7	1 = Protestant 2 = Catholic 3 = Jewish 4 = None 5 = Other	9 = No answer

To organize things properly, a researcher would use the codebook to make a list of information like that in Table 7.1. The NORC codebook suggests variable names, and these are listed in the first column of the figure. Then, a variable label is listed which will be stored with the system file and displayed by SPSS whenever it prints information about the variable. The third and fourth columns list the all important deck and column locations of the variables. Column 5 provides information on the meanings associated with the codes of categorical variables. Quite conveniently, these value labels are stored in the system file and can be reproduced for the user's information as analysis is done. The rightmost column of Table 7.1 lists missing value codes for each variable. In survey research, there will be questions that respondents did not answer for one reason or another, and codes for these situations are referred to as **missing values**. It is important that analysis packages provide ways of differentiating valid codes from missing values. Imagine, for example, if the 98 and 99 codes for the education (EDUC) variable were included in the computation of a mean of the variable!

Figure 7.5 contains a SPSS-X program which makes use of the information in Table 7.1 to create a system file. The TITLE statement provides a convenient way of labeling the output. The right-hand portion of the statement will be listed at the top of output pages. Output cannot be overlabeled or overdocumented. Researchers tend to amass large amounts of output and any information which helps distinguish one stack of computer paper from another is welcome indeed.

The FILE HANDLE statement assigns a temporary short name to the raw data file (EXAMPLE). The NAME statement identifies the full name of the disk file where the data are stored. The SET BLANKS command in-

```
TITLE   CREATION OF NORCGSS 72-82 SYSTEM FILE
FILE HANDLE   EXAMPLE/
  NAME='DSK_SCRATCH:[APP]3.TAP'
SET BLANKS=0
DATA LIST    FILE=EXAMPLE RECORDS=11
 /1 MARITAL 23 AGE 56-57 EDUC 64-65 SEX 76 RACE 77
 /2 REGION 65 /5 RELIG 7
VARIABLE LABELS MARITAL 'MARITAL STATUS'
 AGE 'AGE' RACE 'RACE' SEX 'SEX'
 EDUC 'HIGHEST YEAR OF SCHOOL COMPLETE'
 REGION 'REGION OF INTERVIEW'
 RELIG 'RESP RELIGIOUS PREFERENCE'
MISSING VALUES MARITAL(9)/AGE(0,98,99)/EDUC(97,98,99)/
 RELIG(0,8,9)/
VALUE LABELS MARITAL 1 'MARRIED' 2 'WIDOWED' 3 'DIVORCED'
 4 'SEPARATED' 5 'NEVER MARRIED' 9 'NA'/
 SEX 1 'MALE' 2 'FEMALE'/
 RACE 1 'WHITE' 2 'BLACK' 3 'OTHER'/
 REGION 1 'NEW ENGLAND' 2 'MIDDLE ATLANTIC' 3 'E. NOR. CENTRAL'
 4 'W. NOR. CENTRAL' 5 'SOUTH ATLANTIC' 6 'E. SOU. CENTRAL'
 7 'W. SOU. CENTRAL' 8 'MOUNTAIN' 9 'PACIFIC' 0 'FOREIGN'/
 RELIG 1 'PROTESTANT' 2 'CATHOLIC' 3 'JEWISH' 4 'NONE' 5 'OTHER'/
FILE HANDLE   KEEPNORC/NAME='NORCSAVE.DAT'
SAVE   OUTFILE=KEEPNORC/MAP
```

Fig. 7.5 SPSS-X Program for Building System File

structs the package to treat blanks as zeros. The DATA LIST statement identifies the variables and their associated deck and column locations. For example, the MARITAL variable is located in deck 1 and column 23. Likewise, the RELIG variable resides in deck 5, column 7, of the file. The VARIABLE LABELS statement allows informative labels to be attached to the sometimes cryptic variable names. Next, the MISSING VALUES statement appears and identifies codes which are to be treated as missing. Specific codes associated with categorical variables are identified in the VALUE LABELS statement.

The last two lines of the program (SAVE FILE) instruct SPSS to store the system file for safe-keeping. The system file is given the handle KEEP-NORC and it will be stored on a disk file named NORCSAVE. DAT. Once the system file has been saved, subsequent programs can be quite a bit shorter. For example, the program in Figure 7.6 reads the system file and produces a contingency table that cross-classifies the RACE and SEX variables. Note that variables are referenced only by their names. This is because other data definition information has already been stored with the system file. Similar programs are executed in the appendices, and readers are encouraged to consult the materials there.

A portion of the output associated with this simple program is reproduced in Figure 7.7. Note the labeling which annotates the output. There is no doubt about the contents of each cell of the table. Thus a system file dispenses with most data definition and clearly provides a convenient way to document analysis output fully and completely.

Data Base Management Systems

Construction and maintenance of system files based on rectangular raw data are quite straightforward with any of the available data analysis packages. However hierarchical files can present problems for standard statistical analysis packages. Users should consult their software documentation regarding the availability of special file handling routines for nonrectangular data sets.

Should an analysis package prove unsatisfactory, those working with

```
TITLE READING NORC SYSTEM FILE
FILE HANDLE  NORCSYS/NAME='NORCSAVE.DAT'
GET FILE=NORCSYS
SET BLANKS=0
CROSSTABS TABLES=RACE BY SEX
STATISTICS ALL
OPTIONS 3,4,5
```

Fig. 7.6 SPSS-X Program that Reads System File

30-NOV-83   READING NORC SYSTEM FILE   Digital VAX   VMS 3.3
             UNIVERSITY OF HARTFORD

- - RACE - - - - RACE - - - - - C R O S S T A B U L A T I O N   O F   S E X - - -
- - RACE - - - - RACE - - - - - - - - - BY SEX - - - - - - - - - - PAGE 1 OF 1

```
                                    SEX
              COUNT  I
              ROW PCT I MALE    FEMALE     ROW
              COL PCT I                    TOTAL
              TOT PCT I    1 I      2 I
             ---------+--------+--------+
RACE
  WHITE          1   I  5442  I  6540  I  11982
                     I  45.4  I  54.6  I  87.9
                     I  88.4  I  87.5  I
                     I  39.9  I  48.0  I
             ---------+--------+--------+
  BLACK          2   I   660  I   879  I   1539
                     I  42.9  I  57.1  I  11.3
                     I  10.7  I  11.8  I
                     I   4.8  I   6.5  I
             ---------+--------+--------+
  OTHER          3   I    52  I    53  I    105
                     I  49.5  I  50.5  I   .8
                     I    .8  I    .7  I
                     I    .4  I    .4  I
             ---------+--------+--------+
            COLUMN     6154     7472     13626
            TOTAL      45.2     54.8     100.0
```

CHI-SQUARE	D.F.	SIGNIFICANCE	MIN E.F.	CELLS WITH E.F.< 5
4.34587	2	0.1138	47.422	NONE

STATISTIC	SYMMETRIC	WITH RACE DEPENDENT	WITH SEX DEPENDENT
LAMBDA	0.00000	0.00000	0.00000
UNCERTAINTY COEFFICIENT	0.00029	0.00040	0.00023
SOMERS' D	0.01229	0.00880	0.00038
ETA		0.01071	0.01786

STATISTIC	VALUE	SIGNIFICANCE
CRAMER'S V	0.01786	
CONTINGENCY COEFFICIENT	0.01786	
KENDALL'S TAU B	0.01339	
KENDALL'S TAU C	0.00872	0.0583
PEARSON'S R	0.01071	0.0583
GAMMA	0.01126	0.1056

NUMBER OF MISSING OBSERVATIONS = 0

Fig. 7.7 Output Listening from SPSS-X Program

hierarchical files on mainframes will want to acquaint themselves with a data base management system (DBMS) such as the U.S. Bureau of the Census' **CENSPAC** or the Scientific Information Retrieval (**SIR**) system. Both of these packages facilitate the analysis of hierarchical files. SIR allows the file to read at any of the specified levels of the hierarchy (e.g., SMSA, household, or family) and provides elementary analysis capability. SIR also produces subfiles which can be interfaced with SPSS for more sophisticated analysis of portions of the hierarchical file.

Researchers with hierarchical files small enough to process on microcomputers will be very pleased with a DBMS such as dBase II, Lotus 1-2-3, or DataStar. Each of these is a user-friendly DBMS which greatly facilitates the handling of small nonrectangular files. The term **relational data base management** is sometimes used in conjunction with these packages to indicate that records can be linked together in a variety of ways. The user is not restricted to a single hierarchical pattern of relationships among records.

Thus the structure of social science data files can range from simple arrays to complex hierarchies. No doubt the reader has noticed the continual reference to data files collected by agencies such as the Bureau of the Census. As it turns out, a great deal of data exists in machine-readable form and is archived for the use of researchers throughout the social science community. In the final section of this chapter, some of the more prominent secondary data files are noted.

SECONDARY DATA ANALYSIS

There is an important tradition of secondary data analysis in the social sciences. Secondary data analysis refers to analysis done by someone other than the original researcher who collected the data (Hyman, 1972). Such analysis is therefore distinguished from primary data analysis which is carried out by the person who gathered the data. Secondary data analysis is facilitated by the widespread availability of machine-readable data files (**MRDF**) written on magnetic tape or diskettes. Important social science data bases can thus be used by many researchers who can undertake replications or use previous research as a point of departure for their own work.

Secondary data analysis has become routine in the social sciences, and the increasing popularity of this kind of research can be directly traced to advances in computing (Babbie, 1983). Once research data have been recorded on machine-readable media such as tapes or diskettes, it is quite simple to make multiple copies of a file for distribution. This ease in duplication promotes sharing of data among individual researchers and

Machine-Readable Data Files [MRDF]
Authors analyzing data available in this format should indicate producers and distributors as in these examples:

Louis Harris and Associates. 1975. *Harris 1975 Nuclear Power Survey #2515* [MRDF]. New York: Louis Harris and Associates [producer]. Chapel Hill: Louis Harris Data Center, University of North Carolina [distributor].

Miller, W., A. Miller, and G. Kline. 1975. *The CPS 1974 American National Election Study* [MRDF]. Ann Arbor: Center for Political Studies, University of Michigan [producer]. Ann Arbor: Inter-University Consortium for Political and Social Research [distributor].

U.S. Bureau of Census. 1979. *1970 Census of Population and Housing, Fourth Count Population Summary Tape* [MRDF]. Washington: U.S. Bureau of the Census [producer]. Rosslyn, Va.: DUALabs [distributor].

Fig. 7.8 Excerpt from *Social Forces* Author's Guide
(Source: *Social Forces*, 1983, Vol. 61, p. 910)

the archiving of files for general use. Indeed, making research data public through archives has become such an accepted practice that library procedures have been established procedures for cataloging data files and codebooks (Dodd, 1979). Similarly, scholarly journals have specified cita-

Table 7.2 Selected Cross-sectional National Surveys

Name of Survey	Dates	Organization
General Social Surveys	1972–83	National Opinion Research Center
American National Election Studies (bi-annual)	1948–82	Institute for Social Research, Univ. of Michigan
1900 U.S. Census Public Use Sample (PUS)	1900	U.S. Bureau of the Census and Center for Studies in Demography and Ecology, University ofWisconsin
1970 U.S. Census Public Use Sample Files (PUS)	1970	U.S. Bureau of the Census
1980 U.S. Census Public Use Microdata Samples (PUMS)	1980	U.S. Bureau of the Census
Current Population Surveys (CPS)	1968–83	U.S. Bureau of the Census
Surveys of Consumer Attitudes and Behavior	1953–76	Survey Research Center, Univ. of Michigan

tion formats which ensure that readers can locate the source of an MRDF used in an article. The instructions for authors of articles in *Social Forces* are reproduced in Figure 7.8.

As the foregoing suggests, it is important for those in the social science community to be aware of the sources and the range of secondary data available. Two listings of survey data sets distributed as MRDFs are provided here. Table 7.2 lists some major cross-sectional survey data files. Although these surveys may be carried out more than once, they are classified as cross-sectional because the same respondents are surveyed only once. Table 7.3 lists some major longitudinal data files that have been widely used by researchers in the social sciences. These studies involve repeated surveys of the same individuals.

Table 7.3   Selected National Longitudinal Surveys

Name of Survey	Dates	Organization
National Surveys of Labor Market Experience (NLS)	1966–present	Center for Human Resources, Ohio State University
Panel Study of Income Dynamics (PSID)	1968–80	Survey Research Center, Univ. of Michigan
High School and Beyond, 1980	1980–present	National Center for Education Statistics

Table 7.4   Other National and International Secondary Data Files

Name of Data File	Organization
Macro-economic Time Series for U.S., U.K., Germany, and France	National Bureau of Economic Research
Historical Supplement to the Demographic Yearbook 1948–70	United Nations
The County and City Data Book	U.S. Bureau of the Census
Voting Scores for Members of Congress	Congressional Quarterly
U.S. Historical Election Returns (1788–1980)	Inter-university Consortium for Political and Social Research
Annual Uniform Crime Report	Federal Bureau of Investigation
Health and Nutrition Examination Surveys 1971–75	National Center for Health Statistics
Health Interview Surveys 1975–79	National Center for Health Statistics
Student Achievement Study 1971–74	International Association for the Advancement of Educational Achievement
Dictionary of Occupational Titles	Department of Labor
Quality of Employment Surveys	Employee Standards Administration

Not all of the MRDFs available for researchers fit the conventional model of social science interview surveys. Table 7.4 lists a number of secondary data files ranging from aggregate social and economic indicators to statistics on occupations. These are but a few of the secondary data files that social scientists employ routinely. The archives which serve as sources for these data are noted in the next section.

Sources of Secondary Data

One way to obtain secondary data for computer analysis is to approach those who originally collected the data. Although there is nothing wrong with this, a great number of requests for data would clearly burden the original investigators. Moreover, most researchers are reluctant to release their data to others until they have finished their own analyses. The best way to obtain secondary data is through data archives which routinely make their holdings available at modest costs to researchers. These collections house data files which have been put in the public domain by the primary users. Some of these archives are affiliated with universities and others with government or private agencies. An example of the university-based archive is the Inter-University Consortium for Political and Social Research (**ICPSR**) which is housed at the Institute for Social Research at the University of Michigan. College and universities across the country are members of ICPSR, and one important service provided by the Consortium is the distribution of MRDFs to member universities. Nearly every MRDF listed in Tables 7.2, 7.3, and 7.4 is available at minimal costs through ICPSR. The consortium's extensive holdings are detailed in its *Guide to Resources and Services* which is published annually by ICPSR.

Sobal (1981) provides a listing of other U.S. and international archives along with their addresses, and readers are encouraged to consult his directory. It is likely that a nearby data archive already houses enough information to keep a social scientist busy for a long time. Now that we have identified readily available data sets, it is time to outline procedures of computer analysis of such data. These analyses are the subject of Chapter 8.

SUGGESTED READINGS

1. A good primer on system files can be found in Chapters 7 and 8 of *SPSS-X Basics* (New York: McGraw-Hill, 1984).
2. The NORC General Social Survey *Cumulative Codebook* (see, e.g.,

Davis, 1982) is an example of well-prepared documentation, and, as such, is highly recommended reading. A new edition is published each year by the National Opinion Research Center, University of Chicago.
3. An authoritative source on secondary data analysis is Hyman (1972).
4. The annual *Guide to Resources and Services* published by ICPSR details the holdings of this data archive. Readers will be impressed with the scope and quality of the secondary data available there.

SUGGESTED EXERCISES

1. Before getting on the computer: Inquire about secondary data files available locally or in a nearby archive.
   a. How are the data stored?
   b. Where can the documentation be accessed?
   c. Choose one file to use in Exercise 2.
2. On the computer: Using a text editor, build a simple program which reads a secondary data file and creates a system file. Store the program as a permanent file for use with exercises in Chapter 8.

CHAPTER EIGHT

Strategies for Mainframe Statistical Analysis

Most of the necessary concepts and procedures associated with social science computing have now been introduced. The remaining chapters focus on concepts and procedures specific to data analysis and the maintenance of large social science data files. In this chapter, statistical analysis on mainframes is considered. Chapter 9 contains information on efficient and economical handling of large data files on mainframes. In Chapter 10, problems and procedures associated with data analysis on microcomputers are discussed. Each of these chapters builds on fundamentals introduced in earlier chapters. Readers who are unfamiliar with basic hardware and software concepts, text editing, and data structures will want to review the chapters in which these topics are discussed.

BASIC MODES OF COMPUTER ACCESS

In principle, statistical data analysis consists of providing a mainframe a set of instructions (a program) for one of a handful of powerful software packages. This accessing of a computer takes place in one of two basic ways: batch or interactive time-sharing modes. As the name suggests, **batch processing** means that all of a job's instructions are grouped and executed as a unit, an approach that maximizes efficiency of the system.

Many jobs can be run concurrently in a multiprocessing environment. Jobs are differentiated from one another on the basis of their requirements for system time and resources. Some operating systems defer the execution of high-demand jobs while allowing low-demand jobs to run. The extent of involvement of the operating system in regulating job execution is considerable in batch processing. Individual users typically have little or no control over the execution of their jobs once they have "batched" them into a system. As a matter of fact, in a prototypical batch system, users have no further contact with the computer after submitting their jobs.

Just the opposite situation prevails in an **interactive time-sharing** system. Interactive time-sharing means that many online users access and communicate with the system on an on-going basis. The configuration of an interactive time-sharing system typically corresponds to a distributed network with a central mainframe and terminals in remote locations. Interactive access modes include **remote batch** or remote job entry (**RJE**) in which batch job processing is accomplished in a much more convenient way from a remote terminal. While the job still waits its turn in various queues, the user has the advantage of staying in touch with the system, checking the status of the job, and completing other computing tasks in the interim. The user also typically retains control over the scheduling of printing and can elect not to print output if errors are detected. Remote batch processing in a time-sharing system thus retains for users considerably more control over their jobs and adds a measure of convenience.

Another type of interactive access is characterized as **conversational** because the pattern of interaction follows a question and answer format. Single instructions are evaluated and responses are immediately provided by the computer. In **nonconversational interactive access** the computer is asked to execute a set of instructions immediately. If a system is not saturated with users, use of either of these interactive time-sharing modes greatly improves turnaround time. In the sections that follow, strategies and procedures for batch access and interactive time-sharing are detailed. At the end of the chapter, emphasis will be placed on factors that should be taken into account in choosing one of these modes of access.

BATCH ACCESS

With the possible exception of the operator's console, early computers could only be accessed in batch mode. The capacity of the hardware was easily taxed and programs were typically processed one at a time. Likewise, early versions of operating systems were not sophisticated enough to manage the simultaneous execution of a large number of programs. Batch access is still used today because the use of central system and peripheral resources can be maximized. Indeed, some mainframe installations require that tapes and removable disk packs be accessed by batch jobs only. Since these storage media are frequently used by social scientists, it is important to introduce some basics of batch processing. In this section, four stages in the batch access process are detailed: job preparation, job submission, output retrieval, and output assessment.

Job Preparation

The first step in batch access for data analysis is the construction of a job and this is typically done on standard 80-column punched cards. A simple job structure is represented in Figure 8.1 as a deck of cards. The first few cards are known as job control statements, and these introduce the program to the operating system. Standard parts of this introduction include user identification for accounting purposes, passwords for security, estimated system resources required for execution, and information on any software packages to be accessed. With this information, the operating system can schedule the job for execution and arrange for appropriate billing of charges.

The second portion of the job deck consists of a program of instructions to the software package that will analyze a raw data file. These

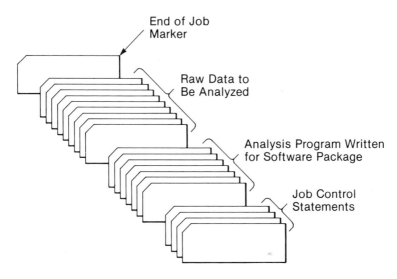

Fig. 8.1 Example of Conventional Batch Card Deck

statements must include data definition instructions which, at a minimum, consist of information on the columns in which the variables are located. This portion of the program is also likely to contain recoding commands as well as other instructions for transforming existing variables and creating new ones. The last part of the software instructions indicates the kinds of data analysis to be done.

In the simple job structure depicted in Figure 8.1, the raw data immediately follow the software package instructions. Of course, large data files that are cumbersome to handle on cards are often stored on magnetic tape or disk. In that event, the job control statements are expanded to include instructions to the operating system for accessing the data. Once system files have been created, the data will always reside on tape or disk, and the program will not contain a lengthy data definition section. The final card is the end-of-job marker which simply identifies the end of the job deck.

Job Submission

Once a program has been prepared on cards, it is entered into the computer system on a peripheral device known as a card reader. The lucky batch user is the one who has a card reader near his or her desk. However, many social scientists can recall trips across campus to a central site card reader and, for some, these journeys are still routine. Barring a mangled or warped card, the physical task of reading the cards has been facilitated by high-speed card reading devices. But the operation of the card reader is the most contact a typical batch user ever has with a computer system. From that point on, the operating system manages the execution and printing of output from the program.

When entered into the system, a job is placed in a queue or waiting list for execution at the discretion of the operating system. Ordinarily, jobs that require the least execution time and central memory will run before jobs that need more system resources. However, these are not the only criteria used by the operating system in job scheduling. Most installations define classes of users and assign different priorities to the different classes. Unfortunately, this usage of the word class will do nothing to allay the social sciences' obsession with class and inequality. Systems analysts who oversee the computer system's operation may have top priority and their jobs will likely execute immediately. Administrative processing such as payroll and billing may also take precedence over routine research applications. Jobs submitted by external users paying premium commercial rates may also execute ahead of jobs belonging to the common user. In university settings, it is not unusual to find that certain forms of instructional computing are given priority over other programs. Some schools have gone so far as to ban word processing during certain peak periods of the day. In any event, a sophisticated operating system mediates the various priorities and schedules jobs for execution. After jobs have run, the results of the computing are placed in yet another queue for printing.

Output Retrieval

After the job has printed, the user can retrieve the output. The time this takes depends on the speed of the system and the level of activity. The actual time that a program is running in the CPU is ordinarily a few seconds (or less); this is known as execution time. The fact that **execution time** is typically very brief offers little consolation to a user who has been cooling his or her heels for several hours. **Turnaround time**, or amount of elapsed time from job entry to output retrieval, is usually much longer than the execution time. The concept of **real time** is also used to refer to the total clock time it takes to use the computer to solve a problem.

If printers are only located at the central site, the user is obliged to remain there or return to retrieve output from jobs. Veteran batch computer users become quite proficient at estimating the real time a job is likely to require. Fortunately, interactive time-sharing computing has greatly reduced the inconvenience associated with slow turnaround. To be sure, the batch access process is not complete when output is retrieved. The user still must examine the output for errors and be prepared to make any necessary corrections.

Output Assessment

It is rare that a program runs successfully on the first try and, the longer the program, the more likely it is that it will contain errors. The last stage of batch processing consists of an examination of the output. If errors are found, the original setup must be corrected and resubmitted. Even if there are no execution errors, there are often user errors which can render any computed statistics useless. Suppose, for example, the wrong columns of a raw data file have been defined for a variable. Any analysis based on that variable would have to be redone. Thus, even when there are no apparent execution errors, careful examination of computer analysis output is always in order.

The batch access process is summarized in Figure 8.2. The process begins with program preparation, and proceeds through job submission, output retrieval, and terminates with review of the output. Note that the figure implies a cycle; the review of output can result in initiating the process once again. As errors are detected, the job is corrected and then resubmitted. Only after the analyst is satisfied that the results are acceptable does the batch process end. In recent years, cumbersome punch cards, slow turnaround, and the general inconvenience of batch access have led many social scientists to turn to interactive time-sharing modes of analysis. In the next section, it will be apparent that remote batch analysis at a computer terminal is a marked improvement over conventional batch access.

INTERACTIVE TIME-SHARING ACCESS

Interactive time-sharing access allows many online users to use a mainframe from terminals at remote sites. Three access modes are identified here: remote batch, nonconversational interaction, and conversational interaction. Strategies and procedures associated with these three access modes are discussed in the next few sections. It should be amply evident to the reader that these interactive access modes are to be preferred over conventional batch analysis.

Remote Batch Access

One important aspect of an interactive time-sharing system is remote batch access. Users at terminals in many different locations can submit jobs and follow their progress through the system. Although the phases of this analysis process are the same (program preparation, job submission, output retrieval, and output assessment), virtually every aspect of remote batch access is easier than conventional batch access. Readers are encouraged to refer to the appendices for extended examples of each of these steps on a variety of mainframes.

Program Preparation. Remote batch jobs are generally prepared at computer terminals with text editors. Job files are created, listed, corrected, and saved like any other text file. Since the job file is to be submitted to a batch queue, the job structure will appear virtually identical to a conventional batch setup (recall Figure 8.1). One possible difference is operating system instructions to delay printing until the user has had a chance to review the results of the job.

Job Submission.   After a job file has been edited and saved, it is submitted to the batch queue to wait its turn to execute. Just as if a deck of cards had been read into the system, a copy of the job file residing in the user's catalog is moved into an execution queue. After the job is submitted, the user can prepare other programs or log off the terminal and return later to check on the job. While still logged on, the status of the job can be checked, and the job can usually be cancelled by the user if something goes awry. Each of these tasks—job submission, status checking, and job cancellation—is quite straightforward on an interactive time-sharing system and typically requires only a few simple commands.

Output Retrieval. Like any other submitted job file, a remote batch job is routinely controlled by the operating system until it is printed. It is frequently possible, however, for users to retain some control over their remote batch jobs. Most operating systems have provisions which allow interactive users to view disk files containing the results of jobs and to determine whether or not output should be printed. This can be done at a computer terminal by editing and displaying portions of the output file. This can result in a substantial reduction in printing, as jobs containing errors or unwanted output are purged rather than printed. If the user determines that the output is worth printing, it can be routed to a printer and retrieved.

Output Assessment. As was noted, an initial review of job output in a remote batch environment is typically done on a terminal. If the output is subsequently printed, the user is obliged to study the results carefully for the many kinds of human errors that the computer cannot detect. If the initial review of the output file reveals errors, the user edits the original job file, makes whatever changes are necessary, and then resubmits the job. Thus, printing is done only when a review of job output indicates no further execution errors. Remote batch access facilitates analysis by expediting the resubmission of corrected jobs. If the user must travel some distance to retrieve printed output, he or she can make that trip confident that there will be something worthwhile to pick up.

Remote batch access is thus a substantial improvement in efficiency and convenience over conventional batch access. Even so, a diagram of the process would appear much the same as the conventional outline of Figure 8.2. The important difference is that the remote batch process is accomplished on a computer terminal. Each of the appendices contains examples of remote batch access, and readers are encouraged to consult them.

The remaining interactive time-sharing access modes enhance the analysis process even more by effectively bypassing the batch execution queue altogether. Conversational and nonconversational interactive modes produce immediate results and—quite understandably—are to be preferred for many routine analysis tasks.

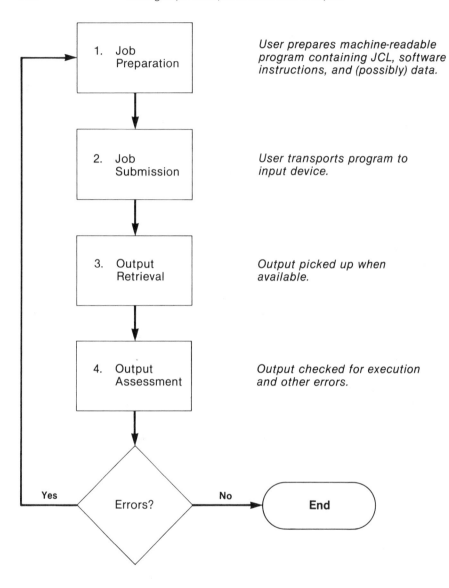

Fig. 8.2 Batch Analysis Process

Nonconversational Interaction

There is no doubt that immediate execution of a set of instructions is a great convenience, and nonconversational interactive access provides just that. The user edits a program file that contains commands written for a software package and then calls the software package to execute the program. Unlike a batch program, the prepared set of instructions does not include commands to the operating system. These statements, if needed, are issued by the user prior to calling the software program. These job control-like commands identify data sets needed as input to the program and those that will be created as a result of its execution.

A typical program requires an input data set (raw or system file), an output data set into which the analysis results are written and, possibly, an output data set which stores a modified version of the original data. The user must provide the system with information on these input and output files before analysis can begin. This file specification is known as **allocation**. Many large systems now facilitate this communication process between the user and the operating system with **command procedures**. A command procedure is a special file containing a set of standard allocation and other operating system statements. By executing the command procedure, the user essentially issues all the commands contained in the file.

Figure 8.3 summarizes the nonconversational interactive access process. At the outset, a program file is edited. Then a command procedure is used to call a software package and execute the program. Next the results are reviewed, and the output file is printed if all appears to have gone according to plan. Although a similarity between this process and remote batch access is apparent, it is important to remember that the interactive user is not delayed while the job waits in an execution queue. Moreover, the cumbersome job control statements that must be included in a batch job are replaced by a series of time-sharing commands which can be repeated in the event that they are issued incorrectly. The interactive mode means that immediate feedback is provided for each command issued by the user. In contrast, a batch job with a single job control error will doom the entire job. There is obviously much to be gained in the way of convenience by using nonconversational interactive access. Still, there are disadvantages as well.

The execution of nonconversational interactive programs is characterized here as immediate. And, as far as the computer is concerned, the execution does take place as quickly as possible. Just how much real time elapses depends on the level of system activity. During periods outside the nine to five workday, the real time associated with most interactive jobs will be within a few seconds of the required execution time. But users who attempt large interactive analyses during peak hours may encounter substantial delays as the operating system defers parts of their program execution until sufficient system resources are available. Under conditions of heavy system activity, the difference between batch and interactive processing becomes a bit blurred. Although a large, demanding interactive program would execute very slowly, the same batch job probably would not be allowed to run at all.

To complicate matters, a user is obliged to stay at a computer ter-

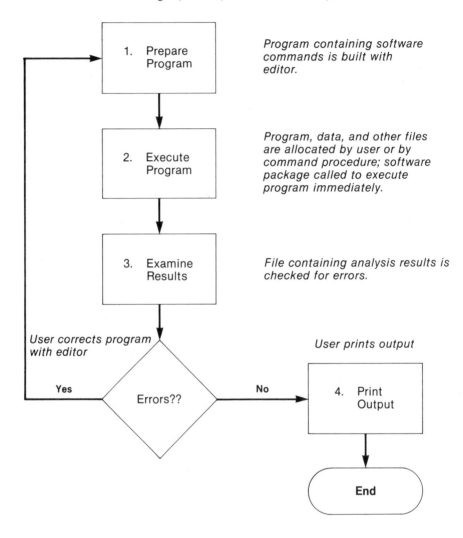

Fig. 8.3 Nonconversational Interaction

minal until an interactive session is completed. Moreover, while an interactive program is executing, the terminal typically cannot be used for anything else at all. Thus, there is something to be said for submitting certain large analysis tasks to batch queues. While the user is waiting for a job to execute, the terminal can be used in other ways.

Another possibly disadvantageous aspect of interactive analysis involves the allocation of files residing on magnetic tape. Tape files are best accessed in batch mode where the operating system can be relied on to open and close data sets correctly and securely. While veteran users sometimes request that tapes be allocated to their terminals, they run the risk of ruining existing files and improperly creating new data sets. Also, a tape drive dedicated for any length of time to a single terminal is not available to the rest of the user community. Thus, mounting tapes for interactive access is somewhat risky and certainly a privilege not to be abused.

Conversational Interaction

Like batch analysis, nonconversational interactive analysis requires the editing of a program file (albeit one without job control statements). In contrast, conversational interaction consists of a dialogue between user and computer. As such, no prepared program is necessary. Like its nonconversational counterpart, conversational interaction requires that necessary operating system instructions be issued prior to beginning the analysis. Unlike nonconversational interaction, however, commands to software packages are entered one at a time. The system responds after each command, informing the user of any errors and providing the requested analysis results. Essentially, a conversation takes place between the user and the computer.

Conversational interaction is clearly a most attractive mode of access for statistical analysis. Still, a number of prior analysis steps are usually required to reach the point where data are analyzed so easily. Not the least of these is the construction of a system file which eliminates the need for lengthy data definition. Typically, a system file analyzed conversationally is the latest in a series of files that began as raw data and went through successive modifications and refinements. To anticipate subsequent recommendations, conversational interaction is best employed on very clean and well-developed system files of modest size.

One other factor associated with conversational interaction regards the number of commands to the software necessary to do the desired analysis. Once the conversation begins, the commands tend to build sequentially on one another. That is, an undetected syntax error in, say, statement 2 can doom all ten statements in a hypothetical program. This will be the case when the software package does not interpret each statement, but waits to interpret a set of several instructions. When the analysis calls for a conversation of more than five lines, users would do better to build the statements with an editor and execute them in a nonconversational interactive fashion.

Short command structures prove more successful because most of the existing conversational packages are based on older batch packages. As properly designed packages for interactive analysis are introduced, much of this inconvenience will likely be eliminated. In the final section of the chapter, the various access modes are reviewed, and recommendations are made regarding appropriate situations for choosing one mode over another.

WHICH ACCESS MODE?

By now it should be clear that conversational and nonconversational modes of access are usually preferred because of the substantially reduced real time required to carry them out. But this is not always the case. Remote batch access is a much better mode of computing for some situations. The purpose of this final section is to provide the reader with some criteria for choosing among the access modes reviewed here.

Perhaps the best indication of the appropriate mode of access is the analysis phase. As noted on several occasions, a standard social science computer analysis typically progresses from large raw data files, through initial system files, to refined and sometimes smaller working system files that contain only those variables most critical to the analysis. As it turns out, this process lends itself nicely to a parallel progression from remote batch to interactive access modes. Table 8.1 summarizes the relation between analysis phases, data file types, and access modes. Social science secondary data are nearly always distributed on magnetic tape and, as discussed in the next chapter, tape is an ideal permanent storage medium for such data. Thus it is quite likely that the first phase of the analysis will require the mounting of a tape (or tapes). It is wise to make the initial system file large so that it contains every variable and every case even remotely relevant to the research topic. In this way it should not be necessary to return to the original raw data at all. Of course, if this initial file construction requires tape mounting, it is best done in remote batch mode.

In the unlikely (but nevertheless convenient) event that the original data are stored on disk, nonconversational interactive mode could be used, depending on the time of day and the local criteria used to discount the costs associated with analysis. Although many installations encourage off-peak hour usage by offering substantial discounts at night, this sometimes applies only to batch processing. Assuming that all users are concerned with curtailing computer expenses, we will return to the subject of discounting in the next chapter. In the interim, suffice it to say that the choice between remote batch and nonconversational interaction modes may well depend on local discounting policies.

As suggested in Table 8.1, the second phase of computer analysis typically consists of further refinements and modifications of the original

Table 8.1 Suggested Access Modes

Likely Analysis Phase	Type of File To Be Analyzed	Remote Batch	Interactive Access Nonconversational	Conversational
1st Phase: Creation of initial, large system file	Raw Data File			
	-stored on tape	X		
	-stored on disk	X	X	
2nd Phase: Creation of second and subsequent generation working system files	Initial System File			
	-stored on tape	X		
	-stored on disk		X	
3rd Phase: Analysis of small working system files	Working System File (stored on disk)			
	-lengthy analysis		X	
	-brief analysis			X

Note: Recommendations do not assume any discount policy. Users may find remote batch more economical and use it on that basis.

system file. This usually results in a smaller working file that can be easily analyzed. For example, a researcher studying labor force participation may begin with an original system file containing all persons in a survey who ever held a job. In the course of the analysis, the researcher may decide to limit the sample further to currently employed respondents of a certain age range (say, 25–64). Variables should be dropped as they are no longer needed, leading to increasingly smaller system files that contain only the most important variables.

Once the analysis enters the third phase and working system files are the primary data sources, interactive access modes are clearly to be preferred. As Table 8.1 suggests, the choice between nonconversational and conversational interaction is based on the kind of analysis to be done. On the one hand, analysis can be lengthy in that it requires a good deal of execution time. On the other hand, analysis can require a series of steps to be completed. In either instance, nonconversational interaction is recommended over remote batch access where discounts are not a consideration. In finishing a research report, a researcher may need a single figure or some small set of statistics. Conversational interaction is ideal for this kind of brief analysis which quickly retrieves small bits of information needed to complete a larger analysis.

In sum, the choice of access modes for mainframe statistical analysis lies in large measure on the progress of the research. Earlier phases generally require more of a computer's resources and are best managed by the operating system (with the user keeping a close tab). Later phases are less taxing on the system and are best managed by the researcher alone.

Should suitable data present themselves in the form of a well-developed system file, some of the earlier steps will obviously not be necessary. Finally, local policies may influence a researcher's choice of access modes and analysis procedures. Whatever the prevailing regulations, there is no substitute for a carefully planned analysis strategy.

By now, the significance of research data files is amply apparent. For example, it has been noted that famous social science data files are available for analysis. In addition, it has been suggested that the nature of a data file largely determines the way a user will access a mainframe for statistical analysis. It is appropriate, then, to return to further consideration of data storage and maintenance. This is done in Chapter 9, where emphasis is placed on handling the large data bases that characterize much social science research.

SUGGESTED EXERCISES

Before getting on the computer:
1. Determine the procedures for submitting a remote batch job at your installation. If your mainframe is one of those covered in the appendices of this book, your remote batch procedures should parallel those illustrated at the end of the book.
2. Review the program built in conjunction with exercises in Chapter 7. The program should read a raw data file and create a system file ready for further analysis. Check to make sure that the raw data you want to use are readily accessible on disk or tape.
3. Build another program which will read the system file and analyze the data. Prepare this second program for nonconversational interactive execution. A simple frequency distribution or contingency table analysis will suffice for practice.

On the computer:
1. Submit the batch job and follow its progress. If errors are apparent, resubmit the job.
2. Once the system file has been created, execute the second program. After a successful execution, retrieve the output associated with both jobs and study it carefully.
3. To maintain your word processing skills, prepare a brief writeup of the analysis you have conducted. Try to make your report as neat as possible and append tables as appropriate.

CHAPTER NINE

Storage, Maintenance, and Use of Large Data Files

This chapter has several objectives. Perhaps the most important of these is a discussion of special strategies for storing and maintaining large social science data files for mainframe analysis. To do this, some technical detail on magnetic tapes and disk drives is introduced in the first section of the chapter. Another objective here is to detail various approaches to the maintenance of documentation associated with social science data files. There must be mechanisms to access information on files, and some advice along these lines is provided in the second section of the chapter. The final section is devoted to a consideration of economy in computing. Large data files employed by social scientists make computing costs a prime concern, and several tips are provided in the concluding section for reducing costs associated with mainframe analysis.

MORE ON STORAGE MEDIA

To this point very little technical detail has been provided on storage devices so that emphasis could be placed on basic aspects of computing. With that fundamental knowledge in place, a closer examination of magnetic tapes and disks is now in order. Physical characteristics of storage devices are discussed here, and the organization of multiple data files on the same unit is considered. Advantages and disadvantages of storing social science data bases on each medium are indicated. Then some important kinds of system utilities or special-purpose software for handling disk and tape files are noted. Finally, security measures are considered for data files residing on magnetic tape and disks.

Magnetic Tape

Physical Characteristics. Magnetic tapes are so widely utilized that some industry standards have emerged, and tapes written by one computer can sometimes be read by another machine. Tapes are typically one-half inch wide and up to 2400 feet long. Figure 9.1 illustrates one method of writing data on a nine-track tape. (There are other methods for recording nine-track tapes and, additionally, seven-track tapes are occasionally used.) In this example, each character is represented by an 8-bit byte. The eight read-write heads of the tape drive write this pattern, one bit per head. The ninth track is used for error checking. Several bytes taken together make up a record, and the records in the figure consist of 80 bytes as if they were card image data. Records can be grouped in **blocks** which have a fixed length in bytes that is a multiple of the record length. In the illustration, the block length is 12960 which is 162×80 (i.e., each block contains 162 80-byte records). Each block is followed by a short, unwritten space known as an **interblock gap**. The size of a block may be

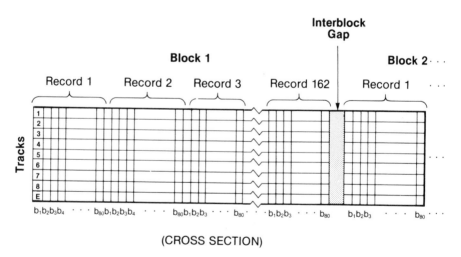

(CROSS SECTION)

Fig. 9.1   Diagram of Nine-Track Tape

anything up to the maximum allowed by the operating system (sometimes as high as 32,000 bytes).

Block size is one factor that affects how much data can be stored on a tape. Since the interblock gaps contain no data, it follows that the fewer there are, the more room there is for data. Thus, one rule of thumb for getting more data on a tape is to use a large block size. When data are to be stored on tape but frequently moved to disk, the optimal tape block size is determined, in part, by considering optimal block size to be used on the system's disks. It is best to check with the local computer center regarding optimal block sizes. In Figure 9.1, the 12960 block size is the highest multiple of 80 that can fit in one track of length 13030 as found on some disk storage devices.

Another factor that can dramatically affect the amount of data stored on a tape is **density**. Tape density refers to the concentration of bits in a given linear area of the tape. The standard measure of density is referred to as **bpi** (bits per inch), and densities of 800, 1600, and 6250 bpi are common. The 12960 8-bit characters in Figure 9.1 would be recorded on 16.2 inches of tape at 800 bpi, 8.1 inches at 1600 bpi, and 2.1 inches at 6250 bpi. Obviously, the recording density makes a striking difference in the amount of data that can be contained on a single tape. Large social science data files are typically written at the highest possible density. The maximum density depends on the tape drives at a particular computer installation and on the quality of tape used.

Organization of Data Files.   Along with standards for construction and recording of magnetic tapes, the computer industry has developed some straightforward principles for organizing data files on magnetic tape. A typical structure of a multifile, **labeled tape** is illustrated in Figure 9.2. The first set of information on a tape is called the **volume header**, and it contains information about the tape as a whole. Tapes are generally

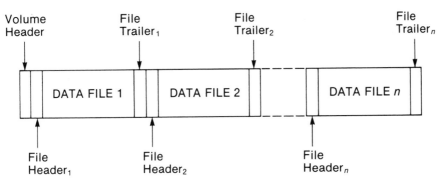

Fig. 9.2   Organization of Data Files on Magnetic Tape

assigned a volume name or internal label that is written on the header. As will be noted in the section on tape security, this encoded header is an important factor in protecting data sets from accidental or intentional misuse.

Following the volume header is the first data file. Note that it is preceded by its own **header** and followed by what is known as a **trailer**. These headers and trailers contain information specific to the data file such as the date the file was written, the name of the file, the record length, the block size, the number of blocks, the name of the job that created the file, and documenting information supplied by the user. These headers and trailers thus become very important in any attempt to determine the contents of a tape.

Following the first file in the figure, the header for the second file appears. This same structure is repeated until the last tape file (file *n*) is encountered. The order of the files is very significant on a tape. The second file cannot be read without passing over the first file. Likewise, rewriting file one is likely to destroy file two. This is because data files on magnetic tapes are organized in **sequential** fashion (i.e., the files are lined up one after another on the reel of tape). To find the appropriate file, the computer must search through the tape until it encounters the header label of the file to be used. This can prove to be disadvantageous for those who frequently update and correct files. Such applications are better done on disk drives where files are not necessarily organized sequentially. In general, however, most social science research applications are not affected by the sequential ordering of files.

Social Science Data on Tape. Due to their enormous capacity and relatively low cost ($15–25), magnetic tapes are by far the best storage medium for large files that social science researchers often use. As noted in earlier chapters, researchers generally work with smaller extracts taken from original raw data files on tape. The smaller working files can be stored on disk where access is faster and more convenient. Tapes also serve an important function as **backup** storage (duplicate copies) for other disk and tape files. A good rule of thumb is never to use any data set that has not been "backed up" for safe-keeping.

Readers should also be aware of some potential disadvantages of magnetic tapes. Since an operator must mount a tape, there is a possibility of deterioration and contamination. Moreover, there is always a delay while the tape is located and brought to a tape drive. Much worse, the wrong tape could be mounted with disastrous consequences. Fortunately this particular problem can generally be avoided through the use of security measures. The sequential structure of files on tape can add to the time required for a job since a tape drive must bypass files at the beginning of a tape to reach a file near the end. This can be minimized, however, by carefully organizing files on a tape so that frequently read files are positioned near the beginning of a tape. One other drawback associated with the use of magnetic tapes is that some software packages cannot read and write on a tape at the same time.

Important Tape Utilities. Most installations provide utilities for handling tapes. One of the most notable of these is a procedure that will search through a labeled tape and list out names of files contained on the tape. Despite all the best efforts at documentation, it is occasionally necessary to do a good bit of detective work on a tape to verify its contents. A **tape contents utility** provides a summary report by reading headers and trailers encountered on a labeled tape. Another very useful utility is a **tape-to-tape copy** routine which provides an easy way for routine backing up of files. The software copies everything on one tape to another tape regardless of the number of files or their content. In choosing such utilities, look for ones in which executing the programs requires minimal effort on the part of the user. Sometimes the utilities contained in analysis packages are superior to those provided with the operating system. For example, SAS has a tape contents procedure called TAPELABELS and a tape-to-tape copy utility called TAPECOPY. There may also be locally written utilities that are better than those written elsewhere. Although there are many other utilities that expedite the handling of tapes, contents and copy routines are among the most important, and all computer users should be acquainted with local equivalents of these programs.

Security Considerations. A number of things must be kept in mind about storing tapes. Although they may charge a small fee for their services, computer centers maintain near-perfect environmental conditions for tape storage. In these days of campus power shutdowns, brownouts, and other related problems, it seems well worth the minimal charge to keep important tapes in a specially designed environment. Once tapes are stored properly in a computer center tape library, a number of other things still can be done to ensure the security of tape files.

Another of the industry standards for magnetic tapes is a **write ring** which must be placed around the center hub of the reel before a tape can be written on. When an original copy of a data set is stored at a computer center, it is a good idea to put an external, stick-on label on the tape requesting that it *never* be mounted with a write ring. Another strategy is to insert a **read-only tape ring** into the hub which prevents a write ring from being mounted. A tape is identified by computer operators on the basis of an **external label** attached to the tape reel which indicates a number or other tape library coding scheme. Some computer centers provide an additional measure of security by allowing (or requiring) users to specify a password on the external label. This code is displayed along with the external label on the face of the tape reel. This password and the tape library number must be supplied each time the tape is used.

The operating system provides further security by insisting that the user provide the internal label which has been prerecorded on the volume header of the tape. Before a tape can be used, it should be **initialized** or have an internal label written on the volume header. Although restricted to a few characters, the content of the internal label is typically left to the user. It is good practice to establish a cataloging procedure so that each new tape belonging to a user has a different internal label. It makes even more sense to choose an internal label that implies something about the contents of the tape.

It is not a good practice to give a tape the same internal label as the external label assigned by the computer center tape library. The reason for this is that considerable confusion can be caused when tapes are checked out of a computer center tape library only to be checked back in at a subsequent point. Most computer centers use a standard external labeling scheme and reuse the codes as tapes are checked in and out. Considerable confusion can result when a tape has an internal label that is exactly like an external label.

Magnetic Disks and Drives

Physical Characteristics.   The recording medium for a disk drive is the magnetic disk. Typically, disk drives use a stack of disks (called a **pack**) similar to a stack of records on a stereo. Also somewhat like a record's spiral rings, each disk's surface is divided into concentric areas known as **tracks**. Some disk drives are constructed so that their read/write heads can be positioned simultaneously on the same track on each disk in the pack. The area composed of all the first tracks on a pack is referred to as the first **cylinder**. The size and number of tracks vary by type of drive and manufacturer, but some standards have emerged with respect to disk packs. Whatever the overall capacity, a single track can typically hold a considerable amount of data.

Organization of Data.   A disk pack has a volume name, just as a tape does. The operating system maintains a **catalog** which keeps track of data stored on the system's disk packs. Records in files on disk packs can be accessed sequentially or randomly (known as **random access**). In the latter case, like a phonograph record, certain bands (tracks) can be skipped. This implies that any record in any data file can be directly accessed without having to read through either a sequence of records in other files or preceding records in the desired file. The random access feature provides much faster access to data stored on a disk pack. Like tapes, files continue to be made up of records which can be blocked, and the inter-block gaps can also be present.

Social Science Data on Disk.   Disk data files are characterized as being **online** when they are located on disk packs that are always in place on disk drives directly under the control of the computer. The luxury of online access is typically well worth the expense. Data can be read faster and without the chance of human error such as that possible in the mounting of a tape. As the drives have increased in capacity and sophistication, these devices have become a mainstay for most computer users. Partly as an attempt to discourage saturation of the available storage space and also to defray the substantial costs of the hardware, most computer installations charge users for space used on disk drives. Thus, some caution is in order with respect to disk storage. As indicated in the previous chapter, it is advisable to keep only small working system files on disk. Large files that are not accessed routinely are best stored on magnetic tape. When needed, these files can be read into the system and, if necessary, stored on disk as well. Program files are usually small enough that there is no major expense associated with their storage. A typical user's catalog contains a number of program files and a handful of system files currently being analyzed. As an analysis project progresses, it is best to migrate older versions of system files to tape for storage.

Disk files can be read and written on at virtually the same time, but this is both an advantage and a disadvantage. On the one hand, existing files can be updated or modified without creating a different file (see, e.g., the SAS procedure EDIT). On the other hand, once changes have been made to a file, there is no going back to the earlier version since it has been replaced by an updated file. Such problems can be avoided by maintaining backups of all important disk files.

Important Disk Utilities.   Just as is the case for magnetic tapes, there are a number of very useful utilities that can be employed to maintain disk files. Disk drives are sensitive to power failures and other mechanical problems. Thus it is mandatory that backups of important files be maintained. This backup is most economical when done on magnetic tape. One useful disk utility is a program that automatically backs up all the user's catalogued data sets to a magnetic tape. Then, in the event of data loss, the files can be returned to disk from the tape where they are stored. Some installations provide local utilities that perform these functions in response to straightforward interactive commands issued from terminals. Another very useful utility copies a single file to a tape. Still another important utility is one that reports summary information on the files residing in a user's catalog. This catalog listing typically includes file sizes (usually measured in tracks) and other file attributes.

Security Considerations.   With the exception of removable disk packs, no operator intervention is required for use of disk files. Thus the chances of operator errors are greatly minimized. Most operating systems provide further security by allowing users to specify passwords which must be issued before their disk files can be used. It is usually possible to specify that a password is necessary only when an attempt is made to write on a file. Maximum protection can be achieved by specifying that a password is necessary even to read a file. Some operating systems routinely provide a measure of overall security by making it impossible for one user to access another user's files. If a user wants others to have access to a file, the file owner must specifically grant permission for the data set to be used.

MAINTAINING DOCUMENTATION

By far the best arrangement for maintaining documentation for social science data files is a library-like facility in which codebooks are cataloged and easily accessible to the user. Some larger universities have social science data librarians affiliated with research centers to expedite the use of social science data by researchers. Another way to ensure ready access to documentation is the creation of machine-readable codebooks which can be viewed from computer terminals and, if necessary, printed for subsequent use. Another helpful facility is an online data catalog which lists names of files available, disk or tape volumes, and file sequences on tape. Such a listing provides information necessary to locate and copy the data of interest. It is also a good idea for individual researchers to keep a small data file on disk in which they list their tapes, volumes, data set names, and sequences. These listings are very handy when a user is working at a remote facility without documentation and must have information on data files.

ECONOMY CONSIDERATIONS

The large data files that characterize much social science research are costly to analyze because of the execution time required to transfer data from tape or disk to central memory where it can be used by an analysis package. In addition, iterative algorithms for the analysis of discrete data can consume large amounts of CPU time and central memory space. These factors lead to a general concern in the social science research community for the expense of computing. The purpose of this section is to bring together a number of the economy measures that have been mentioned throughout this book and to suggest a few more.

High-level language programmers place considerable emphasis on **efficient code** or programming that accomplishes a task as economically as possible. Every attempt is made to eliminate redundant portions of programs and to use as few system resources as possible. Even though they do not write the analysis algorithms themselves, those who use the applications languages found in software packages ought to share a similar concern for programming economy. One way to economize is to minimize passes through large raw data files. Similarly, where they prove to be economical alternatives, system files should be used routinely. Another cost-cutting measure is to have an analysis package compute only those statistics which are likely to be used in a research project. For SPSS users, this means resisting the temptation to simply request all available calculations and specifying only those statistics which are appropriate in light of measurement assumptions and other prevailing analysis conventions. Still another way to reduce costs associated with processing time in SPSS is to use **integer mode** as opposed to **general mode**. To keep things here as simple as possible, the examples in this book have used general mode. Nonetheless, users should be aware that calculations in integer mode can result in substantial savings. In addition to these strategies for the efficient use of software packages, there are a number of other economy measures that social scientists can use.

Many computer installations have substantial discount policies for work done at night and on weekends. It is incumbent upon the user to find out how these discount policies work to maximize the benefits to be derived from them. One strategy is to delay batch jobs until the hours that discount rates apply. A program can be constructed and submitted during office hours, but scheduled to run at night when the rates are lower. Whether or not this results in a substantial savings depends on the magnitude of the job. It may not be efficient at all to delay research operations to save a few cents on a small program that requires very few system resources.

As noted on several occasions, there is no substitute for careful planning of analysis, including the construction of system files. As a rule of thumb, passes through large raw data files should be avoided whenever possible. Many systems provide **scratch disk space** which is disk area that is available for users on a temporary basis. Ordinarily, this disk space is free, but the space is erased daily. One strategy to avoid excessive charges for disk storage is to transfer data sets from tapes to scratch disk space for a brief period of time while analysis is done. Of course, one must be careful to back up important data files that have been created in scratch disk space. Otherwise, the files will be lost during periodic computer center housecleaning.

Other economy measures include minimizing permanent disk file storage and reducing printing. Catalogs should be reviewed from time to time, and inactive files should be moved to tape storage or deleted. To save paper expense, lengthy output can be reduced to microfilm or microfiche. Finally, just as users should be acquainted with discounting policies, they should also be aware of the structure of the billing algorithm at their computer installation. Some systems place a premium on seconds of central processor time consumed. Other systems reduce this charge and proportionately increase charges for input and output. As a rule, this latter scheme puts social science computing applications at a substantial cost disadvantage. It may well be necessary to study the total system configuration in detail and work for changes in local policies which will lead to economical social science computing.

Computing policies that do not work to the advantage of social science research are rather common. Indeed, a large measure of the enthusiasm about microcomputers is a product of researchers' frustration with mainframe installations which are oriented to facilitate research in the physical sciences. How realistic are the prospects that a good deal of social science analysis can be done on microcomputers? This issue is addressed in the final chapter of this book. For some, the chapter will amount to a somewhat disappointing dose of reality therapy. Others will be convinced that they can indeed abandon the mainframe and conduct data analysis on microcomputers.

CHAPTER TEN   Statistical Analysis on Microcomputers

In earlier chapters, a number of social science microcomputer applications were discussed including word processing, data collection, and small data base management. Statistical analysis with microcomputers is the topic of this chapter, and considerations of hardware, software, and analysis strategies are included. Two related themes guide the discussions. The first of these is that recent hardware and software advances have removed virtually all technological barriers restricting the scale and sophistication of statistical analysis on microcomputers. A second and more sobering theme is that corresponding cost barriers remain in place and that mainframes will continue to be the optimal environment for some social science data analysis. But there is much that can be done on microcomputers, and this final chapter reviews the current analytic capabilities of small computers.

HARDWARE CONSIDERATIONS

Internal Modifications

The popularity of 16- and 32-bit microprocessors has been an impetus for other recent hardware innovations that make microcomputer statistical analysis a more realistic possibility for most social scientists. Not the least of the improvements is a trend toward larger central memories with

16-bit processors providing the basis for such expansions. That portion of a computer's memory that is available as work space is called random access memory (**RAM**). In general, the more RAM available, the greater the capacity of the machine to process large data sets. Some 8-bit machines can use **bank switching** which allows the microprocessor to access more than 64,000 bytes of memory (i.e., 64K), but only up to 64K at any one time. To be useful, however, software must be written to take advantage of bank switching. Most 8-bit processors are slow in comparison to 16-bit processors, and it may make more sense to modify an older system by adding a 16-bit coprocessor. The result is faster processing and much larger memory addressing capability. Cards or circuit boards that permit these kinds of enhancements are available from numerous sources.

Even with a large RAM, all data must still be transferred into central memory from auxiliary storage, slowing the analysis process considerably. The most common form of mass storage, the floppy disk drive, is rather slow in its transfer of data to central memory. One solution to this transfer delay, known as **RAM disk emulation**, uses a portion of memory as if it were a disk drive. Add-on circuit boards can also be used as disk emulators. With such strategies, data access and transfer times are reduced to virtually zero because, unlike ordinary disk drives, these boards have no moving parts. The drawback to RAM disks is that data are stored only as long as the computer is operational. This type of storage is referred to as **volatile** because data are lost when the power is interrupted or terminated. RAM disk emulation thus requires an initial **booting** or loading of the pseudo drive from permanent mass storage (most likely a floppy disk) and a transfer back to that storage medium of any data that are to be saved.

Another solution to the transfer time problem involves storing information permanently in central memory (i.e., **nonvolatile** storage). The permanent portion of a microcomputer's memory is known as read only memory (**ROM**), and it typically contains such basic information as definitions of console keys. In a 128K or larger memory, ROM can be expanded (relative to RAM) and used to store software without substantially depleting available memory resources. Some computers incorporate removable **ROM cartridges** much like those used by video games. Nonvolatile **bubble memory** cards are also available which could presumably be used to store not only analysis software, but data files as well.

External Modifications

Data analysis on a microcomputer also requires some concern for peripheral devices. Although floppy disk drives vary a great deal in their speed, capacity, and accuracy, none rivals a hard disk drive which is recommended for most analysis packages. **Hard** or **fixed drives** transfer data to central memory at very high rates and can hold five to fifty **megabytes** (millions of bytes) of data (the equivalent in some cases of hundreds of diskettes). A cross between the floppy and hard disk is a cartridge disk drive which operates on interchangeable cartridges that approach small hard disks in storage capacity. Intended as backup storage for hard drives, cartridge drives have slightly lower speeds of data transfer than their fixed counterparts. But this disadvantage is offset to a certain extent by the more reasonable cost of the cartridge drive.

Interfaces between nine-track tape drives and microcomputers are now available. Though rather expensive, tape drives provide ready access to the extensive tape data archives maintained for social science research and solve the problem of getting large files to microcomputers. Small cartridge tape drives called **streaming tape drives** are also available for microcomputers. Although they are used primarily to back up hard disk files, these devices could be used in much the same way as large nine-track tape drives.

These kinds of elaborate peripherals are necessary to get large data bases from mainframes to microcomputers for analysis purposes. Another alternative is to use asynchronous communications (probably phone lines at a communication rate of 300 or 1200 BAUD). Barring occasional phone line failures, a file of any consequence can require a considerable amount of time to transfer even at the higher rate of data interchange. When diskette drives are interfaced synchronously with mainframes, transfer time is greatly minimized. Of course, the mainframe and the microcomputer must read and write diskettes with a corresponding operating system. Getting large data files to microcomputers need not be a painstaking process. For example, Mathematica Policy Research is distributing the 1980 Census data on diskettes. In addition, most microcomputing magazines contain advertisements for tape-to-diskette transfer services. Similarly, secondary data sets could be distributed on diskettes.

New hardware is constantly appearing which makes it more likely that statistical analysis of social science data can be done on microcomputers. As time passes, the assessment of microcomputers here will appear increasingly conservative. Nonetheless, it is important to note that an over-the-counter personal computer probably cannot be reasonably used for statistical analysis. The recommended hardware configuration illustrated in Figure 10.1 includes a 32-bit CPU with at least 256K of RAM and another 32–128K of ROM, some of which is on cartridges or bubble memory cards. System peripherals include hard and floppy disk drives, a printer, a nine-track tape drive, and a monitor. It is unlikely at the present time that many social scientists could afford to have such expensive configurations at their disposal. Nonetheless, a wide range of analysis software is available. Some criteria for choosing among the available software packages are suggested in the next section.

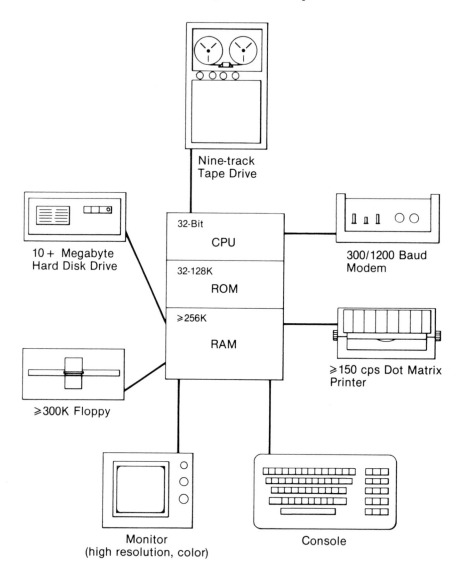

Fig. 10.1 Microcomputer System for Statistical Analysis

MICROCOMPUTER ANALYSIS SOFTWARE

The first analysis packages that appeared for 8-bit machines were quite limited in their capacity to handle data sets of more than a few hundred

Table 10.1   Checklist of Desirable Features in Analysis Package

General Characteristics:	*Baseline Statistical Features:*
•Conversational interaction •Online help •Menu-driven (with bypass option) •User-friendly •Language precision •Graphics •Educational discount •No copy protection •Integration of DBMS and analysis	•Univariate descriptive statistics •Comparison of groups' descriptive statistics •*t*-tests, ANOVA •Contingency table analysis •Correlation •OLS regression
DBMS Features:	*Advanced Multivariate Procedures:*
•Large files (many variables, cases) •Data stored as system files •Direct data entry with form mode •Reads other raw data files •Outputs raw data, system files •Nonrectangular, relational files •Match-merging, other file merges •Missing data provisions	•*n*-way ANOVA •GLS regression •Factor analysis •Log-linear algorithms •Multidimensional scaling •Cluster analysis •Time-series procedures

cases and a few dozen variables. The early packages also included, at most, only a few statistical procedures. Many spreadsheets such as VisiCalc and SuperCalc available then (and now) were actually superior to the early special-purpose analysis software. A second generation of analysis software is now appearing with substantially extended capabilities. Although these newer packages are aimed at 16- and 32-bit microcomputers, some can be used on 8-bit machines. Software developers have recognized the large market for analysis packages, and many are available (some are listed at the end of the chapter). Indeed, a comprehensive review of such software is beyond the scope of this brief introduction. Provided instead are several suggestions that can guide the selection of an analysis package (summarized in Table 10.1). These recommendations pertain to general characteristics, data base management features, baseline analytical capabilities, and advanced multivariate analysis procedures.

General Characteristics

Since microcomputers are dedicated to a handful of users at most, it follows that a microcomputer analysis package should be very responsive and supportive of the user(s). Conversational interaction ought to be the rule, and extensive online help and prompting facilities should be available. The package should be **menu-driven**; that is, it should be prompted by lists of appropriate commands. Once experience has been gained with the package, the user should also be able to bypass basic menus and issue commands without prompts. To borrow a phrase from popular microcomputing jargon, the analysis package should be **user-friendly**.

Microcomputer analysis packages are written in several high-level languages. Because of its precision, FORTRAN is generally preferred over most others. Schrodt (1983) argues convincingly that any microcomputer analysis software should be **benchmarked** against a mainframe analysis package. That is, the same analysis should be run on a small and a large computer for comparison purposes. Users should pay close attention to any rounding errors or apparent inefficiencies in calculations.

Microcomputers excel at color graphics, and many analysts will begin to rely much more on presentations of statistical information in graphic formats. Thus, another consideration in choosing an analysis package has to be the quality of graphics provided by the software. Copyrights, licensing restrictions, and copy protection also need to be considered. Many software vendors sell their products only for use on a single machine (Pournelle, 1983). Thus a research or instructional laboratory with ten microcomputers would technically be required to purchase ten copies of a software packge. More reasonable arrangements include software licensing for multiple machines or substantial discounts for nonprofit agencies and institutions. The latter approach has resulted in numerous educational discounts, and readers are encouraged to inquire about such arrangements. But inexpensive software that cannot be copied poses other problems. Much to many researchers' chagrin, copy-protected software generally cannot be loaded onto hard disk drives.

One final general characteristic is the integration of data base management and analysis capabilities. Just as integrated text editing and formatting packages facilitate word processing, combined data manipulation and analysis software enhances statistical computing. Users would be wise to choose an analysis package that incorporates data entry and file management capabilities.

Data Base Management Features

The large data files employed by social scientists make it imperative that an analysis package have the capacity to handle files with many cases and variables. As a rule of thumb, the package should be able to process the largest secondary data file a user can conceive of using. This appraisal should take into account the researcher's substantive interests and prevailing standards for research in his or her area of expertise. The package should store files as system files, eliminating the need for repeated data definition. Direct data entry should be possible with provisions for form construction and completion similar to those found in general-purpose DBMS packages. So that existing machine-readable data can be analyzed, it is imperative that data entry also be possible by the reading of raw data files. A package should also have facilities for the output of raw data and system files. Likewise, the package should be able to handle nonrectangular and relational files. Match-merging and other recombinations of files should be possible as well. Finally, there must be provisions for missing data. Packages that integrate many of these DBMS features with the statistical analysis procedures that follow are clearly preferable to those that have few data base management capabilities.

Baseline Statistical Features

At a minimum, an analysis package should incorporate basic descriptive statistics (means, standard deviations, and the like). In addition, group comparisons on descriptive statistics should be possible. Likewise, *t*-tests and analysis of variance (ANOVA) procedures are indispensable. Elementary contingency table analysis capacity should also be present along with correlation and ordinary least squares (OLS) regression. A full-feature package would contain a variety of advanced multivariate procedures such as those mentioned in the next section.

Advanced Multivariate Procedures

To rival their mainframe counterparts, microcomputer statistical analysis packages should provide for a number of sophisticated multivariate procedures. These include *n*-way ANOVA, generalized least squares (GLS), factor analysis, log-linear algorithms, multidimensional scaling, cluster analysis, and time-series procedures. Most researchers will use only one of these programs at any given time. Thus, Schrodt (1983) recommends that these kinds of sophisticated procedures be packaged and sold separately. In this way, the total cost of an analysis system is minimized, and precious RAM remains free for working space and data. Packages integrating advanced features like these with DBMS facilities are quite valuable to the researcher.

Fortunately more than just a handful of microcomputer analysis packages incorporate many of these desirable features. But those that do may well require elaborate hardware configurations like that in Figure

10.1. For example, SPSS-Pro for the DEC Professional relies on that machine's 16-bit microprocessor and its 10-megabyte hard disk drive. Likewise, the BMDP StatCat is a complete system, consisting of the familiar BMDP analysis package stored on the hard disk drive of a very powerful microcomputer. The dilemma that many users face is one of reconciling the relatively meager power of an ordinary microcomputer with their data analysis needs. One resolution would be to choose software with as many as possible of the guidelines suggested here (and summarized in Table 10.1) in view of hardware limitations.

PROSPECTS FOR MICROCOMPUTING

As the foregoing suggests, researchers with ample funds can configure a microcomputer system that will meet most of their analysis requirements. In the near future, however, the majority of researchers and students who cannot afford the new equipment will continue to do analysis on mainframes. In this final section, some developments are noted which could bring down costs and expedite a widespread interdisciplinary transition from mainframes to microcomputers.

Most of the necessary hardware for sophisticated statistical analysis already exists. The new generations of 16- and 32-bit processors promise to provide virtually all the computing power any analysis would require. Fallik and Brown (1983) describe a social science computing laboratory organized around a 32-bit microcomputer and contend that such a configuration eliminates the need for a large mainframe.

With sophisticated hardware available, cost and software factors inhibit statistical analysis on microcomputers. Software developments that make microcomputer analysis more cost effective will be slower to take hold than the hardware innovations that have made such analysis technically possible. At today's prices, dedicating a $10,000 system to a single user makes no economic sense. Recognizing this, the industry is developing **multiuser** operating systems for powerful microcomputers which allow several researchers to work simultaneously on the same computer. In view of their large data sets, social scientists will need rather sophisticated versions of such systems.

Other developments make use of the distributed processing concept and network a variety of microcomputing devices. Presumably, one analyst could take advantage of unused capacity on a neighboring machine to complete an especially large job. One approach to this sharing of resources is referred to as local area networking (**LAN**). LAN configurations that include tape drives and large capacity hard disk drives could well become cost-effective solutions to statistical analysis on microcomputers. We are certain to see a number of exciting developments along these lines in the next few years.

List of Sources for Microcomputer Analysis Packages

ABSTAT	Anderson-Bell, P.O. Box 191, Canon City, CO 81212.
AIDA	Action Research Northwest, 11442 Marine View Dr. S.W., Seattle, WA 98146.
A-STAT	Rosen Grandon Associates, 7807 Whittier St., Tampa, FL 33617.
BMDP	BMDP, Statistical Software, 1964 Westwood Blvd., Suite 202, Los Angeles, CA 09925.
Daisy	Rainbow Computing Inc., 19517 Business Center Dr., Northridge, CA 91324.
ELF	Winchendon Group, P.O. Box 10114, Alexandria, VA 22310.
HSD	Human System Dynamics, 9249 Reseda Blvd., Suite 107, Northridge, CA 91324.
MATHSTAT	Mathematica Policy Research, P.O. Box 2393, Princeton, NJ 08540.
MDA	MicroData Analyzer, Cambridge Information International Inc., 238 Main St., Suite 310, Cambridge, MA 02142.
MICROSTAT	Ecosoft Inc., P.O. Box 68602, Indianapolis, IN 46268.
Micro TSP	Micro-TSP Associates, 928 Mears Court, Stanford, CA 94305.
SPSS	SPSS, Inc., Suite 3300, 444 N. Michigan Ave., Chicago, IL 60611.
STATPAK	Northwest Analytical, Portland, OR.
STATPRO	Wadsworth Electronic Publishing Company, Statler Office Bldg., 20 Providence Street, Boston, MA 02116.
Stats Plus	Human Systems Dynamics, 9249 Reseda Blvd., Suite 107, Northridge, CA 91324.
SYSTAT	Systat, 1127 Asbury Avenue, Evanston, IL 60202.

SUGGESTED READINGS

On hardware considerations:
1. A good review of available products and their capabilities can be found in "Microcomputers: Basic Choice Factors" by Gregory A. Marks of the Inter-university Consortium for Political and Social Research, The University of Michigan. This informative document is updated reg-

ularly to reflect the introduction of new hardware and changing market conditions.

2. Philip A. Schrodt discusses some hardware innovations which may soon be useful to social scientists in "Microcomputers in Statistical Work," pp. 4–6 in *News for Teachers of Political Science*, No. 38, Summer 1983.

On analysis software:

1. Analysis software for public administrators is discussed by G. David Garson in "Microcomputer Applications in Public Administration," pp. 453–458 in *Public Administration Review*, September/October 1983.

2. Benchmarking microcomputer statistical programs is the topic of Peter A. Lachenbruch's "Statistical Programs for Microcomputers," pp. 560–570 in *Byte*, Vol. 8, No. 11, November 1983.

3. Suggestions for choosing statistical software are provided by Phillip A. Schrodt in "Microcomputers in Statistical Work," *News for Teachers of Political Science*, No. 38, Summer 1983.

4. Jerome A. Katz reviews several statistical packages in "Statistical Packages for Apple Computers," *The ICPSR MicroNews*, Vol. 1, No. 1, September 1983.

5. A comprehensive review of many analysis packages can be found in "Statistical Software for Microcomputers" by James Carpenter, Dennis Deloria, and David Morganstein (*BYTE*, April 1984, pp. 234–264.)

APPENDIX I Applications on an IBM VM/CMS System

Norman L. Weatherby

This appendix illustrates CMSBATCH and CMS access on Columbia University's IBM 4341 system. We first describe the operating system and the text editor that is used to build files. This will help the reader to understand the details of the CMSBATCH and SPSS-X programs that are used to process the NORC General Social Survey data introduced in Chapter 7.

THE OPERATING SYSTEM

In the past, users competed for time on one large computer and its resources. Under the IBM/370 CMS operating system, each user has access to and controls his or her own virtual machine (VM), a simulated but completely operational computer system. Users appear to have and

Dr. Norman Weatherby is Assistant Professor of Clinical Public Health at the Center for Population and Family Health, Columbia University, 60 Haven Avenue, B-3, New York, NY 10032.

operate their own computers, just as if they had sophisticated personal computers on their desks (Helm, 1981:9).

The Control Program (CP) is used to assemble the type of computer system needed by the user. As Helm (1981:13) explains, this virtual computer typically includes

- A Central Processing Unit (CPU) with 512 to 1024 kilobytes of memory
- Disks for user programs and data storage
- System disks for system files such as WYLBUR and SPSS-X
- A terminal or console
- A printer
- A "card" reader
- A "card" punch

The virtual machine may be difficult to understand unless we consider how input and output is handled on most older mainframes. When cards are used to enter data or programs into mainframes, the card reader is connected to a disk that temporarily stores as files the decks of cards that users submit. Users' files are then sent to their own disks for permanent storage. Similarly, when users want to print or punch files, the files are sent first to a system disk that queues them for output. The card punch or printer takes files from the system disk and punches them or prints them. In CP, a user's printer, reader, and punch devices are connected to part of the mainframe's printer, reader, and punch disks. For example, the reader is a system disk that temporarily stores files that the user will later read and store on his or her own disk.

The simulated (virtual) console, printer, reader, and punch devices are connected to each other or to their real counterparts through spooling. In this context, think of spooling as the sending of files from one device to another device. For example, it is possible to spool (i.e., send) a print file that was generated on a working disk by an SPSS-X program to a user's reader device or to a system printer.

Whereas CP is used to build and interconnect the pieces of the virtual machine, the Conversational Monitor System (CMS) operating system is used to control the system. The user works with CMS or CMSBATCH to load and run programs, manage disk space and files, supervise input and output to the virtual devices, and perform the other tasks of an operating system (Helm, 1981).

Three examples may help to illustrate the use of CP and CMS. (1) CP commands are used to spool a print file to a reader device, and CMS commands are used to read the file and save it to a disk. (2) Tape drives are rewound with a CP command, and files are moved from tape to disk using CMS commands. (3) CP is used to connect or link a disk to a virtual computer, and CMS is used to access this disk and create, delete, copy, or modify files.

CMSBATCH processing is more efficient and less costly than CMS access. Essentially, BATCH is a user on the IBM system that has access to a virtual machine with at least 2048 kilobytes of memory and substantially larger disk space. The user submits to BATCH a file containing the CP and CMS commands that would be issued at the terminal if one were working in CMS. BATCH is also instructed to save its output on the user's disk or to spool its output to the user's reader device or to a printer so that results can be retrieved.

THE TEXT EDITOR

Although there is a text editor available in CMS, most users of the IBM system at Columbia University use WYLBUR. This line-oriented text editor was developed at Stanford University and has been upgraded here and at other installations to be a powerful system tool. In this section, we briefly describe major WYLBUR commands, and then we will create and edit programs for running the NORC data.

WYLBUR has three major modes: command, collect, and modify. The collect and modify modes are entered from the command mode. When the user wants to edit an existing file, the first WYLBUR command is to use the file. In this command mode, WYLBUR can be instructed to list portions of the file, search the file, delete lines, move or copy lines from one part of the file to another, change text globally or in specified ranges, save or replace the file, and do a host of other tasks. To build a new file or to add lines to an existing file, the user enters collect mode. In modify mode, specified lines can be edited by deleting, replacing, and inserting characters.

CMSBATCH ACCESS

In this section, a CMSBATCH job is submitted from a terminal. The batch file sets up an SPSS-X program which reads an SPSS system file from a tape, saving an SPSS-X system file for further analysis. Note that the Virtual Machine that is used in this example has two disks on which to store programs and data. The first disk may be referred to as disk A, at address 191 of the user's computer. Although most IBM CMS users work on their A disks, a second disk B, at address 198, is used here. This disk was added to the system to ensure that enough disk space is available for the SPSS-X program, the batch file, the printouts or listings that are generated, and the new SPSS-X system file.

Program Preparation

To run SPSS-X through CMSBATCH on the IBM system, two programs have to be built: a batch job control file and an SPSS-X program. In Figure A1.1, WYLBUR is called, and collect mode is entered to write the SPSS-X program. Commands that the user types appear in lowercase and responses from the system in uppercase. Comments that help to explain the listing appear on the right in italics. In the program, SPSS-X is instructed to read the NORC GSS7282 SPSS system file; the batch program listed in Figure A1.2 will define the location of that file. Seven variables will be saved in a new SPSS-X system file with a file name of NORC7282 and a file type of SPSSXFIL. This file will be on BATCH's B disk which, as we will show, is the user's B disk.

The batch job control program is listed in Figure A1.2, using the CMS command TYPE. Note that CP commands are differentiated from CMS commands by a "CP." The two records of the program with only /* entered in columns 1 and 2 signify its beginning and end. The user's I.D. is given first in the /JOB record, and the password is last. The name of the account to be billed for the job—NORC—is shown, and NORC1 is the job name, corresponding to the name of the SPSS-X program. Recall that CMSBATCH is just another user that has a console or terminal. In line 4 of the batch program, a CP spool command is used to establish a connection between BATCH's console and the user's reader. At the end of the job, a step-by-step listing of what BATCH did (the console file) is sent to the user's computer.

Several lines of the batch program concern the tape that contains the SPSS system file to be read. Line 3 is a request to the operator to mount the NORC tape. In line 5, a CMS command defines for SPSS-X the characteristics and location of the SPSS system file. To be consistent with the SPSS-X program, this file is named GSS7282. This system file is the eighth file on the standard-labeled (SL) tape that the operator mounts on tape drive TAP1, which is at CP address 181. The system file has records that are a maximum of 20008 characters long, and 7200 records are found in each block on the tape. CP commands rewind the tape before (line 6) and after (line 10) the SPSS-X job. Finally, on line 11 a CP command requests that the tape be taken off of the tape drive; that is, detached from the system.

The SPSS-X program is saved on the user's disk B, at address 198. BATCH must connect to and access this disk in order to find and run the

```
.wylbur                                                    (start WYLBUR after the CMS prompt ".")

COMMAND?.collect                                           (enter collect mode to add lines)

                                                           (the user types in the lines after each !.)
   1.    ?.TITLE   READING GSS7282 SPSS SYSTEM FILE FROM TAPE
   2.    ?.GET FILE=GSS7282/
   3.    ?.  KEEP=MARITAL AGE EDUC SEX RACE REGION RELIG
   4.    ?.COMMENT
   5.    ?.FILE HANDLE NORC7282/NAME='NORC7282 SPSSXFIL B'
   6.    ?.SAVE OUTFILE=NORC7282
   7.    ?.FENISH                                           (typing =attn= or using "break" gets WYLBUR
   8.    ?.=ATTN=                                            back to command mode)

COMMAND?.change "fenish" to "finish" in 7

   7.      FINISH                                           (a misspelled word is corrected, and WYLBUR
                                                            verifies the correction)

COMMAND?.list                                              (list what has been entered)

   1.      TITLE   READING GSS7282 SPSS SYSTEM FILE FROM TAPE
   2.      GET FILE=GSS7282/
   3.        KEEP=MARITAL AGE EDUC SEX RACE REGION RELIG
   4.      COMMENT
   5.      FILE HANDLE NORC7282/NAME='NORC7282 SPSSXFIL B'
   6.      SAVE OUTFILE=NORC7282
   7.      FINISH

COMMAND?.save norc1 spssx b                                (save the file that was built on the user's
                                                            B disk)

NORC1 SPSSX B1 SAVED                                       (CMS reports that the program file was saved)

COMMAND?.quit clear                                        (quit WYLBUR, clear WYLBUR's working file,
                                                            and return to CMS)

R;                                                         (CMS acknowledges our return)
```

Fig. A1.1 Building a Program File with WYLBUR

149

```
.type norc1 batch b                     (A CMS command types the BATCH program, which
                                        was built with WYLBUR on the user's B disk)

/*                                                                          (1)
/JOB USRID NORC NORC1 PSWD                                                  (2)
*SETUP VOL TAPE01 EXT TAPE01                                                (3)
CP SPOOL CONSOLE TO USRID                                                   (4)
FILEDEF GSS7282 TAP1 SL 8 (LRECL 20008 BLKSIZE 7200 RECFM VBS              (5)
CP REW 181                                                                  (6)
CP LINK USRID 198 298 WR WTPSWD                                             (7)
ACCESS 298 B                                                                (8)
SPSSX NORC1                                                                 (9)
CP REW 181                                                                 (10)
CP DET 181                                                                 (11)
RELEASE 298                                                                (12)
CP DETACH 298                                                              (13)
/*                                                                         (14)

R;                                      (CMS returns from typing the program)
```

Fig. A1.2   Listing of Batch Job Control File

program and to save the SPSS-X system file. In line 7, we issue a CP command that tells BATCH to link to the user's 198 disk as its disk at address 298. This command also gives BATCH the ability to write (WR) the SPSS-X system file and the SPSS-X program listing on the user's disk and verifies this ability by giving the write password (WTPSWD). In line 8, the CMS command tells BATCH that its 298 disk (the user's 198 disk) should be called its B disk. Lines 13 and 14 of the listing instruct BATCH to release its 298 disk and, using a CP command, detach it from its virtual machine. Finally, on line 9 we instruct BATCH to run the SPSS-X program named NORC1. BATCH will look first on its own A disk for this program, and then it will find the program on its B disk. BATCH will run this program that reads the SPSS system file on the tape, and the new SPSS-X system file and the SPSS-X listing will be written on the B disk.

Job Submission

Once the SPSS-X and batch programs have been written, the job is submitted to the IBM system. Since BATCH has been given write access to the user's disk, it is best to release it and detach it from the virtual machine so that no one will accidentally use the disk when BATCH is writing to it. Figure A1.3 shows the commands that are issued from the user's terminal and the messages that are received at the terminal from the system.

```
.release 198                      (tells CMS to release the "B" disk)
R;

.cp detach 198                    (tells CP to detach the disk from the user's
                                   virtual machine)

DASD 198 DETACHED                 (CP replies that the disk is detached, giving
R;                                 the completion code R;)

.submit norc1                     (the batch program is submitted)

PUN FILE 7880 TO BATCH COPY 001 NOHOLD   (the system replies that the batch
                                          file is punched to CMSBATCH)

[Job NORC1 sent to BATCH]
                                  (again, the system shows that the batch program
R;                                 is sent to BATCH, and it sends the completion
                                   code R;)

.sleep                            (the user's terminal is put to sleep so that it
                                   can receive messages from the system as the
                                   job progresses)

JOB 7880-USRID ACCEPTED BY BATCH.   (the system checks the syntax of the
                                     batch program and finds no mistakes,
                                     so CMSBATCH accepts the job)

JOB 7880-USRID SUBMITTED TO CMSBAT01   (the system shows that the job is sent
                                        to CMSBATCH; there is a pause while
                                        the operator mounts the tape)

16:20:18                          (at 4:20 PM, CMSBATCH sends a
MSG FROM CMSBAT01: JOB 'NORC1' STARTED.  message that the job has started)

16:23:53                          (at 4:23 PM, CMSBATCH sends a
MSG FROM CMSBAT01: JOB 'NORC1' ENDED.    message that the job has ended)

                                  (BATCH's console file is sent
CON FILE 7899 FROM CMSBAT01 COPY 001   NOHOLD  to the user's reader as file
                                                number 7899)

                                  (the user types "return" to take the terminal
R;                                 out of sleep mode, and the completion code
                                   is returned)
```

Fig. A1.3   Submission of Batch Job

Output Retrieval

The next step is to retrieve the console file from the reader. This is done from the terminal by using WYLBUR to read the console file that was sent from BATCH. In the listing in Figure A1.4, we look for error messages that may indicate trouble with the tape, the linking and accessing of the user's disk, or the SPSS-X program.

The console file restates the commands that were submitted in the batch job and adds some that the system issued. The job took less than

(recall that BATCH sent its console file, number 7899, to the user's "card" reader; WYLBUR is used to read the file)

```
.wylbur cardread file 7899

COMMAND? list

 1.   CP QUERY TIME
 2.   TIME IS 16:20:19 EST FRIDAY 02/17/84
 3.   CONNECT= 00:00:02 VIRTCPU= 000:00.01 TOTCPU= 000:00.06
 4.   CP SET SECUSER
 5.   * JOB 7880-USRID SUBMITTED TO CMSBAT01 ON FRIDAY,
        17 FEBRUARY 1984  16:19
 6.   CP SP CON START CLASS W TO USRID
 7.   R; T=0.01/0.01 16:20:19
 8.   CP SP P CLASS V FOR USRID
 9.   R; T=0.01/0.01 16:20:19
10.   *SETUP VOL TAPE01 EXT TAPE01
11.   CP SPOOL CONSOLE TO USRID
12.   R; T=0.01/0.01 16:20:19
13.   FILEDEF GSS7282 TAP1 SL 8 (PERM LRECL 20008 BLKSIZE 7200 RECFM VBS
14.   R; T=0.01/0.01 16:20:20
15.   CP REW 181
16.   REWIND COMPLETE
17.   R; T=0.01/0.01 16:20:20
18.   CP LINK USRID 198 298 WR WTPSWD
19.   R; T=0.01/0.03 16:20:21
```

```
20.  ACCESS 298 B
21.  R; T=0.01/0.01 16:20:24
22.  SPSSX NORC1
23.  SPSSX Release 1.1.
24.
25.  END OF JOB: 9 COMMAND LINES  0 ERRORS  0 WARNINGS  25 CPU SECONDS
26.                                          (the SPSS-X system disk is detached)
27.  DASD 315 DETACHED
28.  R; T=25.36/45.39 16:23:53
29.  CP REW 181
30.  REWIND COMPLETE
31.  R; T=0.01/0.01 16:23:53
32.  CP DET 181
33.  TAPE 181 DETACHED
34.  R; T=0.01/0.01 16:23:53
35.  RELEASE 298
36.  R; T=0.01/0.01 16:23:53
37.  CP DETACH 298
38.  DASD 298 DETACHED
39.  R; T=0.01/0.02 16:23:53
40.  /*
41.  CMSBATCH ENDED.

COMMAND?.quit clear

R;
```

Fig. A1.4 System Messages from Batch Job

153

```
.cp link usrid 198 198
R;

.access 198 b
R;

.listfile * * b (date

FILENAME FILETYPE FM FORMAT LRECL  RECS  BLOCKS   DATE      TIME
NORC1    LISTING  B1 V        133    38       1  2/17/84 16:23:52
NORC1    SPSSX    B1 V         47     9       1  2/17/84 15:34:37
NORC1    BATCH    B1 F         80    14       1  2/17/84 15:26:42
NORC7282 SPSSXFIL B1 F       1024   125      32  2/17/84 16:23:51
R;

.type norc1 listing b

17 FEB 84   SPSS-X RELEASE 1.1  FOR IBM VM/CMS              PAGE 1
16:20:34    COLUMBIA UNIVERSITY C. C. A.  IBM 4341    VM - SP/CMS

            SPSS INC LICENSE NUMBER:    323

PARM FIELD: 48K

    1  0          TITLE  READING GSS7282 SPSS SYSTEM FILE
    2  0          COMMENT
    3  0          GET FILE=GSS7282/
    4  0           KEEP=MARITAL AGE EDUC SEX RACE REGION RELIG
    5  0          COMMENT

FILE CALLED GSS7282 :
GSS7282  IS AN OLD-FORMAT SYSTEM FILE NAMED GSS7282
  THE VARIABLE CASWGT IS USED FOR CASE WEIGHTING.
  THE FILE'S SUBFILE STRUCTURE HAS BEEN LOST.
  LABEL:
  CREATED 13 JUL 82     537 VARIABLES     13626 CASES
CASES ARE WEIGHTED BY CASWGT

    6  0          FILE HANDLE NORC7282/NAME='NORC7282 SPSSXFIL B'
    7  0          SAVE OUTFILE=NORC7282
    8  0          COMMENT

17 FEB 84 16:21:54         8 VARIABLES,     64 BYTES PER CASE
17 FEB 84 16:23:51     13626 CASES SAVED

17 FEB 84   READING GSS7282 SPSS SYSTEM FILE              PAGE 2

16:23:52 COLUMBIA UNIVERSITY C. C. A. IBM 4341 VM -SP/CMS

PRECEDING TASK REQUIRED     21.25 SECONDS CPU TIME;
                           117.36 SECONDS ELAPSED.

    9  0          FINISH

     9 COMMAND LINES READ.
     0 ERRORS DETECTED.
     0 WARNINGS ISSUED.
    25 SECONDS CPU TIME.
   198 SECONDS ELAPSED TIME.
       END OF JOB.
```

Fig. A1.5 Output Listing from Batch Job

four minutes, mainly because the operator was very quick in mounting the tape. Most significantly, line 25 of the console file shows that there were no warnings and no errors in the SPSS-X program. In fact, there are no system messages which indicate any problems.

Since the console listing indicates that things seem to be in order, we now turn to the SPSS-X listing. This printout of the job was not sent to a printer; BATCH wrote it on the user's B disk. Since there is always a possibility that a programming error has gone undetected by the system, a careful review of the output file is advisable. The steps involved in examining the SPSS-X output are detailed in Figure A1.5. First we have to link to and access the user's 198 disk since it was detached prior to the batch job. All of the files on this B disk are shown to make sure that the listing and the system file exist. Then, the output listing file NORC1 LISTING is displayed at the terminal. At the end of the listing, we find again that there were no warnings and no errors.

Output Review

As noted in Chapter 8, the analyst's job is not finished when the printed results of a successfully executed program have been obtained. The output must be carefully examined for evidence of errors that the computer cannot detect. Unless the user specifically instructs the package otherwise, SPSS-X lists back the program (see Figure A1.5). The rest of the output contains information about reading the SPSS system file, saving the SPSS-X system file, and executing the job.

One important item to check is whether SPSS-X encountered any problems reading and processing the SPSS system file. In Figure A1.5, we see that the large GSS7282 file was read and the new NORC7282 system file was saved with eight variables. SPSS-X created one variable that keeps track of the cases. The user specified the seven variables of interest, and it is worthwhile to check the spelling of these variables. This is important because the variables must be referenced in subsequent analyses precisely by these names. Note that the subfile structure of the old SPSS (not SPSS-X) system file was lost. In this particular case, this means that the data are no longer subdivided by the year in which the interview occurred. Although this does not affect the illustrative analysis here, it may be a serious problem for those planning to convert old SPSS system files with subfiles to SPSS-X system files.

A second important item is the number of cases read by SPSS-X. Does that number match the number of respondents reported in the NORC codebook? SPSS-X encountered 13,626 cases, and this corresponds exactly to the number of respondents listed in the codebook. Finally, users should always be concerned with the amount of execution time a program requires. Here the job consumed 25 expensive seconds of CPU time. In this section of the appendix, we used CMSBATCH access to transform an SPSS system file to an SPSS-X system file. In other appendices, raw data were used as input on other kinds of systems, so the CPU times are not directly comparable. Nonetheless, it is interesting to note the wide variations in processing times across different mainframes. Now that the smaller SPSS-X system file exists, subsequent CMS runs will require much less execution time on the computer's part.

CMS ACCESS

Nonconversational interactive (or CMS) access closely parallels CMSBATCH access. First, an SPSS-X program is built with an editor. Instead of providing operating system instructions in a separate batch file of CP and CMS commands, the user issues the necessary statements at the terminal before running the program. Because it can be difficult to prepare a batch file, CMS is easier to use. After execution, the output is reviewed at the terminal for errors, and the cycle is repeated until errors have been eliminated.

As noted at the beginning of this appendix, one important difference between CMS and CMSBATCH access is that BATCH typically has a virtual machine with a larger CPU and larger working disks. Thus, if the user were processing the entire NORC dataset, it is likely that CMSBATCH would be used. Another important difference is that the operating system is not allowed to intervene and schedule the job at its convenience. Instead, the system is instructed to execute the user's program at once. Of course, just how fast the computer can finish the task depends on the level of activity on the system. Even though it is more costly than CMSBATCH access, careful and efficient use of CMS access represents a substantial improvement in turnaround time over CMSBATCH.

Program Preparation

In this section, we build a simple SPSS-X program which reads and analyzes the NORC7282 system file created in the previous section. In Figure A1.6 the program NORC2 SPSSX is created with WYLBUR. We illustrate the use of the command, collect, and modify modes. The reader is referred to the earlier WYLBUR listing for basic procedures. Comments that explain additional editing procedures are enclosed on the right in italics.

Program Execution

To run a program in CMS from the terminal, the user needs the system file NORC7282, the program NORC2 SPSSX B, and the SPSS-X package. All virtual machines have an A disk at address 191, and users typically work on this disk. Here, a B disk at address 198 is used since, as noted above, a rather large system file is used. It is also desirable to keep the NORC work separate from other files. Therefore, the user must use CP and CMS commands to connect to and access the B disk before running the job.

The "name =" portion of the file handle statement in line two of NORC2 SPSSX tells CMS that the system file is on the B disk. In line 2, this system file is given the short name or handle of NORCSYS. When the user commands CMS to run SPSS-X, the SPSS-X package is automatically called by CMS from its system disk number 315. The output or listing file will automatically be written on the user's B disk.

Since the user's terminal can receive messages from CMS, there is no need to spool the console file as we did in the CMSBATCH job. Thus, as shown in the following program, the user has to enter only one command from the terminal to run the SPSS-X job and then wait for messages from CMS. Explanatory comments are shown in italics.

```
.cp link userid 198 198                  (connect the B disk to the virtual machine)

R;                                       (the system returns the completion code)

.access 198 b                            (tell CMS to use it as the B disk)

R;

.spssx norc2                             (run the SPSS-X job)

SPSSX Release 1.1 - VERSION CURRENT.     (SPSS-X begins by showing its version
                                         number)
                                         (the user waits while the job is running;
                                         nothing appears on the terminal unless
                                         the system is instructed to send occasional
                                         "blips" as CPU time is used)

END OF JOB:    14 COMMAND LINES   0 ERRORS    0 WARNINGS    21 CPU SECONDS

DASD 315 DETACHED                        (the system's SPSS-X disk is detached)

R;                                       (the job is finished)
```

```
.wylbur

COMMAND?.collect

   1.    ?.title  reading norc system file on ibm cms system

   2.    ?.file handle  norcsys/name='norc7282 spssxfile b'
```

                                            (the name of the spssxfile may be incorrect, so
```
   3.    ?.=attn=
```
                                            the break key is used to get back to command
                                            mode)

                                            (from within WYLBUR, CMS is asked
```
COMMAND?.listfile norc* spssxfi* b (date
```
                                            to list the correct name of the
                                            file; asterisks are used in place
                                            of the unknown characters, and
                                            CMS replies in the next lines)

```
FILENAME FILETYPE FM FORMAT LRECL   RECS  BLOCKS   DATE      TIME
NORC7282 SPSSXFIL B1 F        1024   125      32  2/17/84  16:23:51


COMMAND?.modify 2
```
                                            (modify mode is entered to correct line 2)
```
   2.    FILE HANDLE  NORCSYS/NAME='NORC7282 SPSSXFILE B'
ALTERS?.                                             d
```

                                            (the terminal's cursor is moved under the "E" in
                                            "SPSSXFILE", and a "d" is typed to delete the
                                            character)
```
   2.    FILE HANDLE  NORCSYS/NAME='NORC7282 SPSSXFIL B'
ALTERS?.
```
                                            (WYLBUR shows the modified line, asking for more
                                            alterations; a carriage return is used to get
                                            back to command mode)
```
COMMAND?.list

   1.    TITLE  READING NORC SYSTEM FILE ON IBM CMS SYSTEM
   2.    FILE HANDLE  NORCSYS/NAME='NORC7282 SPSSXFIL B'

COMMAND?.collect 3
```
                                            (begin collecting again at line 3)
```
   3.    ?.get file=norcsys
   4.    ?.set blanks=0
   5.    ?.crosstabs  tables=race by sex
   6.    ?.statistics  all
```

Fig. A1.6   Building Program File with WYLBUR

From the information given in the end-of-job line, it seems that there were no warnings or errors in the job. The next step is to examine the output or listing file that was written on the B disk for more subtle errors in programming or execution.

Output Retrieval

CMS routinely names the output file with the file name of the program (NORC2) and the file type "listing." There are three ways to retrieve this output. First, WYLBUR can be used to search the file for error messages and to list the file. Second, if the listing is long it may be searched with

```
 7.    ?.options      3,4,5
 8.    ?.comment
 9.    ?.condescriptive  educ
10.    ?.comment
11.    ?.breakdown   tables=educ by race
12.    ?.commennt
13.    ?.comment
14.    ?.finish
15.    ?.=attn=
```

COMMAND?.delete 12   *(delete the line where "comment" is misspelled)*

```
12.    COMMENNT
```
(WYLBUR lists the deleted line)

COMMAND?.collect 4.1   *(for readability, a comment record is added between lines 4 and 5; the line numbers for insertion range from 4.001 to 4.999)*

```
4.1    ?.comment
4.2    ?.=attn=
```

COMMAND?.number   *(the program is renumbered for readability)*

```
14.    - LAST LINE.
```
(WYLBUR replies with the number of lines)

COMMAND?.list   *(the program is listed)*

```
 1.    TITLE   READING NORC SYSTEM FILE ON IBM CMS SYSTEM
 2.    FILE HANDLE   NORCSYS/NAME='NORC7282 SPSSXFIL B'
 3.    GET FILE=NORCSYS
 4.    SET BLANKS=0
 5.    COMMENT
 6.    CROSSTABS   TABLES=RACE BY SEX
 7.    STATISTICS   ALL
 8.    OPTIONS      3,4,5
 9.    COMMENT
10.    CONDESCRIPTIVE   EDUC
11.    COMMENT
12.    BREAKDOWN   TABLES=EDUC BY RACE
13.    COMMENT
14.    FINISH
```

COMMAND?.save norc2 spssx b   *(it is saved on the user's B disk)*

NORC2 SPSSX B1 SAVED   *(CMS replies that it is saved)*

COMMAND?.quit clear   *(quit WYLBUR, clear WYLBUR's working file, and return to CMS)*

R;   *(CMS acknowledges our return)*

Fig. A1.6 (continued)

WYLBUR for errors and then sent to the system printer. Since this example's listing is fairly short and the user is relatively sure that there are no errors, the third method is used here—the file is listed at a hardcopy terminal. This is usually the quickest way to get printed results when the output is not lengthy. The listing is shown in Figure A1.7.

Output Review

The output in Figure A1.7 contains the requested cross-tabulation of the variables RACE and SEX, the condescriptive procedure for the variable EDUC, and the breakdown of EDUC by RACE. One indication that the

```
.type norc2 listing b

21 FEB 84   SPSS-X RELEASE 1.1  FOR IBM VM/CMS                                          PAGE  1
21:26:08    COLUMBIA UNIVERSITY C. C. A.  IBM 4341      VM - SP/CMS


            SPSS INC LICENSE NUMBER:   323

PARM FIELD: 48K

     1  0       TITLE  READING NORC SYSTEM FILE ON IBM CMS SYSTEM
     2  0       FILE HANDLE  NORCSYS/NAME='NORC7282 SPSSXFIL F'
     3  0       GET FILE=NORCSYS
FILE CALLED NORCSYS :
 LABEL:
 CREATED 17 FEB 84 16:21:54      8 VARIABLES

     4  0       SET BLANKS=0
     5  0       COMMENT
     6  0       CROSSTABS  TABLES=RACE BY SEX
     7  0       STATISTICS  ALL
     8  0       OPTIONS    3,4,5
     9  0       COMMENT

THERE ARE   944416 BYTES OF MEMORY AVAILABLE.
THE LARGEST CONTIGUOUS AREA HAS   944416 BYTES.
 ***** GIVEN WORKSPACE ALLOWS FOR 31480 CELLS WITH    2 DIMENSIONS FOR CROSSTAB PROBLEM *****


21 FEB 84   READING NORC SYSTEM FILE ON IBM CMS SYSTEM                                  PAGE  2
21:26:36    COLUMBIA UNIVERSITY C. C. A.  IBM 4341      VM - SP/CMS

- - - - - - - - - - - - - - - - - -  C R O S S T A B U L A T I O N   O F  - - - - - - - - - - - - - - - - - -
    RACE                                          BY SEX
- - - - - - - - - - - - - - - - - - - - - - - - - - - - - - - - - - - - - - - - - -  PAGE 1 OF 1

                  SEX
          COUNT  :
          ROW PCT :MALE    FEMALE    ROW
          COL PCT :                  TOTAL
          TOT PCT :     1:      2:
RACE      --------+--------+--------+
            1  :  5442  :  6540  : 11982
WHITE        :  45.4  :  54.6  : 87.9
             :  88.4  :  87.5  :
             :  39.9  :  48.0  :
             +--------+--------+
            2  :   660  :   879  :  1539
BLACK        :  42.9  :  57.1  : 11.3
             :  10.7  :  11.8  :
             :   4.8  :   6.5  :
             +--------+--------+
            3  :    52  :    53  :   105
OTHER        :  49.5  :  50.5  :  .8
             :   .8  :   .7  :
             :   .4  :   .4  :
             +--------+--------+
           COLUMN   6154    7472   13626
           TOTAL    45.2    54.8   100.0

CHI-SQUARE    D.F.    SIGNIFICANCE      MIN E.F.    CELLS WITH E.F.< 5
----------    ----    ------------      --------    ------------------

 4.34587       2       0.1138           47.422      NONE
                                                   WITH RACE        WITH SEX
          STATISTIC              SYMMETRIC         DEPENDENT        DEPENDENT
          ---------              ---------         ---------        ---------

LAMBDA                             0.0               0.0              0.0
UNCERTAINTY COEFFICIENT            0.00030           0.00040          0.00023
SOMERS' D                         0.01229           0.00880          0.02038
ETA                                                 0.01071          0.01786
```

Fig. A1.7   Output Listing from SPSS-X Program

160

```
          STATISTIC              VALUE      SIGNIFICANCE
          ---------              -----      ------------


CRAMER'S V                       0.01786
CONTINGENCY COEFFICIENT          0.01786
KENDALL'S TAU B                  0.01339       0.0583
KENDALL'S TAU C                  0.00872       0.0583
PEARSON'S R                      0.01071       0.1056
GAMMA                            0.04126
NUMBER OF MISSING OBSERVATIONS =      0
```

21 FEB 84   READING NORC SYSTEM FILE ON IBM CMS SYSTEM   PAGE   3
21:26:36   COLUMBIA UNIVERSITY C. C. A. IBM 4341   VM - SP/CMS

PRECEDING TASK REQUIRED   10.71 SECONDS CPU TIME;   27.08 SECONDS ELAPSED.

   10 0   CONDESCRIPTIVE EDUC
   11 0   COMMENT
THERE ARE   944576 BYTES OF MEMORY AVAILABLE.
THE LARGEST CONTIGUOUS AREA HAS   944568 BYTES.
      74 BYTES OF MEMORY REQUIRED FOR CONDESCRIPTIVE PROCEDURE.
       2 BYTES HAVE ALREADY BEEN ACQUIRED.
      72 BYTES REMAIN TO BE ACQUIRED.

21 FEB 84   READING NORC SYSTEM FILE ON IBM CMS SYSTEM   PAGE   4
21:26:48   COLUMBIA UNIVERSITY C. C. A. IBM 4341   VM - SP/CMS

NUMBER OF VALID OBSERVATIONS (LISTWISE) =   13578.00
VARIABLE   MEAN   STD DEV   MINIMUM   MAXIMUM VALID N   LABEL

EDUC   11.745   3.252   .000   20.000   13578   HIGHEST YEAR SCHOOL COMPLETED
21 FEB 84   READING NORC SYSTEM FILE ON IBM CMS SYSTEM   PAGE   5
21:26:48   COLUMBIA UNIVERSITY C. C. A. IBM 4341   VM - SP/CMS

PRECEDING TASK REQUIRED   4.43 SECONDS CPU TIME;   11.54 SECONDS ELAPSED.

   12 0   BREAKDOWN TABLES=EDUC BY RACE
   13 0   COMMENT

THERE ARE   944584 BYTES OF MEMORY AVAILABLE.
THE LARGEST CONTIGUOUS AREA HAS   944584 BYTES.
 ***** GIVEN WORKSPACE ALLOWS FOR 26238 CELLS WITH   1 DIMENSIONS FOR BREAKDOWN PROBLEM *****

21 FEB 84   READING NORC SYSTEM FILE ON IBM CMS SYSTEM   PAGE   6
21:27:00   COLUMBIA UNIVERSITY C. C. A. IBM 4341   VM - SP/CMS

- - - - - - - - - - - - - - - - - D E S C R I P T I O N   O F   S U B P O P U L A T I O N S - - - - - - - - - - - - - - - - -
CRITERION VARIABLE   EDUC   HIGHEST YEAR SCHOOL COMPLETED
   BROKEN DOWN BY   RACE
- -
```

| VARIABLE | CODE | VALUE LABEL | SUM | MEAN | STD DEV | VARIANCE | N |
|----------|------|-------------|-----|------|---------|----------|---|
| FOR ENTIRE POPULATION | | | 159479.0000 | 11.7454 | 3.2524 | 10.5780 | ( 13578) |
| RACE | 1. | WHITE | 142231.0000 | 11.9092 | 3.1499 | 9.9217 | ( 11943) |
| RACE | 2. | BLACK | 15932.0000 | 10.4131 | 3.6672 | 13.4486 | ( 1530) |
| RACE | 3. | OTHER | 1316.0000 | 12.5333 | 3.7572 | 14.1167 | ( 105) |

```
   TOTAL CASES =   13626
MISSING CASES =      48 OR   0.4 PCT.
21 FEB 84   READING NORC SYSTEM FILE ON IBM CMS SYSTEM                                    PAGE   7
21:27:01    COLUMBIA UNIVERSITY C. C. A.  IBM 4341        VM - SP/CMS

PRECEDING TASK REQUIRED       5.78 SECONDS CPU TIME;     12.76 SECONDS ELAPSED.


   14  0        FINISH
   14 COMMAND LINES READ.
    0 ERRORS DETECTED.
    0 WARNINGS ISSUED.
   21 SECONDS CPU TIME.
   53 SECONDS ELAPSED TIME.
     END OF JOB.

R;                        (the system returns from listing the output)
```

Fig. A1.7   (continued)
```

analysis has been carried out correctly is that the marginal frequencies are the same as those reported in the NORC codebook for these variables. The mean level of EDUC for the entire population is 11.7 and the range is from 0 through 20. These figures and the race differences in mean schooling produced by the breakdown procedure seem reasonable enough. The calculations for the many statistics that were generated seem satisfactory but, in actual analysis, we would not request that all statistics be computed. Instead, only those specific items needed for the research would be calculated.

In this appendix, we illustrated CMSBATCH and CMS access to SPSS-X analyses of NORC data from the 1972 through 1982 surveys. We used the text editor WYLBUR to build and edit files, and the output was produced and listed for examination. As always, it is incumbent upon the user to examine and interpret output from statistical packages that is rather easily produced on computers. This can be done by following the examples provided here and in other appendices of this book.

COMMUNICATION WITH THE IBM VM/CMS SYSTEM

A major emphasis of the Columbia University Center for Computing Activities is to develop communications among mainframe computers and between microcomputers and mainframes. This appendix was written on a Heath/Zenith microcomputer using WordStar, a word processing package. The communications package KERMIT developed at Columbia was used to connect the microcomputer to the mainframe for editing files and analysis. KERMIT performed well in transferring output and files of terminal sessions from the mainframe to the microcomputer so that they could be incorporated into the text. Thus, this appendix also illustrates the effective use of a combination of a microcomputer, an excellent communication package, and the IBM mainframe.

APPENDIX II Applications on a DEC VAX

Richard P. Briggs

This brief appendix demonstrates remote batch and nonconversational interactive access on a Digital Equipment Corporation (DEC) VAX 11-780 at the University of Hartford. The operating system used for these illustrations is VAX VMS version 3.4. The SPSS-X command files are constructed using the full-screen text editor capabilities available with EDT and DEC's VT-100 terminal. SPSS-X release 1.0 and the combined 1972 through 1982 NORC General Social Survey Cumulative File are used for examples in this appendix. Running SPSS-X on the VAX is relatively straightforward, requiring only two files, the SPSS-X command file and a data file. No separate operating system command file is necessary for either remote batch or nonconversational interactive access. All of the information necessary for execution is provided by the user in response to prompts and queries issued after SPSS has been called.

THE EDT EDITOR

Building the SPSS command file with EDT is accomplished by accessing the line editor, specifying the name of the program file, switching on the

Dr. Richard P. Briggs is Assistant Chief Statistical Analyst, The Travelers Insurance Companies, 5MS, 1 Town Square, Hartford, CT 06115.

full-screen editor mode, and using the terminal (VT-100) as you would a typewriter. This sequence of commands is illustrated as follows:

```
$ EDT

Filename:        PRG1.CC

Input file does not exist.

[EOB]

* Change
```

(*The terminal screen clears,
and the cursor is positioned
in the upper left, first line
on the left bracket of the
[EOB] (end of buffer)
marker. The terminal
keyboard now functions like
a typewriter. Carriage
returns end lines and open
new lines. Control Z
returns the editor to the line
mode prompted by an '*'.
EXIT saves the editor
session and returns to the
operating system.*)

```
CTRL-Z

* Exit

$
```

Figure A2.1 lists an SPSS-X program named PRG1.CC built with EDT. In SPSS-X, the name of the data file to be analyzed is referenced in the command file PRG1.CC. The command FILE HANDLE "tags" a file name with a handle and any reference to this file is made subsequently with the tag, and not the file name as it exists on the operating system. Note that the file name may contain as many specifications as necessary. In this example, the data file 3.TAP does not reside in the user's directory, but in a temporary disk scratch area under the user's name of APP. The other file referenced, NORCSAVE.DAT, is given a different tag in another

```
TITLE   CREATION OF NORCGSS 72-82 SYSTEM FILE
FILE HANDLE   EXAMPLE/
  NAME='DSK_SCRATCH:[APP]3.TAP'
SET BLANKS=0
DATA LIST       FILE=EXAMPLE RECORDS=11
  /1 MARITAL 23 AGE 56-57 EDUC 64-65 SEX 76 RACE 77
  /2 REGION 65 /5 RELIG 7
VARIABLE LABELS MARITAL 'MARITAL STATUS'
  AGE 'AGE' RACE 'RACE' SEX 'SEX'
  EDUC 'HIGHEST YEAR OF SCHOOL COMPLETE'
  REGION 'REGION OF INTERVIEW'
  RELIG 'RESP RELIGIOUS PREFERENCE'
MISSING VALUES MARITAL(9)/AGE(0,98,99)/EDUC(97,98,99)/
  RELIG(0,8,9)/
VALUE LABELS MARITAL 1 'MARRIED' 2 'WIDOWED' 3 'DIVORCED'
  4 'SEPARATED' 5 'NEVER MARRIED' 9 'NA'/
  SEX 1 'MALE' 2 'FEMALE'/
  RACE 1 'WHITE' 2 'BLACK' 3 'OTHER'/
  REGION 1 'NEW ENGLAND' 2 'MIDDLE ATLANTIC' 3 'E. NOR. CENTRAL'
  4 'W. NOR. CENTRAL' 5 'SOUTH ATLANTIC' 6 'E. SOU. CENTRAL'
  7 'W. SOU. CENTRAL' 8 'MOUNTAIN' 9 'PACIFIC' 0 'FOREIGN'/
  RELIG 1 'PROTESTANT' 2 'CATHOLIC' 3 'JEWISH' 4 'NONE' 5 'OTHER'/
FILE HANDLE   KEEPNORC/NAME='NORCSAVE.DAT'
SAVE   OUTFILE=KEEPNORC/MAP
```

Fig. A2.1 SPSS-X Program PRG1.CC

FILE HANDLE command. This SPSS-X system file will be created and stored on disk in the user's catalog in this example. Another option would be to store the file in a temporary disk scratch area with the proper specification.

SPSS-X NONCONVERSATIONAL INTERACTIVE SUBMISSION

Running SPSS requires the user to respond to a series of questions after calling SPSS-X. First, the user must determine whether the output generated by SPSS is to be sent to a disk file or displayed on the terminal screen during processing. Second, the name of the file that contains the SPSS commands (the control file) must be supplied to SPSS. Finally, the amount of workspace required for processing can be specified. A fourth query must be answered if the user directs the SPSS generated output to the terminal.

SPSS is accessed by typing the command SPSS in response to the operating system prompt $. An example of this process using the SPSS

command file PRG1.CC and directing the SPSS output to a file names
PRG1.OUT is as follows:

```
$ SPSS

Please enter the output filename (<a

$ SPSS

Please enter the output filename (<RET> for screen):   PRG1.OUT

Please enter the control filename:   PRG1.CC

Please enter workspace in Kbytes (80 = 80K):  <RETURN>
```

(Responding with only a
<RETURN> to the
workspace query uses the
default allocation of 80K.
The actual processing of the
SPSS command file now
takes place. When the pro-
cessing is finished another
operating system prompt
('$') is displayed.)

The results of processing the commands in PRG1.CC are contained in the
file PRG1.OUT (Figure A2.2).

Using nonconversational interactive execution and screen display of
output allows the user immediate access to the results of an SPSS-X run.
However, the results are not captured simultaneously in a file and no
hardcopy can be obtained. Statistical results are displayed on the terminal screen as SPSS-X processes the command file.

The program file PRG2.CC (listed in Figure A2.3) reads the SPSS
system file NORCSAVE.DAT created in PRG1.CC and requests processing
of several statistical procedures. The careful reader may notice that the
CONDESCRIPTIVE command keyword is misspelled in the program. SPSS-
X is more flexible that earlier SPSS versions and, in this case, will assume
that the user intends to employ the CONDESCRIPTIVE procedure.

The execution of SPSS is done much the same way as before, but with
two minor changes: no response to the first query and additional information on terminal type. See the following example.

```
$ SPSS

Please enter the output filename (<RET> for screen):  <RETURN>

Please enter the control filename:  PRG2.CC

Please enter workspace in Kbytes (80 = 80K):  <RETURN>

Is this terminal a VT-100? YES
```

The terminal screen clears and shifts display width from 80 columns to 132 columns, and the output is shown on the screen the same way it would appear in printed form. The results of running PRG2.CC are displayed in Figure A2.4.

BATCH PROCESSING OF SPSS-X WITH INTERACTIVE SUBMISSION

Batch processing of SPSS-X command files is a matter of answering the same queries as nonconversational interactive requests, but issuing a different SPSS operating system command (SPSSB rather than SPSS). See the following example.

```
$ SPSSB

Please enter the output filename (<RET> for screen):  EXAMPLE.OUT

Please enter the control filename:  EXAMPLE.CC

Please enter workspace in Kbytes (80 = 80K): <RETURN>

    Job #### entered on queue UHABATCH

$
```

The output generated by SPSS will be captured in EXAMPLE.OUT, and an additional file BATCHSPSS.LOG will be created to capture the system's output. If the user neglects to specify a file for the SPSS generated output, this output is also directed to the BATCHSPSS.LOG file. This convenient feature keeps the SPSS output from disappearing into the nether world of the computer never to be seen again. The user periodically checks on the progress of the SPSS batch job and issues a print command to produce a hardcopy once the job has run.

SPSS INC LICENSE NUMBER: 6919

```
1   0       TITLE CREATION OF NORCGSS 72-82 SYSTEM FILE
2   0       FILE HANDLE EXAMPLE/ NAME='DSK$:[APP]3.TAP'
3   0       SET BLANKS=0
4   0       DATA LIST FILE=EXAMPLE RECORDS=11
5   0        /1 MARITAL 23 AGE 56-57 EDUC 64-65 SEX 76 RACE 77
6   0
7   0        /2 REGION 65 /5 RELIG 7
```

THE ABOVE DATA LIST STATEMENT WILL READ 11 RECORDS FROM FILE EXAMPLE .

VARIABLE	REC	START	END	FORMAT	WIDTH	DEC
MARITAL	1	23	23	F	1	0
AGE	1	56	57	F	2	0
EDUC	1	64	65	F	2	0
SEX	1	76	76	F	1	0
RACE	1	77	77	F	1	0
REGION	2	65	65	F	1	0
RELIG	5	7	7	F	1	0

END OF DATALIST TABLE.

```
8   0   VARIABLE LABELS MARITAL 'MARITAL STATUS'
9   0   AGE 'AGE' / SEX 'SEX'
10  0   EDUC 'HIGHEST YEAR OF SCHOOL COMPLETE'
11  0   REGION 'RESP YEAR OF INTERVIEW'
12  0   RELIG 'RELIGIOUS PREFERENCE'
13  0   MISSING VALUES MARITAL(9) AGE(0,98,99)/EDUC(97,98,99)/
14  0   RELIG(0,8,9)/
15  0   VALUE LABELS MARITAL 1 'MARRIED' 2 'WIDOWED' 3 'DIVORCED'
16  0   4 SEPARATED 5 'NEVER MARRIED' 8 'NA' 9 'OTHER'/
17  0   SEX 1 'MALE' 2 'FEMALE'/
18  0   RACE 1 'WHITE' 2 'BLACK' 3 'OTHER'/
19  0   REGION 1 'NEW ENGLAND' 2 'MIDDLE ATLANTIC' 3 'E. NOR. CENTRAL'
20  0   4 'W.NOR.CENTRAL' 5 'SOUTH ATLANTIC' 6 'E. SOU. CENTRAL'
21  0   7 'W. SOU. CENTRAL' 8 'MOUNTAIN' 9 'PACIFIC' 0 'FOREIGN'/
22  0   RELIG 1 'PROTESTANT' 2 'CATHOLIC' 3 'JEWISH' 4 'NONE' 5 'OTHER'/
23  0   FILE HANDLE KEEPNORC/NAME='NORCSAVE.DAT'
24  0   SAVE OUTFILE=KEEPNORC/MAP
```

```
30-NOV-83    CREATION OF NORCGSS 72-82 SYSTEM FILE
             UNIVERSITY OF HARTFORD          Digital VAX         VMS 3.3


OUTPUT FILE MAP

RESULT
------
MARITAL    MARITAL
AGE        AGE
EDUC       EDUC
SEX        SEX
RACE       RACE
REGION     REGION
RELIG      RELIG

30-NOV-83  10:52:43         7 VARIABLES,        56 BYTES PER CASE
30-NOV-83  12:16:58     13626 CASES SAVED


30-NOV-83    CREATION OF NORCGSS 72-82 SYSTEM FILE
             UNIVERSITY OF HARTFORD          Digital VAX         VMS 3.3


PRECEDING TASK REQUIRED     461.48 SECONDS CPU TIME;    5066.54 SECONDS ELAPSED.


      24 COMMAND LINES READ.
       0 ERRORS DETECTED.
       0 WARNINGS ISSUED.
     464 SECONDS CPU TIME.
    5144 SECONDS ELAPSED TIME.
         END OF JOB.
```

Fig. A2.2   Output Listing from SPSS-X Program PRG1.CC

```
TITLE READING NORC SYSTEM FILE
FILE HANDLE  NORCSYS/NAME='NORCSAVE.DAT'
GET FILE=NORCSYS
SET BLANKS=0
CROSSTABS TABLES=RACE BY SEX
STATISTICS ALL
OPTIONS 3,4,5
CONDESCRPITIVE EDUC
BREAKDOWN TABLES=EDUC BY RACE
```

Fig. A2.3   Program NORCXTAB.CC

SOME TIPS ON USING SPSS-X

Several features of SPSS-X are significantly different than those found in version 9. These include the way data are read, limitations on field widths, and the use of upper- and lowercase characters in both the command and data files. Some of the default settings on parameters can be changed. These include page length, format of variables for the WRITE (WRITE CASES in earlier versions) command, recognizing card numbers on SPSS-X command lines, and the way blank characters are handled in data files. In particular, blanks are not automatically assigned a zero (0), but depending on the set-up at time of installation can default to a SYSMIS value of $-0.1698089E+39$. If SPSS-X encounters several blanks in a row, it will begin to misread the position of subsequent variables. For the example run PRG1.CC, the raw data file DSK SCRATCH: APP 3.TAP contained several series of blanks. When the first attempt was made to read the NORC data using PRG1.CC without the SET BLANKS = 0 command, the fields containing each variable were not read correctly. After considerable detective work on the part of this writer, it was determined that the errors were the result of the blanks being set automatically to the SYSMIS value.

Another system parameter to check is the NUMBERED feature. If this parameter is set to YES, SPSS-X *expects* to encounter line numbers in columns 72 through 80 and will *not* recognize continuations of commands beyond column 71. This feature can lead to a great deal of frustration which did not occur with version 9 of SPSS. To determine the default setting of these parameters, the user can invoke a new SPSS-X command SHOW without accessing any data or performing any procedures. In addition, another command INFO has been implemented which allows the user to obtain information on SPSS-X, changes from version 9 or earlier, local processing information, and other information pertinent to the use of the SPSS-X. This feature is particularly important since there are no longer appendices in the SPSS-X User's Guide on operating SPSS in cer-

```
30-NOV-83     SPSS-X RELEASE 1.1 FOR VAX/VMS      Digital VAX          VMS 3.3
              UNIVERSITY OF HARTFORD

              SPSS INC LICENSE NUMBER:     6919

   1    0         TITLE READING NORC SYSTEM FILE
   2    0         FILE HANDLE NORCSYS/NAME=NORCSAVE.DAT'
   3    0         GET FILE=NORCSYS

FILE CALLED NORCSYS :
   LABEL:
   CREATED 30-NOV-83 10:52:43        7 VARIABLES

   4    0         SET BLANKS=0
   5    0         CROSSTABS TABLES=RACE BY SEX
   6    0         STATISTICS ALL
   7    0         OPTIONS 3,4,5

THERE ARE 81160 BYTES OF MEMORY AVAILABLE.
THE LARGEST CONTIGUOUS AREA HAS  81160 BYTES.

***** GIVEN WORKSPACE ALLOWS FOR  2705 CELLS WITH    2 DIMENSIONS FOR CROSSTAB PROBLEM *****
```

Fig. A2.4 Output Listing from SPSS-X Program PRG2.CC

30-NOV-83   READING NORC SYSTEM FILE   Digital VAX   VMS 3.3
            UNIVERSITY OF HARTFORD

- - - RACE - - RACE - - RACE - - C R O S S T A B U L A T I O N   O F - - - - - - - - - - -
- - - RACE - - RACE - - RACE - - - - - - - - B Y   S E X - - S E X - - S E X   O F - - - - - - -
                                                                                   PAGE 1 OF 1

RACE by SEX

	SEX		
COUNT ROW PCT COL PCT TOT PCT	MALE 1	FEMALE 2	ROW TOTAL
RACE			
WHITE 1	5442 45.4 88.4 39.9	6540 54.6 87.5 48.0	11982 87.9
BLACK 2	660 42.9 10.7 4.8	879 57.1 11.8 6.5	1539 11.3
OTHER 3	52 49.5 .8 .4	53 50.5 .7 .4	105 .8
COLUMN TOTAL	6154 45.2	7472 54.8	13626 100.0

CHI-SQUARE	D.F.	SIGNIFICANCE	MIN E.F.	CELLS WITH E.F. < 5
4.34587	2	0.1138	47.422	NONE

STATISTIC	SYMMETRIC	WITH RACE DEPENDENT	WITH SEX DEPENDENT
LAMBDA	0.00000	0.00000	0.00000
UNCERTAINTY COEFFICIENT	0.00029	0.00040	0.00023
SOMERS D	0.01229	0.00880	0.02038
ETA		0.01071	0.01786

STATISTIC	VALUE	SIGNIFICANCE
CRAMER'S V	0.01786	
CONTINGENCY COEFFICIENT	0.01786	
KENDALL'S TAU B	0.01339	0.0583
KENDALL'S TAU C	0.00872	0.0583
PEARSON'S R	0.01071	0.1056
GAMMA	0.04126	

NUMBER OF MISSING OBSERVATIONS = 0

```
30-NOV-83    READING NORC SYSTEM FILE          Digital VAX        VMS 3.3
             UNIVERSITY OF HARTFORD

PRECEDING TASK REQUIRED       57.52 SECONDS CPU TIME;     643.44 SECONDS ELAPSED.

      8   0        CONDESCRPITIVE EDUC

THERE ARE    81208 BYTES OF MEMORY AVAILABLE.
THE LARGEST CONTIGUOUS AREA HAS    81200 BYTES.

      74 BYTES OF MEMORY REQUIRED FOR CONDESCRIPTIVE PROCEDURE.
      72 BYTES HAVE ALREADY BEEN ACQUIRED.
      72 BYTES REMAIN TO BE ACQUIRED.

30-NOV-83    READING NORC SYSTEM FILE          Digital VAX        VMS 3.3
             UNIVERSITY OF HARTFORD

NUMBER OF VALID OBSERVATIONS (LISTWISE) =      13578.00

VARIABLE       MEAN      STD DEV    MINIMUM    MAXIMUM   VALID N    LABEL

EDUC          11.745      3.252       0.0       20.000    13578    HIGHEST YEAR OF SCHOOL COMPLETE

30-NOV-83    READING NORC SYSTEM FILE          Digital VAX        VMS 3.3
             UNIVERSITY OF HARTFORD

PRECEDING TASK REQUIRED       25.87 SECONDS CPU TIME;     881.85 SECONDS ELAPSED.

      9   0      BREAKDOWN TABLES=EDUC BY RACE

THERE ARE    81216 BYTES OF MEMORY AVAILABLE.
THE LARGEST CONTIGUOUS AREA HAS    81216 BYTES.
***** GIVEN WORKSPACE ALLOWS FOR    2256 CELLS WITH    1 DIMENSIONS FOR BREAKDOWN PROBLEM *****
```

Fig. A2.4 (continued)

173

30-NOV-83   READING NORC SYSTEM FILE   Digital VAX   VMS 3.3
            UNIVERSITY OF HARTFORD

CRITERION VARIABLE   EDUC   - - - - D E S C R I P T I O N   O F   S U B P O P U L A T I O N S - - - -
BROKEN DOWN BY   RACE   HIGHEST YEAR OF SCHOOL COMPLETE
                             RACE

VARIABLE	CODE	VALUE LABEL	SUM	MEAN	STD DEV	VARIANCE	N
FOR ENTIRE POPULATION			159479.0000	11.7454	3.2524	10.5780	(13578)
RACE	1.	WHITE	142231.0000	11.9092	3.1499	9.9217	(11943)
RACE	2.	BLACK	15932.0000	10.4131	3.6672	13.4489	(1530)
RACE	3.	OTHER	1316.0000	12.5333	3.7572	14.1167	(105)

TOTAL CASES =   13626
MISSING CASES =   48 OR   0.4 PCT.

30-NOV-83   READING NORC SYSTEM FILE   Digital VAX   VMS 3.3
            UNIVERSITY OF HARTFORD

PRECEDING TASK REQUIRED   27.42 SECONDS CPU TIME;   580.78 SECONDS ELAPSED.

9 COMMAND LINES READ.
0 ERRORS DETECTED.
0 WARNINGS ISSUED.
112 SECONDS CPU TIME.
2124 SECONDS ELAPSED TIME.
END OF JOB.

Fig. A2.4   (continued)

tain mainframe environment. The following is an example of the suggested first run of SPSS to obtain this information.

```
TITLE SHOW INFORMATION ON SPSS-X AND LOCAL DEFAULTS
      FOR 'SHOW' COMMAND
SHOW ALL
INFO ALL
```

A partial listing of the output generated by the SHOW command is presented in Figure A2.5.

If your VAX implementation of SPSS-X does not have the interactive prompts about output, control files, and workspace requirements, docu-

```
29-NOV-83   SPSS-X RELEASE 1.1 FOR VAX/VMS
            UNIVERSITY OF HARTFORD          Digital VAX      VMS 3.3

            SPSS INC LICENSE NUMBER:     6919
    1  0               TITLE SHOW INFORMATION ON SPSS-X AND LOCAL DEFAULTS
    2  0                     FOR 'SHOW' COMMAND
    3  0               SHOW ALL
BLANKS = SYSMIS

BLKSIZE =   3072 BYTES   (FOR WORK AND SYSTEM FILES)

BOX = '-I+++++++++'   (X'2049282B2B2B2B2B2B2B2B')

BUFNO = 2

CASE = UPLOW   (UPPER AND LOWER CASE)

COMPRESSION = OFF   (WORKFILES ARE NOT COMPRESSED)

DUMP = NO

FORMAT = F8.2

LENGTH = 60   (INCLUDING PAGE HEADERS)

MXERRS = 40   (0 ENCOUNTERED SO FAR)

MXLOOPS = 40

MXWARNS = 80   (0 ERRORS+WARNINGS SO FAR)

N = UNKNOWN

NUMBERED = YES

PRINTBACK = YES

SCOMPRESSION = ON   (SAVED FILES WILL BE COMPRESSED)

SEED = 2000000

SYSMIS = -0.1698089E+39   (X'FFFFFFFF7FFFFFFF')

UNDEFINED = WARN   (CONVERSION ERRORS REPORTED)

THE FILE IS NOT WEIGHTED

WIDTH = 132

$CASENUM =   INAPPLICABLE        $DATE    =   '29-NOV-83'
$JDATE   =       146508          $LENGTH  =           60
$SYSMIS  = -0.1698089E+39        $WIDTH   =          132
    4  0               INFO ALL
```

Fig. A2.5 Listing Generated by SPSS-X SHOW Command

mentation provided from SPSS-X INFO command lists the operating system commands necessary to run SPSS. The following is an example of accessing SPSS-X specifying the operating system parameters for the first example used in this appendix.

```
$ SPSSX / CONTROL = PRG1.CC / OUTFILE = PRG1.OUT / SPACE = 80
```

These hints notwithstanding, it is always a good idea to check with your local SPSS coordinator or computer center for the latest information on SPSS at your installation.

APPENDIX III   Applications on a CDC CYBER

Charles M. Tolbert II

This appendix illustrates remote batch, conversational, and nonconversational interactive access on a Control Data Corporation (CDC) CYBER 170 Model 760 housed at the Florida State University. The operating system is NOS 1.4. Program files are built with the Control Data Text Editor (EDIT) SPSS, and the NORC General Social Survey data introduced in Chapter 7 are also used. Readers are encouraged to review appropriate sections of the main text and the glossary for details on the terminology and strategies employed in this appendix.

CONTROL DATA EDIT

EDIT is a line-oriented editor which, among other things, can be used to build and modify program files. Table A3.1 lists a few fundamental editing commands. These commands are used to build an SPSS program in Figure A3.1. Once the file has been edited, the analysis can proceed.

Table A3.1   Some CDC EDIT Commands

Editing Task	Command	Explanation
Building text	ADD	One way to invoke input mode
Displaying text	LIST;n	Lists n lines
	FIND:/string/	Finds delimited string
	RESET	Moves pointer to beginning of file
	SET;n	Moves pointer n lines
Modifying text	RS:/old/,/new/	Replaces old string of text with new string
	DELETE;n	Deletes n lines beginning at pointer
Saving text	END	Terminates edit
	END TEXT EDITING	
	/replace,lfn	Saves file under batch system

(tab defined)	`/edit,pgm1`
	`BEGIN TEXT EDITING.`
	`? deftab:/;/`
	`? tab:/16/`
(input mode entered;	`? add`
input text delimited	`ENTER TEXT.`
with '%')	`? %run name;creation of norcgss 72-82 sytem file`
	`? file name;norcgss`
	`? data list;fixed(11)/1 marital 23 age 56-57 educ 64-65 sex 76 race 77`
	`? ;/2region 65/5 relig 7`
	`? var labels;marital marital status/`
	`? ;age,age/race,race/sex,sex/`
	`? ;educ highest year school completed/`
	`? ;region region of interview/`
	`? ;relig resp's regligious preference/`
	`? missing values;marital(9)/age(0,98,99)/educ(97,98,99)/`
	`? ;relig(8,9,0)`
	`? value labels;marital(1)married(2)widowed(3)divorced(4)separated`
	`? ;(5)never married(9)na/sex(1)male(2)female/`
	`? ;race(1)white(2)black(3)other/region(1)new england(2)middle atlant`
	`? ;e. nor. central(4)w. nor.central(5)south atlantic`
	`? ;(6)e. sou. central(7)w. sou. central(8)mountain(9)pacific`
	`? ;(0)foreign/relig(1)protestant(2)catholic(3)jewish(4)none(5)other/`
(input ended by final	`? save file%`
delimiter '%')	`READY.`
	`? reset`
	`? list;*`
(file listed)	`RUN NAME     CREATION OF NORCGSS 72-82 SYTEM FILE`
	`FILE NAME    NORCGSS`
	`DATA LIST    FIXED(11)/1 MARITAL 23 AGE 56-57 EDUC 64-65 SEX 76 RACE 77`
	`             /2REGION 65/5 RELIG 7`

Fig. A3.1   Building SPSS Program File with EDIT

REMOTE BATCH ACCESS

In this section, a remote batch job is submitted to the background queue from a terminal, following the steps outlined in Chapter 8. The job runs the SPSS program built in Figure A3.1 and reads the NORC General Social Survey Cumulative File. A small system file is saved for further analysis.

Program Preparation

This illustration of remote batch access on a CYBER uses two program data sets: a job control file and an SPSS program (edited in Figure A3.1). The job control file JOB1 is listed in Figure A3.2. When working on a CDC CYBER, it is convenient to keep a permanent file similar to this one. In many cases, only the names of files need to be changed from one

```
VAR LABELS    MARITAL MARITAL STATUS/
              AGE,AGE/RACE,RACE/SEX,SEX/
              EDUC,HIGHEST YEAR SCHOOL COMPLETED/
              REGION REGION OF INTERVIEW/
              RELIG RESP'S RELIGIOUS PREFERENCE/
MISSING VALUES MARITAL(9)/AGE(0,98,99)/EDUC(97,98,99)/
              RELIG(8,9,0)
VALUE LABELS  MARITAL(1)MARRIED(2)WIDOWED(3)DIVORCED(4)SEPARATED
              (5)NEVER MARRIED(9)NA/SEX(1)MALE(2)FEMALE/
              RACE(1)WHITE(2)BLACK(3)OTHER/REGION(1)NEW ENGLAND(2)MIDDLE ATLANT
              E. NOR. CENTRAL(4)W. NOR. CENTRAL(5)SOUTH ATLANTIC
              (6)E. SOU. CENTRAL(7)W. SOU. CENTRAL(8)MOUNTAIN(9)PACIFIC
              (0)FOREIGN/RELIG(1)PROTESTANT(2)CATHOLIC(3)JEWISH(4)NONE(5)OTHER/
SAVE FILE
 -END OF FILE-
```

(pointer positioned and RS commands used to correct errors)

```
? reset
? rs1/syt/,/syst/
? list
RUN NAME       CREATION OF NORCGSS 72-82 SYSTEM FILE
? set13
? list
               /2REGION 65/5 RELIG 7
? rs1/2r/,/2 r/
? list
               /2 REGION 65/5 RELIG 7
? find1/e. nor/
               E. NOR. CENTRAL(4)W. NOR. CENTRAL(5)SOUTH ATLANTIC
? rs1/e/,/(7)e/
? list
               (7)E. NOR. CENTRAL(4)W. NOR. CENTRAL(5)SOUTH ATLANTIC
```

(EDIT session ended)

```
? end
END TEXT EDITING.
/EDIT,PGM1.
```

(file saved)

```
/replace,pgm1
/
```

Fig. A3.1 (continued)

```
JOB,T100,CM77000.
CHARGE,1234,MASTER.
ATTACH,GSS7282.
GET,PGM1.
DEFINE,NORCGSS.
ATTACH,SPSS/UN=LIBRARY.
SPSS,I=PGM1,D=GSS7282,L=OUT1,S=NORCGSS,LO=ABRV.
SKIP,L1.
EXIT.
ENDIF,L1.
DAYFILE,DF.
RP,DF,OUT1.
```

Fig. A3.2 Job Control File for Batch Job

run to the next. Line 1 of JOB1 is the JOB statement which informs the system that the program will take no longer than 100 seconds and will need no more than 77000 units of central memory. Line 2 is a CHARGE statement which bills a project named "master" under account number 1234. The next four lines allocate various input and output files (or, in CDC jargon, make them "local files"). The ATTACH statement allocates the existing direct access file named GSS7282 which contains the raw NORC data. The GET command allocates the indirect access file PGM1 which is the SPSS program. The DEFINE statement allocates a new direct access file named NORCGSS which will contain the SPSS system file created by PGM1. Finally, line 6 is an ATTACH statement which makes available the SPSS package stored on the system library.

A command procedure file resides on the system which is activated when the user issues the SPSS command in either batch or interactive mode:

/SPSS,   (*other parameters separated by commas*)

In the SPSS execution statement on line 7 of JOB1, the I= parameter identifies the input SPSS program file (PGM1). The D= parameter refers to input raw data (GSS7282), and the L= parameter names the output listing associated with the job (OUT1). The S= parameter identifies the output system file and matches the direct access file name specified in the DEFINE statement. The LO= parameter instructs SPSS to arrange the printed results in 80 columns so that the output can be displayed on a terminal. Omitting the LO= parameter would result in output formatted for a line printer (132 columns wide).

Several other optional parameters could be included on the SPSS execution statement, and these are detailed in the CDC appendix of the SPSS manual (Nie, et al., 1975). Two of the more useful ones are:

G =   *(specifies name of SPSS system file to be read)*
A =   *(specifies name of raw data output file)*

The next three lines of JOB1 ensure that output from the job will not be lost in case of execution errors. The DAYFILE statement on line 11 creates a file named DF into which the dayfile of the job is written. The dayfile contains messages from the operating system about the job and can be useful in detecting problems. The final line of the setup replaces (saves) the two output report files created by the job. After execution is completed, DF can be reviewed for operating system messages at the user's convenience. Likewise, OUT1 can be opened to view SPSS messages and any results of statistical calculations. Ultimately, the output from a successful job is printed. In the interim, however, this job control setup allows the user a good deal of discretion and control over the timing of the printing.

Job Submission

This part of remote batch access on a CYBER is quite straightforward. The job control file JOB1 is allocated and submitted in Figure A3.3. Upon submission, the operating system notes the time and assigns a job name. In the preceding example, the job is submitted at 9:13 AM and is named EWBABFV. The ENQUIRE command followed by JN is a request for status of jobs belonging to the user. As long as the user is logged on, one job will be executing in the system (the terminal session itself). In the illustration, the executing job is the terminal, and the deferred job is the batch job waiting its turn. A second ENQUIRE command indicates that the batch job belonging to the user is now executing as well. The third status inquiry indicates that only the terminal session remains in the system (i.e., the batch job has finished executing). The real time involved

```
/get,job1
/submit,job1
  09.13.40. SUBMIT COMPLETE.  JOBNAME IS EWBABFV
/enquire,jn
  EWBA252  EXECUTING.
  EWBABFV  IN TIMED/EVENT ROLLOUT.
/enquire,jn
  EWBA252  EXECUTING.
  EWBABFV  EXECUTING.
/enquire,jn
  EWBA252  EXECUTING.
```

Fig. A3.3 Results of Job Status Inquiries

in this example was about three minutes, but this will vary depending on the level of activity in the system.

Output Retrieval

The next step is to retrieve the output from the batch job. This is done from a terminal by simply opening the output files with an editor and looking for error messages. The SPSS command procedure terminates with a message that errors have been encountered ("SPSS ERRORS") or a statement that suggests that the SPSS portion of the job has executed successfully ("END SPSS"). Either of these messages will be contained in the dayfile associated with the job. In Figure A3.4, the dayfile DF is opened with EDIT and listed. The dayfile provides useful information on the outcome of the job. Most significantly, line 9 indicates the system report END SPSS, which suggests that the SPSS program ran successfully. In fact, there are no system messages which indicate any problems. Such messages would appear, for example, if the operating system had been unable to find or open one of the files required by the job. Also, any syntax errors in the job control file would be noted in the dayfile.

Since the dayfile indicates that things seem to be in order, the output file OUT1 written by SPSS is examined. There is always a possibility that a programming error has gone undetected by the system, and a careful review of the output file is advisable. In the following example, the file is opened with EDIT, and the FIND command is used to locate any occurrences of the word ERROR:

```
/edit,out1

 BEGIN TEXT EDITING.
? find:/error/
 NUMBER OF ERRORS DETECTED        0
? end
 END TEXT EDITING.
$EDIT,OUT1.
/
```

The only place the word is encountered is on the last line of the file where SPSS always prints an error summary. The line confirms that there were indeed no SPSS errors in the run. At this point, the output is ordinarily routed to a printer. For readers' information, however, the entire output from the job is reproduced in Figure A3.5.

```
/get,df
/edit,df

BEGIN TEXT EDITING
 ? list;*
09.15.40.JOB,T100,CM77000.
09.15.40.USER(      1234***   ,)
09.14.40.CHARGE,1234,MASTER.
09.15.45.ATTACH,GSS7282.
09.15.48.GET,PGM1.
09.15.49.DEFINE,NORCGSS.
09.15.49.ATTACH,SPSS/UN=LIBRARY.
09.15.49.SPSS,I=PGM1,D=GSS7282,L=OUT1,S=NORCGSS,LO=ABRV,NR.
09.17.02.END SPSS
09.17.02.SKIP,L1.
09.17.02.ENDIF,L1.
09.17.02.DAYFILE,DF.
-END OF FILE-
```

Fig. A3.4 Listing of Dayfile with Text Editor

Output Review

The analyst's job is not finished when the printed results of a successfully executed program have been obtained. The output must be carefully examined for evidence of errors that the computer cannot detect. Unless the user specifically instructs the package otherwise, SPSS lists back the program in the upper portion of the output. The latter portion of the output contains information about the execution of the job.

In the example run, there are two important things to check in the lower half of the output. One is the number of cases read by SPSS. Does that number match the number of respondents reported by the NORC codebook? SPSS encountered 13,626 cases, and this corresponds exactly to the number of respondents listed in the code book (look back at the codebook pages reproduced in Chapter 7).

A second important item to check is whether or not the system file NORCGSS was stored properly. Near the bottom of the output file, we see that the system file was indeed stored, and that the variables in the file have been listed for future reference. This listing is valuable because the variables must be referenced in subsequent analysis by precisely these names. Any misspelled variable names will result in error messages. One other useful bit of information concerning the system file NORCGSS is its size. The disk and tape size parameters are conveniently provided near the end of the output. Also, the amount of execution time (17.1 seconds) is listed for the user's information. Now that this system file exists, subsequent illustrations of other access modes will require

```
T                                    83/07/05. 09.15.50. PAGE   1

COMPUTING CENTER
FLORIDA STATE UNIVERSITY

S P S S - -

STATISTICAL PACKAGE FOR THE SOCIAL SCIENCES

VERSION 8.3 (NOS) -- MAY 04, 1982

077000 CM MAXIMUM FIELD LENGTH REQUEST

RUN NAME       CREATION OF NORCGSS 72-82 SYSTEM FILE
FILE NAME      NORCGSS
DATA LIST      FIXED(11)/1 MARITAL 23 AGE 56-57 EDUC 64-65 SEX 76 RACE 77
               /2 REGION 65/5 RELIG 7

THE DATA LIST PROVIDES FOR    7 VARIABLES AND  11 RECORDS PER CASE.
A MAXIMUM OF  77 COLUMNS ARE USED ON A RECORD.

VAR LABELS     MARITAL MARITAL STATUS/
               AGE,AGE/RACE,RACE/SEX,SEX/
               EDUC HIGHEST YEAR SCHOOL COMPLETED/
               REGION REGION OF INTERVIEW/
               RELIG RESP'S RELIGIOUS PREFERENCE/
MISSING VALUES MARITAL(9)/AGE(0.98,99)/EDUC(97,98,99)/
               RELIG(8,9,0)/
VALUE LABELS   MARITAL(1)MARRIED(2)WIDOWED(3)DIVORCED(4)SEPARATED
               (5)NEVER MARRIED(9)NA/SEX(1)MALE(2)FEMALE/
               RACE(1)WHITE(2)BLACK(3)OTHER/REGION(1)NEW ENGLAND(2)MIDDLE ATLANT
               (3)E. NOR. CENTRAL(4)W. NOR. CENTRAL(5)SOUTH ATLANTIC
               (6)E. SOU. CENTRAL(7)W. SOU. CENTRAL(8)MOUNTAIN(9)PACIFIC
               (0)FOREIGN/RELIG(1)PROTESTANT(2)CATHOLIC(3)JEWISH(4)NONE(5)OTHER
```

Fig. A3.5   SPSS Output from Batch Job

much less programming on the user's part and less execution time on the computer's part.

NONCONVERSATIONAL INTERACTIVE ANALYSIS

Program Preparation

Another SPSS program (PGM2) which reads and analyzes the NORCGSS system file is as follows:

```
RAN NAME          READING NORCGSS SYSTEM FILE
GET FILE          NORCGSS
CROSSTABS         TABLES=RACE BY SEX
STATISTICS        ALL
```

```
CPU TIME REQUIRED..      .050 SECONDS

SAVE FILE

DATA COPIED TO SCRATCH FILE

END OF FILE ON FILE GSS7282
AFTER READING  13626 CASES FROM SUBFILE NORCGSS

1CREATION OF NORCGSS 72-82 SYSTEM FILE      83/07/05. 09.15.50. PAGE    2

A SAVE FILE HAS BEEN GENERATED WITH THESE VARIABLES...

SEQNUM   SUBFILE  CASWGT   MARITAL  AGE       EDUC     SEX
RACE     REGION   RELIG

THE SUBFILES ARE..
                 N OF
    NAME        CASES
    NORCGSS     13626

SPSS FILE NORCGSS  WAS WRITTEN ON LOCAL FILE NORCGSS

ITS SIZE IS       2136 DISK PRUS
         OR        268 TAPE BLOCKS

CPU TIME REQUIRED..   17.081 SECONDS

TOTAL CPU TIME USED..   17.131 SECONDS

RUN COMPLETED

NUMBER OF CONTROL CARDS READ  18
NUMBER OF ERRORS DETECTED      0
```

Fig. A3.5 (continued)

Those who are familiar with SPSS will note that one mistake remains in the program. To illustrate the nonconversational interaction process, that error will be ignored for the time being.

Program Execution

Execution of a nonconversational interactive program requires prior allocation of all necessary files. In this case, the system file NORCGSS created earlier, the program PGM2, and the SPSS package all must be local files. Once these have been allocated, the SPSS call statement is issued in exactly the same format as the remote batch procedure. This time, however, the input program file is PGM2, and the output file will be named OUT2. Also, note that a system file is read (G = NORCGSS), and that no raw data file is required; hence, there is no D = parameter. The terminal commands to execute PGM2 are as follows:

```
/get,pgm2
/attach,norcgss
/attach,spss/un=library
/rewind,*
6 FILE(S) PROCESSED.
/spss,i=pgm2,g=norcgss,1=out2,lo=abrv
SPSS ERRORS
/
```

The system response indicates that something went wrong. To determine the problem, the output of the file must be examined.

Output Retrieval

The SPSS call statement identified a file named OUT2 for the program results, and it is opened to look for error messages. One simple method is to use an editor to search for occurrences of the word ERROR. The FIND command of EDIT finds the word ERROR, and the lines immediately around the mistake are listed with a LIST command in Figure A3.6. The error message indicates that the SPSS keyword RUN NAME is misspelled.

```
/edit,out2                                              (OUT2 opened)

 BEGIN TEXT EDITING.
? find:/error/                                          ("error" found)
 ERROR NUMBER..    1. PROCESSING CEASES, ERROR SCAN CONTINUES.
? set;-2                                                (lines around error
? list;5                                                 listed)
 RAN NAME         READING NORCGSS SYSTEM FILE

 ERROR NUMBER..    1. PROCESSING CEASES, ERROR SCAN CONTINUES.

 GET FILE         NORCGSS
? end
 END TEXT EDITING.
$EDIT,OUT2.
/edit,pgm2                                              (program file PGM2
 BEGIN TEXT EDITING.                                     opened and error
? rs:/ran/,/run/                                         corrected)
? list
RUN NAME          READING NORCGSS SYSTEM FILE
? end
 END TEXT EDITING.
$EDIT,PGM2.
/replace,pgm2                                           (new version of program
/                                                        file PGM2 saved)
```

Fig. A3.6   Error Detection and Correction

Now that the nature of the error is known, the edit of OUT2 is terminated, and the original program (PGM2) is corrected and saved with the editor. Now PGM2 is executed again. If all the relevant files are still allocated (i.e., still local files), only a REWIND command is necessary to ensure that all files are positioned properly. The SPSS command is issued and the system responds with END SPSS. The output file OUT2 is edited, and the only occurrence of the word ERROR is in the error summary message:

```
/rewind,*
    5 FILE(S) PROCESSED.
/spss,i=pgm2,g=norcgss,1=out2,lo=abrv
END SPSS
/edit,out2
BEGIN TEXT EDITING

  ? find:/error/
  ? list
NUMBER OF ERRORS DETECTED        0
  ?end
  END TEXT EDITING
/
```

The file is ready to be routed to a printer and is reproduced in Figure A3.7 for the reader's information.

Output Review

The output in Figure A3.7 contains the requested cross-tabulation of the variables RACE and SEX. The marginal frequencies are the same as those reported in the NORC codebook for the two variables (see Chapter 7), and the calculations appear to be satisfactory. In actual analysis, it would be wasteful to compute all of the possible contingency table statistics. They are presented here merely to suggest the range of computations that is available in analysis software.

CONVERSATIONAL INTERACTION

Brief analyses like the preceding one are also quite easily done conversationally. One conversational package that operates on CYBER systems is

```
----------------------------------------------------------------------
                              83/07/04. 17.42.08. PAGE   1

            COMPUTING CENTER
            FLORIDA STATE UNIVERSITY

            S P S S - - STATISTICAL PACKAGE FOR THE SOCIAL SCIENCES

            VERSION 8.3 (NOS) -- MAY 04, 1982

            123700 CM MAXIMUM FIELD LENGTH REQUEST

RUN NAME        READING NORCGSS SYSTEM FILE
GET FILE        NORCGSS

FILE NORCGSS  HAS  10 VARIABLES

THE SUBFILES ARE..

            N OF
   NAME     CASES

   NORCGSS  13626

CPU TIME REQUIRED..      .011 SECONDS

CROSSTABS       TABLES=RACE BY SEX
STATISTICS      ALL

 GIVEN 2 DIMENSIONS,  INITIAL CM ALLOWS FOR    522 CELLS
                      MAXIMUM CM ALLOWS FOR   4605 CELLS

1READING NORCGSS SYSTEM FILE                  83/07/04. 17.42.08. PAGE    2

 FILE - NORCGSS  (CREATED - 83/07/04)

 * * * * * * * *  C R O S S T A B U L A T I O N  O F  * * * * * * * * *

    RACE     RACE
 BY SEX      SEX
 * * * * * * * * * * * * * * * * * * * * * * * * * * * * * * PAGE  1 OF  1

              SEX
      COUNT  I
      ROW PCT IMALE     FEMALE     ROW
      COL PCT I                    TOTAL
  TOT PCT I      1.I       2.I
    RACE    ---I--------I--------I
          1. I   5442  I   6540  I 11982
   WHITE      I   45.4 I   54.6  I  87.9
             I   88.4 I   87.5  I
             I   39.9 I   48.0  I
             -I--------I--------I
          2. I    660  I    879  I  1539
   BLACK      I   42.9 I   57.1  I  11.3
             I   10.7 I   11.8  I
             I    4.8 I    6.5  I
             -I--------I--------I
          3. I     52  I     53  I   105
   OTHER      I   49.5 I   50.5  I    .8
             I    .8  I    .7   I
             I    .4  I    .4   I
             -I--------I--------I
        COLUMN   6154     7472     13626
        TOTAL    45.2     54.8     100.0
```

Fig. A3.7 SPSS Output Associated with Program File PGM2

SPSS-ONLINE. Lines of programs are entered one by one with semicolons used to tab to column 16. The only major syntax difference is that line numbers are entered to indicate the order of the statements (and thereby allow some flexibility in case a line is omitted). Once the statements have been entered, the user types EXECUTE and each command is evaluated. If there are no errors, the results of the requested calculations are presented.

To initiate SPSS-ONLINE, the software package and any required data files must be allocated. In the following example, the system file NORCGSS and ONLINE are made local files, and then ONLINE is called:

```
/attach,norcgss
/get,spsson1/un=library
/spsson1
```

Once ONLINE is called, the user responds to prompts about files and builds a program in AUTO-MODE. This is illustrated in Figure A3.8. The careful reader will no doubt recall that the education variable on the NORCGSS file is named EDUC. That information eluded this writer, however, as he composed this demonstration. Thus, the analysis in

```
RAW CHI SQ =     4.34587 WITH     2 D.F., SIG. =    .1138
CRAMER"S V = .01786
CONTINGENCY COEFFICIENT = .01786
LAMBDA (ASYMMETRIC) =          0 WITH RACE     DEP.
                    =          0 WITH SEX      DEP.
LAMBDA (SYMMETRIC)   =          0
UNCERTAINTY COEF. (ASYMMETRIC) =    .00040 WITH RACE     DEP.
                               =    .00023 WITH SEX      DEP.
UNCERTAINTY COEF. (SYMMETRIC)  =    .00029
KENDALL"S TAU B = .01339, SIG. = .0583
KENDALL"S TAU C = .00872, SIG. = .0583
GAMMA = .04126
SOMERS"S D (ASYMMETRIC) =    .00880 WITH RACE     DEP.
                        =    .02038 WITH SEX      DEP.
SOMERS"S D (SYMMETRIC)  =    .01229
ETA =  .01071 WITH RACE     DEPENDENT.
ETA =  .01786 WITH SEX      DEPENDENT.
PEARSON"S R =  .01071, SIG. = .1056

1READING NORCGSS SYSTEM FILE              83/07/04. 17.42.08. PAGE    3

CPU TIME REQUIRED..     1.497 SECONDS

TOTAL CPU TIME USED..     1.509 SECONDS

RUN COMPLETED

NUMBER OF CONTROL CARDS READ    4
NUMBER OF ERRORS DETECTED       0
```

Fig. A3.7 (continued)

```
SPSS/ONLINE 8.3

USE AN SPSS SYSTEM FILE THIS RUN
? yes
 ENTER FILE NAME
? norcgss
 USE A RAW DATA FILE THIS RUN
? no
 AUTO-MODE.
? 1.0 get file;norcgss
? 2.0 condescriptive;education
? 3.0 breakdown;tables=educ by race/
? execute
 ENTERING SPSS.
        103000 CM MAXIMUM FIELD LENGTH REQUEST



- - - CONDESCRIPTIVE - - -

THE FOLLOWING HAS CAUSED AN ERROR .. EDUCATIO

 ERROR NO.   801 IN GROUP   2

00040600 CM NEEDED FOR CONDESCRIPTIVE

CPU TIME REQUIRED..      .005 SECONDS


- - - BREAKDOWN - - -


GIVEN 1 DIMENSIONS,  INITIAL CM ALLOWS FOR   847 CELLS
                     MAXIMUM CM ALLOWS FOR  2810 CELLS

CPU TIME REQUIRED..      .005 SECONDS


    ERROR NO.. 801
    THE VARIABLE LIST ON A CONDESCRIPTIVE CARD IS INVALID

TOTAL CPU TIME USED..      .026 SECONDS
SPSS/ONLINE AUTO-MODE
```

Fig. A3.8   SPSS-ONLINE Session Including User Error

Figure A3.7 ends on an unfortunate note as the requested variable name is not on the system file.

After the error, the user is returned to AUTO-MODE and can type additional commands. Since line 2 was in error, it is replaced by simply entering another second line. As is evident in Figure A3.9, the resulting statement is executable, and ONLINE begins producing results of the requested calculations.

As always, it is incumbent upon the user to examine the output. The statistics for EDUC indicate that the mean is 11.7 and that the range is 0 through 20. These figures and the race differences in mean schooling levels produced by the BREAKDOWN procedure correspond to conven-

```
? 2.0 condescriptive;educ
? execute
 ENTERING SPSS.
         103000 CM MAXIMUM FIELD LENGTH REQUEST

CPU TIME REQUIRED..      .011 SECONDS

- - - CONDESCRIPTIVE - - -

00040600 CM NEEDED FOR CONDESCRIPTIVE

VARIABLE  EDUC       HIGHEST YEAR SCHOOL COMPLETED

  MEAN         11.745    STD ERR       .028    STD DEV      3.252
  VARIANCE     10.578    KURTOSIS      .857    SKEWNESS     -.348
  MINIMUM          0     MAXIMUM     20.000    SUM      159479.000
  C.V. PCT     27.691    .95 C.I.    11.691         TO      11.800

VALID CASES    13578    MISSING CASES     48

CPU TIME REQUIRED..    1.507 SECONDS

- - - BREAKDOWN - - -

GIVEN 1 DIMENSIONS,  INITIAL CM ALLOWS FOR   1018 CELLS
                     MAXIMUM CM ALLOWS FOR   2981 CELLS

CRITERION VARIABLE   EDUC      HIGHEST YEAR SCHOOL COMPLETED
   BROKEN DOWN BY    RACE      RACE

VARIABLE        CODE      MEAN    STD. DEV.    N VALUE LABEL

FOR ENTIRE POPULATION       11.745    3.252  13578

RACE              1.        11.909    3.150  11943 WHITE
RACE              2.        10.413    3.667   1530 BLACK
RACE              3.        12.533    3.757    105 OTHER

TOTAL CASES =   13626
MISSING CASES =       48 OR    .4 PCT.

CPU TIME REQUIRED..    1.160 SECONDS

TOTAL CPU TIME USED..    2.682 SECONDS
 SPSS/ONLINE AUTO-MODE
? end
 GOOD-BYE.
SPSSONLINE.
```

Fig. A3.9 Analysis with SPSS-ONLINE

tional expectations, and things would thus appear to be in order. Conversational interaction is clearly a handy way to calculate quickly a few statistics. From these brief examples, it should be apparent that a CDC CYBER mainframe is an adequate medium for analysis of social science data.

APPENDIX IV Applications on a DECSYSTEM 10

Alice Abel Kemp

In this appendix, batch and time-sharing modes of access are illustrated on a Digital Equipment Corporation Decsystem 1070 (DEC-10) housed at the University of New Orleans. The first section describes the Lined text editor, and a SPSS program is created which accesses the NORC General Social Survey data (see Chapter 7). The following sections demonstrate batch and interactive time-sharing applications of SPSS on a DEC-10.

LINED TEXT EDITOR

Once logged on the system, the user begins work at the monitor level which is indicated by a period (.) prompt. Lined is a line-oriented editor which offers two ways to enter input mode. In Figure A4.1, an edit ses-

Dr. Alice Abel Kemp is Assistant Professor in the Department of Sociology, University of New Orleans, New Orleans, Louisiana 70148.

```
.edit read.sps
?EDTCNF File not found.          Creating new file

00010   run name        creation of norcgss 72-82 system file
00020   file name       norcgss
00030   data list       fixed(11)/1kmarital 23 age 56-57 educ 64-65
                        sex 76 race 77/2 region 65/5 relig 7
00050   var labels      marital marital status/
00060                   age,age/race,race/sex,sex/
00070                   region region of interview/
00080                   educ highest year school completed/
00090                   relig resp's religious preference/
00100   missing values  marital(9)/age(0,98,99)/educ(97,98,99)/
00110                   relig(8,9,0)/
00120   value labels    marital(1)married(2)widowed(3)divorced(4)
00130                   separated(5)never married(9)na/
00140                   sex(1)male(2)female/
00150                   race(1)qhite(2)black(3)other/
00160                   region(1)new england(2)middle atlantic
00170                   (3)e. nor. central(4)w. nor.central
00180                   (5)south atlantic(6)e. sou. central
00190                   (7)w. sou central(8)mountain(9)pacific
00200                   (0)foreign/relig(1)protestant(2)catholic
00210                   (3)jewish(4)none(5)other
00220   save file       norcgss.sys
00230   finish
00240
[EDTCPT CHECKPOINT taken]
*del 20
*i 20
00020   file name       norcgss.sys
*i 30
00030   data list       fixed(11)/1 marital 23 age 56-57 educ 64-65
*m 150
00150   [ 1) ]          RACE (1)Q/w HITE(2)BLACK(3)OTHER/
00150
```

Fig. A4.1 Building READ.SPS with Lined

sion is begun by specifying a file name that does not exist in the user's catalog. Lined notes the nonexistence of the file and invokes input mode with line number prompts. An alternative way to create a new file is the CREATE command which is issued at the monitor level:

```
.CREATE READ.SPS
```

Once in input mode, the lines of the SPSS program file READ.SPS are entered as illustrated in Figure A4.1. After several lines of the SPSS program are typed in, the escape (ESC) is used to terminate input. The response is an asterisk (*) which is the Lined edit mode prompt. The next step is to inspect the file for typos or errors and to correct them.

For beginners, the easiest way to make corrections is to delete and replace entire lines. The incorrect line 20 is replaced in Figure A4.1 by using delete (DEL) and insert commands (I). Likewise, a corrected version of line 30 is substituted. The MODIFY (M) command is a very flexible command for making changes in a file. It can also be used to search the file for a letter, a series of letters (a string), or numbers. To correct line 150, M is typed along with the line number. Lined responds with the line number and awaits further commands, some of which are issued with control (CNTL) key sequences. In the figure, the text immediately preceding the error on line 150 is located by issuing a control-F (^F) command, then typing "1)", and another ^F. These commands produce brackets which enclose the string of text to be found. Lined supplies the portion of the line up to the bracketed string and awaits further instructions. In this case, a ^B is issued, indicating that a single character forward (or to the left) is to be deleted. The deleted "q" is then indicated with a slash by Lined, and the correct letter "w" is typed by the user. Finally, the RELEASE command (^R) is issued, leaving the remainder of the line unchanged. Had the change involved deleting a character or characters backward (left) on the line, the DELETE key on the terminal keyboard would have been used.

Modify can also be used to search for a particular string without making any corrections. Simply follow the same steps, and use the escape key after the pointer locates the desired string. This interrupts the modify sequence and returns the user to edit mode with an * prompt. Files are listed with the TYPE (T) command as indicated in Figure A4.2. A single line is listed by specifying a line number in the command. When the file is correct, a NOSEQ (N) command is issued to strip off the line numbers, and an EXIT (E) command is used to terminate the edit session and return to the system.

```
*t
00010  run name      creation of norcgss 72-82 system file
00020  file name     norcgss.sys
00030  data list     fixed(11)/1 marital 23 age 56-57 educ 64-65
00040                sex 76 race 77/2 region 65/5 relig 7
00050  var labels    marital marital status
00060                age,age/race,race/sex,sex/
00070                region region of interview/
00080                educ highest year school completed/
00090                relig resp's religious preference/
00100  missing values marital(9)/age(0,98,99)/educ(97,98,99)/
00110                relig(8,9,0)/
00120  value labels  marital(1)married(2)widowed(3)divorced(4)
00130                separated(5)never married(9)na/
00140                sex(1)male(2)female/
00150                race(1)white(2)black(3)other/
00160                region(1)new england(2)middle atlantic
00170                (3)e. nor. central(4)w. nor.central
00180                (5)south atlantic(6)e. sou. central
00190                (7)w. sou central(8)mountain(9)pacific
00200                (0)foreign/relig(1)protestant(2)catholic
00210                (3)jewish(4)none(5)other
00220  save file
00230  finish
*n
*e

EXIT
```

Fig. A4.2 Listing of Edited File

196

REMOTE BATCH ACCESS

The capacity of this particular DEC-10 system is rather limited, and a remote batch job is the wisest method for analysis of a large file (i.e., over 1,000 cases). As noted in Chapter 8, the steps in a batch job are job preparation, job submission, output retrieval, and output assessment.

Job Preparation

A remote batch job control file must be built which contains instructions for the operating system. A sample job control program is listed in Figure A4.3. The first three lines of the job control file provide user identification and system instructions. The job control file also contains commands to mount a magnetic tape containing the raw NORC data (lines 4 and 5). In the MOUNT statement, the tape is given a logical name RAW:. The /WE parameter means the tape is write-enabled (i.e., the write ring is to be inserted by the operator). When SPSS has finished the system file, it will be written as another file on the same tape. The operating system also requires that the blocksize for the dataset be specified. This is done in the SET statement which indicates a blocksize of 4094 (the maximum for this system).

The next statement in the job control file asks that SPSS be executed. The following line contains instructions regarding the job's various input and output files. LPT: directs the output to a line printer, = READ.SPS provides the name of the file containing the SPSS program, RAW:/INPUT indicates that the data for input reside in a file associated with the logical device RAW:. /SPACE:16K allocates additional space (memory) for a

```
00010      $JOB KEMP[9999,999]
00020      $PASSWORD AAK
00030      $TOPS10
00040      .MOUNT MTA:RAW:/REELID:10667/WE
00050      .SET BLO RAW:4094
00060      .R SPSS
00070      LPT:=READ.SPS,RAW:/INPUT/SPACE:16K
00080      .REW RAW:
00090      .SKIP RAW:1 FILE
00100      .SET BLO RAW:4094
00110      .COPY RAW:=NORCGSS.SYS
00120      .DIS RAW:
00130      .DEL NORCGSS.SYS
00140      $EOJ
```

Fig. A4.3 Job Control File ALICE.CNTL

large job. The next commands rewind the magnetic tape, instruct the system to skip the first file (which contains the raw data), reset the blocksize, and copy the newly created NORCGSS.SYS system file onto the tape. The format for the COPY command is the conventional destination = source format. Finally, the tape is dismounted, the system file deleted from the temporary directory on disk, and the last command ends the job.

Job Submission

Once the job control file (here, ALICE.CNTL) is ready, the next step is to submit the batch job:

```
.SUBMIT ALICE.CTL/TIME:59:00
```

On this system the default time is 60 seconds, and this specification overrides that, requesting 59 minutes.

Output Retrieval and Assessment

READ.SPS becomes the header name on the printed output file which can be retrieved the following day, if all goes well. It is important to examine the output carefully to be sure that the system file has been stored properly. The output listing reproduced in Figure A4.4 indicates that there were no execution errors and that the system file was created and stored for further use.

NONCONVERSATIONAL INTERACTIVE ACCESS

The typical user on this system uses nonconversational interactive access. As noted in Chapter 8, this access mode requires an SPSS program file, but not a job control file. The SPSS program CROSS.SPS listed in Figure A4.5 reads the NORCGSS.SYS system file and generates a cross-tabulation of two variables in the data file. In nonconversational interaction, each of the operating system commands in a batch job control file is issued from a terminal. When the analysis is completed, the user can edit the output from the terminal, inspect it for errors, and print it only if the results are satisfactory. This method is more convenient for the user than batch access, provided that the system is not saturated with users and that a tape drive is available.

The first task is to mount the tape containing the NORCGSS.SYS system file and to assign a logical unit name (here ONE). Once the tape has been mounted, the blocksize is set, and the tape is positioned to the proper file. In this case, one file is skipped because the system file is the second file on the tape. Then SPSS is called, and the system provides an * prompt. The user responds by providing names for output and input files. In the following example, the system file is read directly from the tape.

```
.MOUNT MTA:ONE/REELID:10667
.SET BLOCKSIZE RAW:4094
.SKIP ONE:1 FILE
.R SPSS
*OUT.OUT=CROSS.SPS,ONE:/GET/SPACE:16K
```

Note that the system file could also be copied from the tape into the user's temporary directory stored on disk. When the program runs, any error messages from SPSS are listed at the terminal and in the text of the output file. In this way, the user is alerted to problems before the output is printed.

The output of a job, whether batch or interactive time-sharing access, can be sent directly to a line printer. But a more efficient method is to have this output written in a separate data set in the user's temporary directory. This was done in the preceding example with the OUT.OUT parameter (names are the user's choice and can include any eight characters plus a three-letter secondary name). Once the OUT.OUT data set is created, it can be edited and examined at the terminal prior to printing.

Lined can be used to search through an output listing for error messages. The MODIFY command can be employed to find the string ERROR in the output file:

```
.M
00010    [ ERROR ]
```

Since no line number is given, the entire file will be searched, and Lined responds with the first line number (10). When the line containing "ERRORS" is located, the escape key is used to interrupt MODIFY. If

SPSS BATCH SYSTEM

SPSS FOR DECSYSTEM-10, VERSION H, RELEASE 9.1, MAY 1, 1982

ORDER FROM MCGRAW HILL;   CURRENT DOCUMENTATION FOR THE SPSS BATCH SYSTEM
                          SPSS, 2ND ED. (PRINCIPAL TEXT)   ORDER FROM SPSS INC.;   SPSS STATISTICAL ALGORITHMS
                          SPSS PRIMER (BRIEF INTRO TO SPSS)   KEYWORDS; THE SPSS INC. NEWSLETTER
                          SPSS UPDATE 7-9 (USE W/SPSS,2ND FOR REL. 7, 8, 9)
                          SPSS INTRODUCTORY GUIDE; BASIC STATISTICS AND OPERATIONS
                          SPSS PRIMER (BRIEF INTRO TO SPSS)

DEFAULT SPACE ALLOCATION: ALLOWS FOR: 78 TRANSFORMATIONS
WORKSPACE   14336 WORDS   315 RECODE VALUES + LAG VARIABLES
TRANSPACE   2048 WORDS   1262 IF/COMPUTE OPERATIONS

    1 RUN NAME   CREATION OF NORCG8S 72-82 SYSTEM FILE
    2 FILE NAME   NORCG8S.SYS
    3 DATA LIST   FIXED(11)/1 MARITAL 23 AGE 56-57 EDUC 64-65
    4   SEX 76 RACE 77/2 REGION 65/5 RELIG 7

THE DATA LIST PROVIDES FOR   7 VARIABLES AND 11 RECORDS ('CARD6') PER CASE. A MAXIMUM OF   77 COLUMNS ARE USED ON A RECORD.

LIST OF THE CONSTRUCTED FORMAT STATEMENT:
    (22X,F1.0,32X,F2.0,6X,F2.0,10X,2F1.0/64X,F1.0//6X,F1.0,//////)

    5 INPUT MEDIUM   TAPE
    6 VAR LABELS   MARITAL MARITAL STATUS/
    7   AGE,AGE/RACE,RACE/SEX,SEX/
    8   EDUC HIGHEST YEAR SCHOOL COMPLETED/
    9   REGION REGION OF INTERVIEW/
   10   RELIG RESP'S RELIGIOUS PREFERENCE/
   11 MISSING VALUES   MARITAL(9)/AGE(0,98,99)/EDUC(97,98,99)/
   12   RELIG(8,9,0)/
   13 VALUE LABELS   MARITAL(1)MARRIED(2)WIDOWED(3)DIVORCED
   14   (4)SEPARATED(5)NEVER MARRIED(9)NA/
   15   SEX(1)MALE(2)FEMALE/

200

```
16          RACE(1)WHITE(2)BLACK(3)OTHER/
17          REGION(1)NEW ENGLAND(2)MIDDLE ATLANTIC
18          (3)E. NOR. CENTRAL(4)W. NOR. CENTRAL
19          (5)SOUTH ATLANTIC(6)E. SOU. CENTRAL
20          (7)W. SOU. CENTRAL(8)MOUNTAIN(9)PACIFIC
21          (0)FOREIGN/RELIG(1)PROTESTANT(2)CATHOLIC
22          (3)JEWISH(4)NONE(5)OTHER
23 SAVE FILE
```

(SPSSEOF AFTER READING 13626 CASES FROM SUBFILE NORCGSS , END-OF-FILE WAS ENCOUNTERED ON INPUT MEDIUM)

CREATION OF NORCGSS 72-82 SYSTEM FILE   31-AUG-83   PAGE   2

FILE NORCGSS HAS BEEN SAVED WITH   10 VARIABLES:

SEQNUM   SUBFILE   CASWGT   MARITAL   AGE   EDUC   SEX   RACE   REGION   RELIG

THE SUBFILES ARE:

NAME   NO. OF
          CASES

NORCGSS   13626

          24 FINISH

CPU TIME REQUIRED: 597.81 SECONDS

NORMAL END OF JOB
   24 CONTROL CARDS WERE PROCESSED
    0 ERRORS WERE DETECTED

Fig. A4.4   Output Listing from SPSS Program READ.SPS

201

```
RUN NAME        READING NORCGSS SYSTEM FILE
GET FILE        NORCGSS.SYS
CROSSTABS       TABLES=RACE BY SEX
STATISTICS      ALL
FINISH
```

Fig. A4.5 SPSS Program CROSS.SPS

there are no execution errors, the only occurrence of the string ERROR is usually the "0 ERRORS WERE DETECTED" summary provided by SPSS. If the string occurs somewhere else, simply list several lines around that line to determine what has gone wrong. If the results are error-free, the PRINT command can be used to send the output to the main line printer:

```
.PRINT OUT.OUT/DI:RE
```

The /DI:RE switch asks that the output file be deleted from the user's temporary directory and be renamed in the print queue. Available storage on this system is in short supply, and it is best not to use precious disk space for output listings. The DELETE command is used to dispose of output files that will not be printed:

```
.DELETE OUT.OUT
```

The limitations of this system prevent the implementation of sophisticated conversational interaction packages. Nonetheless, batch and nonconversational interactive access are quite straightforward on the DEC-10.

APPENDIX V

Applications on IBM OS/MVS Systems

Charles M. Tolbert II

This brief appendix provides sample procedures for using SPSS-X on IBM mainframes which use the OS/MVS operating system. The first two sections give overviews of the IBM editor (EDIT) and operating system commands (JCL). The final two sections contain sample setups for a remote batch job and for nonconversational interactive access on an IBM/OS mainframe. Although these essentials should be sufficient for some preliminary data processing, the complexity of the OS/MVS operating system requires that readers consult local computer center personnel for details on more sophisticated computing applications.

EDIT

EDIT is a mode- and line-oriented editor which operates quite similarly to the generic editor illustrated in Chapter 4. The examples here represent user input in lowercase letters and computer responses in uppercase. To begin an edit session, EDIT is typed along with the name of the file to be edited:

```
READY
edit pgm1.cntl nonum new
INPUT
(program text typed in here)
```

Carriage returns "<cr>" are used to "toggle" or switch between input and edit modes:

```
INPUT
this is line 1.<cr>
this is line 2.<cr>
this is line 3.<cr>
<cr>
EDIT
<cr>
INPUT
```

Text is listed by the LIST command:

```
EDIT                    (entire file is listed)
list
THIS IS LINE 1.
THIS IS LINE 2.
THIS IS LINE 3.

                        (two lines are listed beginning at pointer)
EDIT
list * 2
THIS IS LINE 1.
THIS IS LINE 2.
```

LIST moves the pointer to the last line listed. Other ways to move the pointer are the TOP, BOTTOM, UP, DOWN, and FIND commands. In the following examples, the position of the pointer is verified because the user turns EDIT's verifier on:

```
verify on
top
THIS IS LINE 1.
bottom
THIS IS LINE 3.
up 1
THIS IS LINE 2.
find /3/
THIS IS LINE 3.
```

One way to modify text is the CHANGE command which is used in the following:

```
list * 1              (pointer line is listed)
THIS IS LLINE 2.
change /lline/line/   (slashes delimit old, new
THIS IS LINE 2.         text; edit verifies
                        change)
```

An edited file is saved by the SAVE command:

```
save
SAVED
```

An edit session is terminated with the END command:

```
end       (session ended and user
READY       receives system prompt)

end       (end and save combined)
SAVED
READY
```

JCL: JOB CONTROL LANGUAGE

Novice users find OS/MVS JCL (job control language) very intimidating and frustrating. Some explanations are provided here for beginning SPSS-X users. Those who anticipate frequent usage of IBM systems would do well to move beyond these rudimentary examples to more detailed accounts that should be provided by computer centers and by IBM.

Figure A5.1 contains a batch job file named PGM1.CNTL which uses SPSS-X to read the NORC General Social Survey data (1972–82) and creates a system file named NORCGSS. The JCL statements appear in the first seven lines of the program file. Line 1 is known as the "job card" because it introduces the job to the system, naming it "PGM1" and providing accounting information. The TIME = 2 parameter estimates two minutes of central processor time for the job. The other parameters on the job card are optional and appear because the job is to be executed by remote batch access. The MSGCLASS = 6 field instructs the operating system to hold all system messages associated with the job so that the user can view them from a remote terminal prior to printing. The NOTIFY = USERID causes a message to be sent to the user upon completion of the job. Quite obviously, the second line of the JCL instructs the system to execute SPSS-X.

The remaining JCL statements are the infamous DD (Data Definition) statements with which many novice OS/MVS users struggle. Unfor-

```
//PGM1 JOB USER=USERID,PASSWORD=XYZ,MSGCLASS=6,TIME=2,NOTIFY=USERID
// EXEC SPSSX
//FT06F001 DD SYSOUT=6
//IN DD DSN=USERID.NORC.DATA,DISP=SHR
//NORCGSS DD DSN=USERID.NORCGSS.DATA,UNIT=SYSDA,DISP=(NEW.CATLG),
// SPACE=(TRK,(100,10)),VOL=SER=VOL001
//SYSIN DD *
TITLE   CREATION OF NORCGSS 72-82 SYSTEM FILE
SET BLANKS=0
DATA LIST     FILE=IN    RECORDS=11
/1 MARITAL 23 AGE 56-57 EDUC 64-65 SEX 76 RACE 77
/2 REGION 65 /5 RELIG 7
VARIABLE LABELS MARITAL 'MARITAL STATUS'
AGE 'AGE' RACE 'RACE' SEX 'SEX'
REGION 'REGION OF INTERVIEW'
RELIG 'RESP RELIGIOUS PREFERENCE'
MISSING VALUES MARITAL (9)/AGE(0,98,99)/EDUC(97,98,99)/
RELIG(0,8,9)/
VALUE LABELS MARITAL 1 'MARRIED' 2 'WIDOWED' 3 'DIVORCED'
4 'SEPARATED' 5 'NEVER MARRIED' 9 'NA'/
SEX 1 'MALE' 2 'FEMALE'/
RACE 1 'WHITE' 2 'BLACK' 3 'OTHER'/
RELIG 1 'PROTESTANT' 2 'CATHOLIC' 3 'JEWISH' 4 'NONE' 5 'OTHER'/
SAVE OUTFILE=NORCGSS/MAP
/*
```

Fig. A5.1 Remote Batch Job PGM1.CNTL

tunately, DD statements are indispensable since they are used to identify files for input and output. The following model statement is listed with user-supplied information in lowercase:

```
//ddname DD DSN=dsname,DISP=status
```

In the DDNAME field, the user supplies a single word which is used to link files referenced in programs to files elsewhere in the system. In the DSNAME (dataset name) field, the user inserts the entire name of the file to be accessed. On many systems, this name is typically multilevel, beginning with an USERID and ending with a "qualifier" which implies characteristics of the file. Valid names in OS/MVS are up to eight characters in length, and each level is separated by periods.

The one-word DDNAME serves as a shorter nickname or label for a longer, multilevel file name. The linkage between a DDNAME and a DSNAME is made on the all important DD statement. The DISP = (disposition) field notes whether the file is new or old and whether exclusive access to the file is required. Note that the DD statement begins with slashes, the DDNAME, and the label DD. All parameters that follow are separated by commas.

In Figure A5.1, the first DD statement (line 3) concerns the output listing from SPSS-X (here given the DDNAME FT06F001). The SYS-OUT = 6 field instructs the operating system to hold the output from the job so that a remote user can view it from a terminal. The second DD statement assigns a name of IN to an input raw data file containing the NORC survey data. The DISP = SHR simply means that the existing file is not needed for exclusive use and can be used simultaneously by other users. DISP = OLD would reserve the file for exclusive use, and other users would not be allowed to use the file until it had been released.

The third DD statement allocates a file labeled with a DDNAME of NORCGSS and a multilevel DSNAME of USERID.NORCGSS.DATA. UNIT = SYSDA tells the operating system that the file is to be stored on disk. The DISP field notes that the file is new and that it should be cataloged. The SPACE parameter allocates 100 tracks of disk space and reserves 10 extra for secondary use if the file exceeds the 100 primary tracks. Finally, the VOL = SER = specifies a particular disk pack on which the data will reside.

The final DD statement refers to a file with a DDNAME of SYSIN and indicates by an asterisk (*) that the contents of a file follow immediately thereafter. In this way, the system looks beyond the JCL to the SPSS-X program that follows. The remote batch job listed in Figure A5.1 ends with a /* end-of-file marker. The execution of such a job is discussed in the next section on remote batch access.

REMOTE BATCH ACCESS

Remote batch access on an IBM OS/MVS system first requires the preparation of a program such as PGM1.CNTL listed in Figure A5.1. EDIT or some other editor is used to create a program file which contains JCL and software package instructions. The job is submitted to the batch queue from a terminal with the SUBMIT command:

```
READY
submit pgm1.cntl
JOB PGM1(JOB9999) SUBMITTED
```

The user can follow the progress of the job with the STATUS command:

```
READY
status
JOB PGM1(JOB9999) WAITING FOR EXECUTION
READY
```

When the job has finished running, the NOTIFY command on the job card causes a message to be sent to the user's terminal. Then the output from the job is checked by using the OUTPUT command and an editor:

```
READY                                    (file printed to disk)
output pgm1(job9999) hold keep print(out)
READY
edit out.outlist nonum
EDIT                                     (output listing searched
find /error/                             searched for "error")
```

If errors are detected, the user purges the job from the output queue and corrects the program file with an editor:

```
READY
cancel pgm1(job9999) purge
READY
edit pgm1.cntl nonum
```

If there are no errors, the file is released for printing:

```
READY
output pgm1(job9999) newclass(a)
```

The printed output will be available at the printer station designated by the code A in the NEWCLASS parameter.

NONCONVERSATIONAL INTERACTIVE ACCESS

As noted in Chapter 8, nonconversational interaction causes the user's program to be executed immediately. Another major difference between remote batch and nonconversational interactive access is that operating system instructions are issued as terminal commands. On an OS/MVS mainframe using IBM's Time-Sharing Option (TSO), this means converting DD statements to ALLOCATE statements. Fortunately, ALLOCATE commands are similar in structure to DD statements:

```
ALLOCATE F(ddname) DA(dsname)      (optional parameters)
```

For example, the input raw data in the previous example required this DD statement:

```
//IN DD DSN=USERID.NORC.DATA,DISP=SHR
```

The equivalent ALLOCATE command issued from a terminal would appear as follows:

```
allocate f(in) da(norc.data) shr
READY
```

Note that the USERID is not listed in the dataset name because the file resides in the user's personal catalog.

Nonconversational interactive access involves issuing a series of ALLOCATE statements and, finally, calling a software package. The following example assumes that the SPSS-X program portion of Figure A5.1 exists in a file called PGM2. Explanations of commands appear in italics.

```
READY
allocate f(ft05f001) da(pgm2.cntl)                                    (input program file allocated)
READY
allocate f(ft06f001) da(out1.data)                                    (output listing file allocated)
READY
allocate f(in) da(norc.data) shr                                      (input data file allocated)
READY
allocate f(norcgss) da(norcgss.data) sp(100) tr vo(vol001)            (output data file allocated)
READY
call 'library.proc(spssx)'                                            (SPSS-X executed; filename will vary
                                                                       from one installation to another)
READY                                                                 (system responds after execution)
```

210

After execution, the file OUT1.DATA can be checked for errors with an editor. If there were errors, the user would correct the program file PGM2.CNTL and re-execute it. All files remain allocated until the user logs off or uses the FREE command:

```
READY
free f(in)
READY
```

To avoid repeating lengthy terminal command sequences, these allocation procedures can be grouped under a command procedure file. Although the construction of such a file requires intermediate programming skills, it would be well worth the effort of frequent SPSS users to seek experienced system programming assistance in building a command procedure file. With or without such an aid, nonconversational interaction is clearly a more convenient mode of access than is remote batch on an IBM OS/MVS system.

Glossary

The terms defined in this glossary appear at one or more points in this book. Italicized terms within the glossary definitions are also defined elsewhere in the glossary. Much larger compendia exist such as C. J. Sippl and R. J. Sippl's *Computer Dictionary and Handbook* (Third edition, Indianapolis: H. W. Sams, 1980).

acoustic coupler: A *modem* that accepts a telephone handset and audibly transfers information between a host computer and a remote device.

allocation: The identification and/or definition of a data file that is to be used. Most computer systems require that files be allocated before they are accessed by a user.

analog computer: A computer that analyzes continuous flows of information as opposed to discrete numerical information (contrast with *digital computer*).

APL: A Programming Language; causes a computer terminal with a special keyboard to become a powerful calculator for mathematical problem solving.

applications language: The easy-to-use language of a *software package*; does not require programming experience.

artificial intelligence: The use of computers for complex problem solving such as simulation of a physician's diagnosis.

ASCII: The American Standard Code for Information Interchange; a widely used 8-bit code for representing characters including all upper-and lowercase letters, numbers, and several special symbols. ASCII is the standard character set for virtually all word processing applications (contrast with *EBCDIC*).

assembler: A program that translates *assembly language* programs into *machine language.*

assembly language: A *low-level language* one step removed from *machine language.*

asynchronous communications: Communications between computers and terminals which start and stop at random intervals; commonly use slower *BAUD* rates of 300 or 1200.

auxiliary memory: Extra memory for a computer system outside the *CPU* proper.

bank switching: A memory expansion strategy in which a *microprocessor* addresses different blocks of memory, but in combinations that do not exceed the maximum limits of the microprocessor.

BASIC: Beginners' All-Purpose Symbolic Instruction Code; an easy *high-level language* used widely on microcomputers.

batch processing: Accessing a computer by turning a set of instructions (a "batch") over to the operating system for execution.

BAUD: The speed with which communication takes place; commonly equated with *bits* per second (BPS) such that 300 BAUD means 30 BPS.

bit: The smallest piece of information processed by a computer; expressed in binary as a one or a zero.

block: A unit of data set organization which consists of a set of complete individual records.

block move: In *word processing*, the "cutting and pasting" of text.

BMDP: Biomedical Data Programs; an analysis software package originally produced at UCLA.

booting: The initial loading of a computer's *RAM.*

BPI: *Bits* per inch; a method of measuring the density at which data are written on magnetic tapes.

briefcase computer: A "lap-size" microcomputer small enough to fit in a briefcase (contrast with *transportable computer*).

BRS: Bibliographic Retrieval Services; an information and retrieval service which operates, among other things, BRS/After Dark.

byte: A set of *bits* used to represent data; 8 bits is the most common number in a byte.

C: A powerful programming language that has characteristics of high-level and low-level languages.

CAI: Computer-Assisted Instruction.

card image data: Data stored on a mass storage device in 80-column, punched card format.

case: The basic unit of analysis in a data set; in the social sciences the cases are often persons from whom data have been collected by interview or questionnaire.

CATI: Computer-Assisted Telephone Interviewing.

CENSPAC: Data management software distributed by the U.S. Bureau of the Census.

central site: the main installation of a *distributed data processing* system.

chip: a small silicon wafer etched with integrated circuits; some widely known chips are microprocessors.

CMI: Computer-Managed Instruction.

COBOL: Common Business-Oriented Language; a high-level language used in business applications.

command procedure: A set of time-sharing operating system commands that are grouped into a program and executed together.

communication protocol: A set of communication rules that provide for error checking between devices and ensure that transmitted data are not lost.

communication software: A program that allows devices to communicate with one another; usually provides one or more *communication protocols*.

compiler: A program that translates a *high-level language* program into *machine language*.

CompuServe: A consumer-oriented data base and information retrieval system.

conditional paging: A word processing feature that causes printing to begin on the next page if a specified block of text will not fit completely within the remaining space on a page.

CONDUIT: A distributor of educational software of interest to social scientists.

console: A typewriter-like keyboard for computer input; frequently used to indicate the main operating station of a computer.

conversational interaction: Interaction with a computer which takes the form of a dialogue between the user and the machine.

coprocessor: A *CPU* that works in tandem with another to increase the computing power of a system. Among microcomputers, one widely used coprocessor is the Intel 8087 which enhances the mathematical computational powers of the 8088 chip.

CP/M: Control Program/Monitor; an operating system used with the 8080 and Z80 family of *microprocessors*.

CPU: Central processing unit; the key central component of a computer system; composed of control, arithmetic/logic, and memory units.

CRT: Cathode ray tube; a terminal that displays on a television-like screen.

CTRL: The Control key found on most terminal keyboards.

cursor: An indicator of location on a *CRT*; plays important role in use of *full-screen editor*.

cylinder: On a *disk pack*, a set of corresponding *tracks*.

daisy wheel printer: A printer that uses a typing element that resembles a flower with characters on extensions (petals) from a center hub; often characterized as producing letter-quality printing.

Datamyte 1000: A data recording device used in structured observation.

data definition: That portion of a software package program which identifies the data to be used in analysis.

DBMS: Data base management system; a *software package* that aids in collecting and organizing data and generating reports on data files.

deck: A portion of a case in a *card image data* file.

dedicated word processor: A computer that is designed to be used exclusively for *word processing*.

DIALOG: An information and retrieval service which operates, among other things, Knowledge Index.

digital computer: A computer that analyzes discrete digital data (contrast with *analog computer*).

disk pack: A set of magnetic disks that are housed so that each can be read at the same time by a disk drive.

diskette: A flexible magnetic recording medium contained in a cardboard or paper liner; the most popular form of mass storage for microcomputers.

distributed data processing: A computing network composed of one or more *central sites* with *mainframes* and numerous remote sites with *minicomputers, microcomputers*, and terminals. Ideally, remote computing power is used only when local computers do not have the capacity required by the application.

dot matrix printer: A printer that represents characters within a matrix of dots; capable of draft-quality printing and, sometimes, correspondence-quality printing.

download: Transfer a file from a mainframe to a microcomputer.

dual processors: Two *microprocessors* in a single microcomputer which allow the use of software designed for either chip.

EBCDIC: Extended Binary Coded Decimal Interchange Code; a way of coding characters employed mostly on mainframes; does not include lowercase letters (contrast with *ASCII*).

E-Com: The U.S. Postal Service's electronic mail system.

floppy disk: see *diskette*.

FORTRAN: FORmula TRANslator; a high-level language used in mathematical and other scientific applications.

full-screen editor: A text editor that operates on entire screens (or pages) of data at a time (contrast with *line-oriented editor*).

General Social Survey: Annual national surveys conducted by the National Opinion Research Center (*NORC*).

hard disk drive: A housing for a magnetic disk mass storage device; faster data interchange and more capacity than floppy disk drive.

hardcopy terminal: A terminal that displays by printing on paper (contrast with *CRT*).

hardware: The machinery by which computing is accomplished.

hardwiring: The practice of directly connecting terminals and computers without using dial-up phone lines.

hierarchical file: A file with records nested according to some hierarchy such as SMSAs, households, families, and persons; records do not necessarily correspond to the same units of analysis (contrast with rectangular file).

high-level language: A programming language so far removed from *machine language* that ordinary words are used instead of cryptic codes or numbers.

ICPSR: The Inter-university Consortium for Political and Social Research; maintains a secondary data archive and provides many other services.

integrated circuit: A method of controlling circuits which improves on transistors; circuits are etched on tiny *chips*.

integrated word processing package: A package that allows text editing and text formatting.

intelligent terminal: A *terminal* (or *microcomputer*) that is capable of exchanging files with another computer system.

interactive time-sharing: Simultaneous interaction of multiple users with a single computer.

interpreter: A program that translates a *high-level language* to *machine language*, one line of code at a time.

I/O: Input/output; usually used to indicate that a *peripheral unit* is capable of reading and writing data.

justification: In *word processing*, the practice of aligning text at the left and, possibly, right margins.

labeled tape: A tape that has a *volume header* and labels preceding and following each file.

LAN: Local area network; a network linking computers that allows sharing of resources among them.

laser printer: A printer that uses a laser to form characters as they are printed.

line printer: A printer that prints an entire line with one strike of a print train; usually associated with a *mainframe*, and very fast.

line-oriented editor: A text editor that operates on text in units of lines (contrast with *full-screen editor*).

loop: A programming strategy that causes sets of program statements to be executed repeatedly.

low-level language: A programming language written in *machine* or *assembly language*.

LSI: Large scale *integrated circuits*; *chips* with thousands of circuits.

machine language: The native code of *digital computers* written in binary.

mainframe: The *CPU* of a large-scale, fourth-generation computer system with many users.

megabyte: A measure of mass storage capacity meaning one million *bytes* (i.e., 1000K).

microcomputer: A small-scale, fourth-generation computer used by no more than a few persons.

microprocessor: The *CPU* of a *microcomputer*.

minicomputer: A mid-sized computer with more power than a *microcomputer*, but less capacity than a *mainframe*.

Mini-Tab: An analysis *software package* developed at the University of Pennsylvania.

missing values: Symbols for variable values that are absent from a data file; for example, codes representing refusals to answer certain questions by respondents in a survey.

modeless editor: A *text editor* that does not have input and edit modes, but differentiates commands from input text by certain keystrokes.

modem: A combination of the words modulate and demodulate; used to send digital data across telephone lines.

mouse: A hand-operated device that facilitates movement of a *cursor*; it is wire connected to a computer and, due to its small size, resembles a rodent.

MRDF: Machine-readable data file; a file that can be directly read by a computer (i.e., stored on tape, disk, or cards).

MS-DOS: Microsoft's Disk Operating System; an operating system for the 8088 family of *microprocessors*.

multiplexer: A communications device that allows several terminals to communicate with a mainframe over a single phone line.

multiprogramming: Several programs can be active in a CPU at the same time.

nonconversational interaction: Interactive time-sharing access of a computer which does not take the form of a question and answer dialogue.

nonvolatile mass storage: Permanent mass storage; that is, data remain stored even when the system is powered down.

NORC: The National Opinion Research Center at the University of Chicago; conducts the *General Social Survey*.

numeric pad: A set of numeric keys on a *terminal* keyboard which facilitates entry of digital data.

OCR: Optical character recognition; conversion of printed or hand-coded data into computer data files.

online: Direct access to a computer.

operating system: Software that regulates the operation of a computer system.

OSIRIS: Analysis software produced at the University of Michigan.

packet switching network: Networks of remote computers available to users by local phone lines or toll-free numbers.

Pascal: A high-level programming language name for the French mathematician Blaise Pascal; renowned for its emphasis on structured programs.

peripheral processor: Small computers that interface *peripheral units* with *CPUs*; faster data interchange results.

peripheral unit: Computer hardware that is not part of the *CPU*; auxiliary equipment such as disk drives, tape drives, and printers.

PLATO: Programmed Logic for Automatic Teaching Operations; a large-scale instructional package originally written for Control Data (CDC) mainframes.

PL/I: Programming Language/1; a *high-level* programming language which builds on *FORTRAN* and *COBOL*.

plotter: A printer that is used for graphing and plotting.

pointer: A concept associated with *line-oriented text editors*; refers ("points") to the line on which the editor is operating.

program: A set of instructions for a computer.

programming language: A language with a specific syntax which must be learned by the user (contrast with *applications language*).

proportional spacing: A printing feature that reserves different amounts of space on a line for characters of differing widths.

P-STAT: An analysis *software package* produced at Princeton University.

RAM: Random access memory; the portion of a computer's memory that is reserved for work space; RAM can be written on and read repeatedly, but is usually erased when the power is turned off ("volatile" memory).

RAM disk emulation: The use of a portion of *RAM* as if it were a disk drive; although this increases the speed of data processing, it is volatile (temporary) memory.

random access file: A file than can be accessed immediately without the necessity of reading over other files (contrast with *sequential file*).

raw data file: An unprocessed data file.

RDD: Random digit dialing; software which generates random telephone numbers for surveying and automatically dials those numbers.

recode: Transformation of original variable values to new codes.

rectangular file: A data file in which all records pertain to the same unit of analysis; e.g., persons or countries (contrast with *hierarchical file*).

relational file: A file which connects records on the basis of specified relationships; can be *hierarchical* or *rectangular*.

remote batch: The submission of a *batch* job from a remote terminal; typically the user checks the output at a terminal and prints it at a remote printer if there are no errors.

remote site: An outpost in a *distributed processing* network.

report generator: A software package which can be used to summarize a data base and to print reports based on the data.

ROM: Read-only memory; that portion of a computer's memory which can only be read and cannot be written on; the contents range from basic system definitions such as *console* keys to entire *software packages* which are permanently stored in the computer's memory.

SAS: The Statistical Analysis System; an analysis *software package* which is a favorite of many quantitative researchers.

secondary data analysis: Analysis of data that have been collected by someone else; often facilitated by use of *MRDF*.

sequential file: A file that is organized on a mass storage medium as if it were in a line with files ahead and files behind; those files in front of the file must be passed through in order to access the desired file.

SIR: The Scientific Information Retrieval System; a *DBMS* that operates on mainframes.

smart terminal: see *intelligent terminal*.

soft hyphen: A *word processing* feature that allows the user to indicate appropriate points for hyphenation of words; the hyphen only appears in the printed product if the word is indeed hyphenated.

software: Instructions which drive computer *hardware*.

software package: An integrated set of *software* routines that allows the use of an *applications language*.

special function keys: *Console* keys that are programmed to produce the effects of several commands; results in economy of keystrokes.

spreadsheet software: A *software package* that allows the user to organize data in rows and columns; arithmetic computation and logical evaluation of cell entries makes such packages extremely useful.

SPSS: Statistical Package for the Social Sciences; a very popular analysis *software package*.

SPSS-X: A major new edition of the analysis *software package SPSS*.

streaming tape drive: A device that holds a continuous tape cartridge and is used primarily for backup of *hard disk drives*.

supercomputer: A fourth-generation mainframe with an extremely fast *CPU* based on *VLSI* architecture.

synchronous communications: Communications are synchronized by a clocking signal, allowing large blocks of data to be sent and received at very fast rates (4800, 9600 *BAUD* or higher).

system file: Data that have been processed by a *software package* and formatted for ease of use with that package.

tape initialization: The practice of encoding a *volume header* and other information on a tape.

task definition: That portion of an analysis *software package* program which specifies the statistics that are to be computed.

terminal: A device that is used to interact with a computer from a remote location.

text editor: A *software package* that is used to create, display, modify, and save text files.

text formatting: In *word processing*, the rearrangement of text so that it is neatly aligned within margins and prepared for final printing.

The General Inquirer: A *software package* that does content analysis.

The Source: A consumer-oriented data base and information retrieval system.

tracks: Concentric rings on the surface of a disk.

transistor: Circuitry in second-generation computers; allowed considerable reduction in size of computers.

transportable computer: A portable computer which is heavy and bulky (contrast with a *briefcase computer*).

undo command: A *word processing* feature that cancels the effects of the most recently issued command.

upload: The transfer of a data file from a microcomputer to a mainframe.

vacuum tube: Glass tubes containing electronic circuitry; used in first-generation computers.

variable: An item that takes on different values ("varies"); social science data files are composed of variables.

VDT: Video data *terminal*; see *CRT*.

verification: The process by which a *line-oriented editor* displays the results of an operation on a line or lines.

videotex: Two-way interchange of information which usually consists of displays from a host computer and responses from a remote user.

VLSI: Very large scale integrated circuits; the basis for circuitry in *supercomputers*.

volume header: A label encoded on a magnetic tape in an *initialization* procedure; serves as a basis for identification of data and security.

widowing: A *word processing* feature that ensures that paragraphs are not begun at the bottoms of pages and that single lines of paragraphs are not carried over to the next page.

wildcard character: A text editing feature which represents any character; allows considerable flexibility in search and replace procedures.

word processing: The manipulation of words and text with a computer to produce neatly formatted and printed results.

word wrapping: A *word processing* feature that automatically moves words that will not fit on a line to the next line as they are entered by the typist; this allows continuous typing without concern for ends of lines.

write ring: A ring inserted in the center hub of magnetic tape reel that enables a tape to be written on.

References

Anderson, Ronald E.
  1981 "Instructional Computing in Sociology: Current Status and Future Prospects." *Teaching Sociology* 8(January):171–195.
American Psychological Association
  1974 *Publication Manual of the American Psychological Association.* Fourth Edition.
Babbie, Earl R.
  1983 *Methods of Social Research.* Third Edition. Belmont, CA: Wadsworth.
Bailey, Kenneth D.
  1982 *Methods of Social Research.* Second Edition. New York: Free Press.
Bassis, Michael S., and Joyce P. Allen
  1977 "Teaching Introductory Sociology with TIPS." *Teaching Sociology* 4(January):141–154.
Becker, Henry J.
  1982 "Microcomputers in the Classroom: Dreams and Realities." Report No. 319, Center for Social Organization of Schools. Baltimore: Johns Hopkins University.
Beckman, Margaret M.
  1982 "Online Catalogs and Library Users." *Library Journal* 107(November):2043–2047.
Bell, Daniel
  1973 *The Coming of Post-Industrial Society.* New York: Basic Books.
Bluestone, Barry, and Bennett Harrison
  1982 *The Deindustrialization of America.* New York: Free Press.
Bradley, Virginia N.
  1982 "Improving Students' Writing with Microcomputers." *Language Arts* 59(September):732–743.
Calhoun, Craig J.
  1981 "The Microcomputer Revolution? Technical Possibilities and Social Choices." *Sociological Methods and Research* 9(May):397–437.

Carpenter, James, Dennis Deloria, and David Morganstein
    1984   "Statistical Software for Microcomputers." *BYTE* 9(April): 234–264.
Coburn, Peter, P. Kelman, N. Roberts, T. Snyder, D. Watt, and C. Weiner
    1982   *Practical Guide to Computers in Education.* Reading, MA: Addison-Wesley.
Cole, Bernard
    1983   "The Family Tree of Computer Languages." *Popular Computing* 2(September):80–88.
Conger, Rand, and R. Douglas McLeod
    1977   "Describing Behavior in Small Groups with the Datamyte Event Recorder." *Behavior Research Methods and Instrumentation* 9(October):418–424.
Cooperband, Alvin S.
    1966   "The Use of a Computer in Conducting Psychological Experiments." *Behavioral Science* 11(July):307–311.
Davis, James A.
    1978   "Teaching Social Facts with Computers." *Teaching Sociology* 4 (April):235–259.
    1982   *General Social Surveys, 1972–1982: Cumulative Codebook.* Chicago: National Opinion Research Center.
DIALOG Information Services, Inc.
    1983   *Database Catalog: January 1983.* Palo Alto: DIALOG Information Services, Inc.
Dodd, Sue A.
    1979   "Bibliographic References for Numeric Social Science Data Files: Suggested Guidelines." *Journal of the American Society for Information Science* 30(March):77–82.
Fallik, Fred, and Bruce Brown
    1983   *Statistics for Behavioral Sciences.* Homewood, IL: Dorsey.
Fallows, James
    1982   "Living With a Computer." *The Atlantic* 250(July):84–91.
    1983   "Computer Romance, Part II." *The Atlantic* 251(March): 107–108.
    1984   "Computers: Behavior Modification." *The Atlantic* 253 (January):90–94.
Freeman, Howard E.
    1983   "Research Opportunities Related to CATI." *Sociological Methods and Research* 12(November):143–152.
Garson, David G.
    1983a   "The First Year of the *Political Science Micro Review.*" *News for Teachers of Political Science* 38(Summer):10–12.

1983b "Microcomputer Analysis in Public Administration." *Public Administration* 43(September/October):453–458.

Galbraith, John K.
1967 *The New Industrial State*. Boston: Houghton Mifflin.

Glossbrenner, Alfred
1983 *The Complete Handbook of Personal Computer Communications*. New York: St. Martins.

Gouldner, Alvin W.
1979 *The Future of Intellectuals and the Rise of the New Class*. New York: Seabury Press.

Heise, David R.
1981 Microcomputers in Social Research. Special issue of *Sociological Methods and Research* 9(May):395–536.
1982a "Teaching with Microcomputers." *The Southern Sociologist* 13 (Winter):26–27.
1982b "Measuring Attitudes with a PET." *BYTE* 7(July):208–246.

Helm, John L.
1981 "Working with VM/CMS." Unpublished manuscript. New York: Columbia University Center for Computing Activities.

Hennings, Dorothy Grant
1981 "Input: Enter the Word-Processing Computer." *Language Arts* 58(January):18–22.

Heywood, Stephen A.
1983 "The 8086—An Architecture for the Future, Part 1: Introduction and Glossary." *BYTE* 8(June):450–455.

Hyman, Herbert
1972 *Secondary Analysis of Sample Surveys*. New York: Wiley.

Johnson, Edward S.
1967 "The Computer as Experimenter." *Behavioral Science* 12(November):484–489.

Jones, Edward
1984 "Electronic Proofreader and Thesaurus." *Popular Computing* 3(January):208–212.

Katz, Jerome
1983 "Statistical Packages for Apple Computers." *The ICPSR MicroNews* 1(September):4–13.

Kirk, Rodney C.
1981 "Microcomputers in Anthropological Research." *Sociological Methods and Research* 9(April):473–492.

Kline, David
1983 "Me and My Ramblin' Osborne: Traveling with Your Computer." *The Portable Companion* 2(August):23–28.

Lachenbruch, Peter A.
1983 "Statistical Programs for Microcomputers." *BYTE* 11(November): 560–570.

Lemmons, Phil
1983 "16-Bit Designs." *BYTE* 8(June):52–53.

Magarrell, Jack
1983 "Dearth of New 'Supercomputers' Called Threat to U.S. Leadership in Science and Technology." *The Chronicle of Higher Education* 26(March 30):8–9.

Mandell, Steven L.
1983 *Computers and Data Processing Today with BASIC.* St. Paul: West.

Markoff, John
1983 "Computers that Think: The Race for the Fifth Generation." *InfoWorld* 5(August 1):25–26.

Marks, Gregory A.
1983 "Microcomputers: Basic Choice Factors." Ann Arbor: Interuniversity Consortium for Political and Social Research, University of Michigan.

Mier, Edwin E.
1984 "Data Communications for Personal Computers." *Popular Computing* 39(February):99–100.

Miller, Darby
1983 "Videotex: Science Fiction or Reality?" *BYTE* 8(July):42–56.

Miller, Michael J.
1984 "The New Word Processors." *Popular Computing* 3(January):113–117.

Molm, Linda D.
1981 "Power Use in the Dyad: The Effects of Structure, Knowledge, and Interaction History." *Social Psychology Quarterly* 44(March):42–48.

Naisbitt, John
1981 *Megatrends.* New York: Warner Books.

Nie, Norman H., C. H. Hull, J. G. Jenkins, K. Steinbrenner, and D. H. Bent
1975 *Statistical Package for the Social Sciences.* Second edition. New York: McGraw-Hill.

Ogburn, William
1922 *Social Change.* New York: Viking.

Orcutt, James D., and Ronald E. Anderson
1977 "Social Interaction, Dehumanization and the 'Computerized Other'." *Sociology and Social Research* 61(April): 380–397.

Osborne, Adam
 1979 *Running Wild: The Next Industrial Revolution.* Berkeley: Osborne/McGraw-Hill.
 1982 "The Need for Standardization." *The Portable Companion* 19 (August/September):9–11.
Pournelle, Jerry
 1983 "User's Column." *BYTE* 8(June):411–442.
Roberts, Nancy, D. Andersen, R. Deal, M. Garet, and W. Shaffer
 1983 *Introduction to Computer Simulation: The System Dynamics Approach.* Reading, MA: Addison-Wesley.
Schrodt, Phillip A.
 1983 "Microcomputers in Statistical Work." *News for Teachers of Political Science* 38(Summer):4–6.
Shanks, J. Merrill
 1983 "The Current Status of Computer-Assisted Telephone Interviewing." *Sociological Methods and Research* 12(November):119–142.
Shanks, J. Merrill, W. Nicholls II, and H. Freeman
 1981 "The California Disability Survey: Design and Execution of a Computer-Assisted Telephone Study." *Sociological Methods and Research* 10(November):123–140.
Shea, Tom
 1983 "Eight and 16-bit Machines: What's the Difference?" *InfoWorld* 5(August 1):18–21.
Shuford, Richard S.
 1983 "Word Processing Tools for the IBM Personal Computer." *BYTE* 8(May):176–216.
Shure, Gerald H., and Robert J. Meeker
 1969 "A Computer-based Experimental Laboratory." *Administrative Science Quarterly* 14(June):286–293.
Sobal, Jeff
 1981 "Teaching with Secondary Data." *Teaching Sociology* 8(January):149–170.
SPSS Inc.
 1983 *SPSSX User's Guide.* New York: McGraw-Hill.
Stern, Nancy, and Robert Stern
 1983 *Computers in Society.* Englewood Cliffs: Prentice-Hall.
Stone, Phillip J., D. C. Dunphy, M. S. Smith, and D. M. Ogilvie and Associates
 1966 *The General Inquirer: A Computer Approach to Content Analysis.* Cambridge, MA: The M.I.T. Press.
Stone, Phillip, and Cambridge Computer Associates, Inc.
 1968 *User's Manual for the General Inquirer.* Cambridge, MA: The M.I.T. Press.

Sykes, Richard E.
  1977 "Techniques of Data Collection and Reduction in Systematic Field Observation." *Behavior Research Methods and Instrumentation* 9(October):407–417.
Toffler, Alvin
  1980 *The Third Wave.* New York: Random House.
Tolbert, Patricia H., and Charles M. Tolbert II
  1983 "Classroom Applications of Electronic Spreadsheets." *Educational Technology* 23(October):20–22.
Turner, Judith Axler
  1983 "How a Carnegie-Mellon Student May Have Crashed a Computer at Columbia U." *The Chronicle of Higher Education* 26(July 27):18.
University of Waterloo
  1978 *Waterloo SCRIPT Reference Manual.* Waterloo, Ontario: University of Waterloo Computer Center.
U.S. Internal Revenue Service
  1972 *Statistics of Income: Corporation Income Tax Returns.* Washington: U.S. Government Printing Office.
van den Eeden, Pieter, and H. J. Huttner
  1982 "Multi-Level Research." *Current Sociology* 30(Winter):31–117.
Wallace, George W.
  1983 "Beginning Microcomputer Instruction on a Shoe-String." *The Southern Sociologist* 14(Spring):25.
Watt, Dan
  1984 "Tools for Writing." *Popular Computing* 3(January):75–78.
Wieting, Stephen C.
  1975 SIMSEARCH. Iowa City, IA: Department of Sociology, University of Iowa.
Wong, William G.
  1983 "The New 16-Bit Super Microcomputers: A Comparative Look at the Intel 80286, Motorola 68000, and National 16032." *Microsystems* 11(November):36–41.

Name Index

Allen, Joyce P., 79
Anderson, D., 78
Anderson, Ronald E., 75, 77, 78

Babbie, Earl R., 72, 106
Bailey, Kenneth D., 72, 73
Bassis, Michael S., 79
Becker, Henry J., 76, 77
Beckman, Margaret M., 80
Bell, Daniel, 1
Bent, D.H., 4
Bluestone, Barry, 1
Bradley, Virginia N., 51
Brown, Bruce, 142

Calhoun, Craig J., 28, 70
Carpenter, James, 144
Coburn, Peter, 76, 77
Cole, Bernard, 31
Conger, Rand, 75
Cooperband, Alvin S., 74

Davis, James A., 4, 32, 78, 100, 110
Deal, R., 78
Deloria, Dennis, 144
Dodd, Sue A., 107
Dunphy, D.C., 74

Fallik, Fred, 142
Fallows, James, 53, 68
Freeman, Howard E., 72

Galbraith, John K., 1
Garet, M., 78
Garson, G. Davis, 78, 144
Glossbrenner, Alfred, 90
Gouldner, Alvin, 1

Harrison, Bennett, 1
Heise, David, 5, 72, 77
Hennings, Dorothy Grant, 51
Heywood, Stephen A., 22
Hollerith, Herman, 8
Hull, C.H., 4
Huttner, H.J., 98
Hyman, Herbert, 106, 110

Jenkins, J.G., 4
Johnson, Edward S., 74
Jones, Edward, 52, 53

Katz, Jerome A., 144
Kelman, P., 76, 77
Kirk, Rodney C., 76
Kline, Davis, 76

Lachenbruch, Peter A., 144
Lemmons, Phil, 23

Magarrell, Jack, 10, 28
Mandell, Steven L., 9
Markoff, John, 11, 26
Marks, Gregory, 28, 143
McLeod, R. Douglas, 75
Meeker, Robert J., 74
Mier, Edwin E., 70
Miller, Darby, 85
Miller, Michael, 68
Molm, Linda D., 75
Morganstein, David, 144
Myers, Thomas, 12

Naisbitt, John, 74
Nicholls II, W., 72
Nie, Norman H., 4

Ogburn, William, 90
Ogilvie, D.M., 74
Orcutt, James D., 75
Osborne, Adam, 22, 23, 28, 89

Pascal, Blaise, 31
Pournelle, Jerry, 140

Roberts, Nancy, 76, 77, 78

Schrodt, Phillip A., 140, 141, 144
Shaffer, W., 78
Shanks, J. Merrill, 71, 72
Shea, Tom, 28
Shuford, Richard S., 68
Shure, Gerald H., 74
Smith, M.S., 74
Smith, Tom, 4
Snyder, T., 76, 77
Sobol, Jeff, 78, 109
Steinbrenner, K., 4
Stern, Nancy, 8, 28, 89
Stern, Robert, 8, 28, 89
Stone, Phillip, 74
Sykes, Richard E., 75

Toffler, Alvin, 1, 70
Tolbert, Charles M., 79
Tolbert, Patricia H., 79
Turner, Judith Axler, 71, 89

van den Eden, Pieter, 98

Wallace, George W., 78
Watt, Dan, 51, 54, 76, 77
Weiner, C., 76, 77
Wieting, Stephen C., 77
Wong, William G., 23

Subject Index

AI, (*see* artificial intelligence)
analysis software, 36, 139, 140
analog computer, 9
archival data collection, 3, 4, 72, 73
artificial intelligence, 11
assembly language, 30, 31
asynchronous communications, 70, 137

bank switching, 136
BASIC, 31–34
batch processing, 111, 113–115
BAUD, 20, 70, 137
bits, 22
BMDP, 36, 37, 98, 143
bpi, 128
briefcase computers, 26, 73
bubble memory, 136
bytes, 22

CAI (*see* computer-assisted instruction)
card image data, 96
card readers and punches, 15
case, 93
cathode ray tube, 20, 24
CENSPAC, 106
census data, 2, 8, 25, 96, 106, 137
Census, U.S. Bureau of, 2, 8, 72
central processing unit, 12, 14, 15, 22, 115
CMI, (*see* computer-managed instruction)
COBOL, 31
codebook, 99–101
coding, 99–101
command procedure, 119 (*see also* macro)
communications, 2, 20, 69–71, 88–90, 137
    equipment, 18
    protocol, 70
    software, 70
compiler, 31
computer-assisted instruction, 76–79
computer-assisted telephone interviewing,
    71, 72, 90
computer-managed instruction, 79
console, 14, 18
conversational interaction, 112, 121, 140
coprocessor, 23
CPU, (*see* central processing unit)
CP/M, 62
crime and computers, 48
CRT, (*see* cathode ray tube)
cursor, 39, 62

data base management, 2, 37, 140, 141
data base management systems, 2, 37,
    73, 106, 140, 141
data bases, online, 80–83

data collection, 21, 25, 71–74, 76
data definition, 98, 141
data structure, 93–106
DBMS, (*see* data base management system)
DDE, (*see* direct data entry) deck, 96
digital computer, 9, 213, 218
direct data entry, 72, 141
disk, magnetic, 14, 15, 130–132
    cartridge drive, 137
    organization of data, 130
    security considerations, 132
    packs, 130, 215
    storage, advantage of, 131
    tracks, 14, 130, 215
diskette, 20, 24, 137
distributed data processing, 14, 27
downloading, 27

EBCDIC, 213
economy considerations, 132–134
edit mode, 40
eight-bit microprocessors, 22, 28, 138, 139
electronic card files, 53
electronic mail, 88
electronic spreadsheet, 81
execution time, 115

fixed drive, (*see also* hard disk drive) 136
floppy disk drive, 20, 137
formatting of text, 51, 54–60, 64, 68
FORTRAN, 31, 34, 36, 140, 219
full screen editor, 39, 215, 217

games, instructional, 77
General Social Surveys, 100, 101, 109, 218
grammar checker, 53

hard disk drive, 136, 137, 220
hardware, 3, 8, 141, 142, 220
hierarchical data files, 37, 96–98, 219
high level language, 31, 34, 140, 214, 215,
    217, 219
history of computers, 3, 7–12

ICPSR, (*see* Interuniversity Consortium
    for Political and Social Research)
information storage and retrieval, 2,
    83–88, 91
input, 12, 32
input mode of text editor, 40
integrated circuit, 9, 101, 215, 217
integration
    analysis packages, 3, 68
    software packages, 3, 68, 140
    word processing packages, 51

intelligent terminal, 27
interactive time-sharing access, 112, 116
interpreter, 31
Interuniversity Consortium for Political
    and Social Research, 109, 110
I/O device, 12, 14

job submission, 114–117, 124
justification of text, 55

laboratory experiment, 38, 74, 75
LAN, (*see* local area network)
large data file, 125–134, 140
laser printer, 15, 64
line-oriented text editor, 39
line printer, 15, 20
local area network, 142
LSI, 10
loop, 32, 47
low-level language, 31

machine language, 30
machine readable data files, 106–109
macro, 47
mainframe, 2, 3, 11, 14, 18, 20, 21, 26,
    27, 30, 37, 51, 65, 66, 71, 72, 106,
    111–124, 137
megabyte, 22, 137
menu-driven software, 140
merging of files, 48, 141
microcomputer, 2–7, 11, 14, 20, 21, 23,
    24, 26, 27, 30, 37, 38, 51, 65, 66, 71,
    106, 135–144
microprocessor, 2, 22–24, 30
minicomputer, 72, 135–144
Mini-tab, 36
modem, 20, 24
MRDF, (*see* machine-readable data files)
MS-DOS, 62
multiplexer, 20
multi-programming, 29
multiuser system, 142

National Opinion Research Center, 4, 32,
    101, 102, 110
networking of computers, 72, 142
nonanalytic applications, 3, 69–91
nonconversational interactive access,
    112, 118–120
    disadvantages of, 119, 120
nonrectangular files, 141
NORC, (*see* National Opinion Research
    Center)

OCR, (*see* optical character recognition)
online information, 80–88, 91
operating system, 29, 113–116
operators, computer, 18
optical character recognition, 14, 72
OSIRIS, 36
output, 12, 32

packet switching networks, 71, 88
Pascal, 31
peripheral processors, 18
peripheral units, 14
PLATO, 91
PL/I, 31
plotters, 15
portable microcomputer, 73
printing, 14, 58, 65, 66, 68

RAM, (*see* random access memory)
RAM disk emulation, 136
random access memory, 136, 137
random digit dialing, 72
raw data files, 94, 98, 99, 102, 141
RDD, (*see* random digit dialing)
read-only-memory (ROM), 136
recoding, 98
rectangular data files, 94, 96
relational data bases, 37, 106, 141
remote batch access, 116, 117, 124
report writing, 67
ROM, (*see* read-only-memory)

SAS, 36, 98, 99, 129, 131
scratch disk space, 133
SCRIPT, 37, 59, 60
secondary data analysis, 106–110
sequential files, 128
simulations, 38, 69–91
SIR, 37, 106
sixteen-bit microprocessor, 22, 23, 28,
    135, 136, 139
Social Science Micro Review, 78, 91
software, 3, 29–31
software package, 34, 35
spelling checkers, 52
spreadsheets, 80, 139
SPSS, 4, 34, 36, 37, 39, 42, 67, 98,
    102–104, 133, 143
SPSSX, 4, 101, 103
supercomputer, 10, 28
survey data, 3, 71, 108
synchronous communications, 70, 137
system files, 94, 98–99, 101, 103, 104,
    109, 124, 133, 141
tape, magnetic, 126–130
    cassette, 24
    density, 127
    drive, 14, 15, 136
    drives, streaming, 137
    external label, 128
    initialization, 130
    labeling, 127
    organization of data files, 127
    ring, read-only, 129
    security considerations, 129
    storage, advantages, 128
    storage, disadvantages, 128
    trailer, 128
    volume headers, 127

task definition, 98
Telenet, 71, 88
terminal, 18
text editor, 3, 39, 51
thesaurus, electronic, 52, 53
thirty-two bit computers, 27, 135, 136,
     139, 142
transportable computer, 26
transistors, 9
Tymenet, 71

undo command, 48
Uninet, 71

United Press International, 89
uploading of files, 27

vacuum tubes, 9
variables, 93
VLSI, 10

word processing, 2, 3, 25, 51–68, 124, 140
WordStar, 38, 62–65, 67
word wrapping, 41